A VICTORIAN TRAGEDY

The extraordinary case of

Banks v Goodfellow

A VICTORIAN TRAGEDY

The extraordinary case of
Banks v Goodfellow

Martyn Frost

Wildy, Simmonds & Hill Publishing

© Martyn Frost, 2018

ISBN: 9780854902538

British Library Cataloguing in Publication Data

A catalogue record for this book is available from the British Library

The right of Martyn Frost to be identified as the author of this Work has been asserted by him in accordance with sections 77 and 78 of the Copyright, Designs and Patents Act 1988.

All rights reserved. No part of this book may be reproduced, stored in a retrieval system, or transmitted, in any form or by any means, electronic, mechanical, photocopying, recording or otherwise, without the consent of the copyright owners, application for which should be addressed to the publisher. Such a written permission must also be obtained before any part of this publication is stored in a retrieval system of any nature.

First published in 2018 by

Wildy, Simmonds & Hill Publishing
Wildy & Sons Ltd
Lincoln's Inn Archway
Carey Street
London WC2A 2JD
www.wildy.com

Typeset by Heather Jones, North Petherton, Somerset.
Printed and bound by CPI Group (UK) Ltd, Croydon, CR0 4YY

For Linda, with love and gratitude for
her encouragement and patience

Contents

Introduction		ix
Chapter One	Who was John Banks the Elder?	1
Chapter Two	John Banks the Elder: His Life, Illness and Death	7
Chapter Three	The Wills of John Banks the Elder	49
Chapter Four	Margaret Banks Goodfellow: The Niece and Beneficiary of the Last Will	73
Chapter Five	The Trials of the Will	99
Chapter Six	John Banks the Younger: The Claimant	137
Chapter Seven	Edward Barron Goodfellow: The Defendant	143
Chapter Eight	The Questions that still Remain	169
Appendix I	Information	181
Appendix II	Biographical Sketches of the Judges and Principal Barristers	189
Appendix III	The Judgment in Queen's Bench	205
Endnotes		225
Index		257

Introduction

This book is a history of the events and people involved a dispute over a will in mid-nineteenth-century Keswick. The story is one of a family of modest wealth and modest attainment – a not untypical mid-nineteenth-century middle-class family. At the heart of the story is the will dispute, but the story is far from just a legal analysis of the issues.

Litigation over a will usually pits two sides of a family against one another and this case was no different. In will disputes there are official winners, because that is what the court is asked to determine in relation to the validity of a will. But the reality is that nearly always everyone loses in some way. The damage that a will dispute inflicts on a family is generally irreparable and the poisoned relationships that result can leave an additional, bitter, legacy to the future generations. The pain of losing and the initial pleasure of winning will also both be affected by the size of each side's lawyers' bills. It has ever been thus and the case that is central to this book seems to have been no exception, but other events within this family leave no doubt that there really were no winners this time.

The case concerned is *Banks v Goodfellow*, and the judgment has been familiar to probate lawyers for almost 150 years. Today, those involved with wills and probate work with its principles regularly. Although handed down in 1870, the appeal judgment in this case is still the leading judicial statement on the test for the mental capacity required for a person to make a valid will – any modern judgment in this area of law will cite this case and use Chief Justice Cockburn's definition of capacity (the mental capacity to make a will is better known to lawyers as testamentary capacity). Not only is Cockburn's test, as set out in *Banks v Goodfellow*, the cornerstone of the current law in this area in England and Wales, but it is also a fundamental part of the law in many other jurisdictions that derive their law from the English common law.

A Victorian Tragedy: The Extraordinary Case of Banks v Goodfellow

Although delivered almost 150 years ago, the judgment sets out sound criteria, in non-medical terms, that still give us an effective test. When looked at in this light, it is a case that deserves to be more widely understood than it actually has been.

Although I have been familiar with the legal principles of this judgment for much of my working life, it is only latterly that my curiosity (some might call it obsession) about the background to the case has grown. So often with famous legal cases the personal histories of the individuals are lost in the judge's findings as to the law. The fates of the winners and losers are usually of no more interest to history (and today the media) after the judgment – when the participants move out of the limelight to continue their lives off-stage. The legal arguments and principles alone live on in law reports and text books. This book is an attempt to explain how this important case came about, how it was resolved and what happened to the main characters involved – a sort of biography of a case rather than a biography of any single individual.

In plain terms, the case was to decide whether or not John Banks the elder's will was valid, or not. Was his mental illness so severe as to deprive him of the level of mental capacity necessary to make a will? On this decision depended which branch of his family would inherit his property. There were two trials of the validity of this will. The first trial was at the Cumberland Spring Assizes held in Carlisle in 1869. The second was by way of an appeal from the first judgment and this was heard in the Court of Queen's Bench in London in 1870. It was in the latter court that the judgment set out what we now know as the test in *Banks v Goodfellow*.

Frustratingly, because of the passage of time, some important aspects of family history are now simply beyond our reach – this is particularly the case with likenesses of the key individuals and family recollections of their lives and characters. However, enough information is available to make some sense of the relationships of the parties involved, why they fought the case and what happened to them afterwards.

It is not only the dispute that made me refer to this as a Victorian tragedy. Madness, fatal illness and early death accounted for most of the principals, but perjury, abandonment and financial ruin also provide a conclusion to the story. There really were no happy endings.

To tell this story properly requires that it be seen in the context of its own time. This is often a difficult task for later generations to understand. LP Hartley's much quoted words:

> The past is a foreign country: they do things differently there[1]

Introduction

have often been used to describe this issue, as they summarise it so well. The nineteenth century is a very foreign country to many twenty-first-century readers. A nineteenth-century story should therefore involve not merely understanding facts and events, but also something of their zeitgeist. Facts and events are easier to establish, but how contemporary society felt about them, and what the events reflected about contemporary society's attitudes, are harder to discover and understand, especially when considering everyday issues. To try to view past events with modern values and sensibilities can distort our understanding of the events or lead to our misunderstanding the impact of what occurred. The narration of this story therefore required some explanation of how the events fitted into, or reflected, life in nineteenth-century England. The lives of the individuals involved in this story bring together issues of the Victorian treatment of mental illness, the White Plague of tuberculosis, the horrors and risks of childbirth, emigration to the British colonies and social reform of the marriage laws – as well as one judge's laudable efforts to reform the law in relation to mental illness.

The reign of Queen Victoria was not a stultifying age of resistance to progress, although it is often represented in that way today – especially when 'Victorian' is wrongly used as shorthand for stuffy reactionary attitudes or obstinate opposition to change. The near 64 years of Victoria's reign constituted an era of huge change not only in Britain, but generally throughout the world. Victoria was born at the tail end of the Regency period and she died not far short of the First World War. Change during her reign was particularly marked as far as science, trade and industry were concerned. The advances in these areas in turn impacted directly on politics, employment and society's values, and the lives of all British people during that time. On the other hand, one cannot pretend that there was no resistance at all to change during this reign. A stout defence of the status quo in society was maintained by some of the more traditional sections of British life (is this not often the case?), but generally the resistance eventually failed. One example in this story of such resistance to change is the long battle fought by the established church over marriage to a deceased spouse's sibling – an issue which first arose two years before Victoria came to the throne and was not resolved until six years after her death. The established church's resistance involved resurrecting a scriptural debate that went back to the divorce of Henry VIII and Catherine of Aragon (his Queen, but also his deceased brother's widow). This legal problem of marriage to his deceased wife's sister was an important element in one character's life in this story.

Acknowledgements

Some of the subjects that this book touches on involve areas that are definitely outside my expertise or they involve issues where a second view was always appreciated. I am hugely grateful for the assistance of others that has been so generously given. My sincere thanks are therefore owed to:

- Title Research, in particular *Claire Langford*, for her work on the genealogy of the Banks and Goodfellow families;
- *Robin Jacoby*, emeritus professor of old age psychiatry at Oxford University, for his most informative attempt at a modern diagnosis of John Banks' illness. His willingness to share his knowledge freely (and answer endless questions from me) has been both generous and invaluable. This book would not be what it is without his support;
- old friends *Gill Brown* and *Wendy Sewell* for their help with nursing and other medical issues;
- *Tom Dumont* of Radcliffe Chambers, Lincoln's Inn for his perceptive review of the two chapters on the wills and trials;
- *Sidney Ross* of Ten Old Square, Lincoln's Inn for reading through the entire text (which cannot have been an easy task with my erratic typing);
- *Andrew Riddoch* and all at Wildy, Simmonds & Hill for bringing this project to fruition.

Despite all the help from the above, the responsibility for any errors must remain mine alone.

Martyn Frost
Carlton Le Moorland
February 2018

CHAPTER ONE

Who was John Banks the Elder?

Keswick in the 1860s was probably most well known to the general public through the works of William Wordsworth, Robert Southey and Samuel Taylor Coleridge, often collectively referred to simply as the Lake Poets. The first two named had both held the post of poet laureate. Their poetry was closely connected to the landscape in which they lived. Wordsworth is most associated with Grasmere, and Southey and Coleridge are more associated with Keswick. The popularity of their poetry and its romantic view of the scenery of the Lake District prompted the moneyed classes to travel there to see this unique part of England – Victoria and Albert might have popularised the Highlands, but the Lake District was more accessible to the nascent tourist industry.

Thomas Cook started in the travel business with trips for temperance campaigners in 1841. He claimed to have arranged trips to the Great Exhibition of 1851 for over 165,000 visitors. In doing so he was exploiting Britain's new railway network and he continued to do so by organising tourist travel. He pioneered the idea of the packaged holiday within this country, and thereby assisted the early growth of tourism. Alongside this appeared tourist guide books to help the traveller seek out the scenery and views of the remoter parts of Britain. *Sylvan's Pictorial Handbook to the English Lakes* was published in 1847. As tourist numbers grew, there was a need for an infrastructure to support the tourism – new hotels, lake cruises, guided tours etc. Jacob Banks the elder,[1] the father of John Banks the younger,[2] prospered in Keswick, as a business man, during the time of the Lake Poets and the beginning of the Lakes tourist trade.

Jacob Banks the elder was more concerned with commerce than poetry – he was a black-lead pencil manufacturer in Keswick. Success in this business had made Jacob a man of some local importance, as, at the time of his son

John's birth, Keswick was not only the centre of pencil manufacturing in England but, in that early part of the nineteenth century, England still enjoyed a global monopoly in black-lead pencil manufacture. Black lead, now known more correctly as graphite, had been first mined in this area of the Lake District in the sixteenth century. Production initially was at the Grey Knotts mine in Borrowdale, just outside Keswick. When first mined, the only known use for graphite was for marking sheep. Originally called plumbago, graphite was believed to be a type of black lead rather than, as was later realised, a form of carbon. Other uses were soon developed and by the late eighteenth century it was mainly being used for lead-pencil making. By the start of the nineteenth century the pencil industry was well established in Keswick and it had become the key manufacturing industry in the area. The mistaken belief that plumbago was lead gave rise to the name 'lead pencil' and this, once established, remained the usual, but incorrect term. The 1811 edition of *Jollie's Guide* lists three pencil manufacturers for Crosthwaite, of which Jacob Banks the elder was one.[3] Crosthwaite, at that time, was the village at the heart of the extensive parish of the same name that contained Keswick, but today, known as Great Crosthwaite, it is a suburb of Keswick.

The early manufacture of pencils was fundamentally a cottage industry. From around 1830, when the English global monopoly was disappearing, the industry had to change to meet the challenge of foreign competition. One of the significant changes to try to keep the Keswick industry competitive was a move towards factory-based manufacturing during the remainder of the nineteenth century. The first of the pencil factories was that of Banks, Son & Co (which later became the Cumberland Pencil Company), but this was not the business of the Banks family that is the subject of this book. The move to factory manufacture created economies of scale, but reduced employment in the industry. Despite the challenge of foreign competition, and the necessity to start importing graphite, in 1866 the *Cumberland Pacquet* of 4th September reported that Keswick production was 250,000 pencils per week, or 13,000,000 per annum.

At the time of Jacob Banks the elder, 'pencil manufacturers' were the businessmen of the industry; they were the organisers of and financiers for the production, marketing, sales and distribution. Those known as 'pencil makers' were the craftsmen of the industry who actually made the pencils on their own small premises, usually part of their homes, on contract from manufacturers such as Jacob Banks. Pencil makers would have employed a small amount of additional labour, but theirs was still a small-scale craft industry.

Who was John Banks the Elder?

The families of the pencil manufacturers seem to have been very aware of the standing that their position in this industry gave them in local society. Jacob's daughter Margaret's marriage announcement in 1847 in the local press refers to her as 'only daughter of the late Jacob Banks, pencil manufacturer, of Keswick'.[4] The death notice for his son, John Banks the elder, in the local press in 1865, also refers, some thirty-five years after Jacob's death, to Jacob as having been a pencil manufacturer. In a similar vein, the headstone on the grave of John Banks the elder's nephew (John Banks the younger) in Crosthwaite Parish Church churchyard records that he too was the son of a pencil manufacturer (Jacob Banks the younger), fifty years after his father died. It was obviously a matter of family pride to have been part of a family that played an important role in Keswick's main industry in the early part of the century.

Jacob Banks the elder was first married to Martha Hurstfield by whom he had one son, Jacob the younger. After Martha's death, Jacob the elder married his second wife, Margaret Newby, in Kendal on 29th May 1810. The *Lancaster Gazette* carried a notice on 2nd June 1810:

> Lately, Mr Jacob Banks, black-lead pencil manufacturer, Keswick to Miss Margaret Newby, daughter of Mr Daniel Newby, of Kendal.

There were two children from this marriage, John Banks the elder and Margaret Banks the younger (later to become Margaret Goodfellow). John was baptised at Crosthwaite Parish Church, Keswick on 6th July 1812 and Margaret on 19th September 1815. John was baptised less than two weeks after Napoleon's Grande Armée had launched its invasion of Russia with the bloody slaughter of Borodino, the burning of Moscow and the horrors of the disintegration of this army in the Winter Retreat soon to come before John reached his first birthday. Margaret was baptised slightly less than three months after the Anglo-Prussian victory at the Battle of Waterloo, the exile of Napoleon and the return of the Bourbons to the throne of France. They were both born during turbulent times for Europe.

Jacob Banks the elder died in December 1829. In his will, made in 1824, he described himself as 'Gentleman (late pencil manufacturer)'. His will opened with the words 'in the name of God Amen'. A not unusual commencement in a will at this time, but certainly this would be less conventional in a will today. The will appointed his widow Margaret and his son John to be Jacob's executors and trustees.

Jacob's will provides some confirmation that he left only three children, as he made provision for only his widow, Jacob the younger, John and

Margaret. If there had been any other surviving issue, one would have expected mention of them. Two further sources point in the same direction: first, Margaret's marriage announcement also describes her as an only daughter and, secondly, the appeal judgment in the trial of John Banks the elder's will clearly refers to Jacob the younger as being John's only brother – albeit his half-brother.

There were no bequests in Jacob Banks the elder's will of any business interests, apparently confirming Jacob's description of himself in his will as being a former pencil manufacturer. However, there is a clue from the terms of this will as to what probably happened to his pencil business when he retired. His will made only relatively minor provision for the child of his first marriage, Jacob the younger. It would be unusual for a man of Jacob the elder's standing to make only minor provision for his eldest child – particularly so when the eldest child was a son. Jacob the younger is also known to have been a pencil manufacturer in his own right around the time of his father's death. It seems to be a reasonable assumption that Jacob the younger took over, or more likely was given, his father's pencil business when his father retired. It was Jacob the younger's son, John Banks the younger, who was to be the claimant (then called the plaintiff) who initiated the legal dispute over John Banks the elder's will. (There is more on Jacob the younger's family in Chapter Six.)

In tracing the history of pencil manufacture in Keswick, a degree of confusion can arise, not only because of the two Jacob Banks but also because there was a second family called Banks involved in the industry. The second family was that of William Banks whose son Joseph (born 1807) became involved in the industry during the 1830s. Under Joseph and then his widow, Ann, this business prospered, while Jacob Banks the younger's business certainly did not prosper as he was declared bankrupt c1835. Thereafter there appears to be no connection between Jacob the elder's descendants and pencil manufacturing. Given the pressures on Kendal pencil manufacturing after its monopoly ended, perhaps Jacob the younger was not able to adapt his business approach to the new commercial reality.

The witnesses to Jacob the elder's will were Michael Ashton and John Birkett; the former was once a Liverpool merchant and the latter described himself simply as a manufacturer. Admittedly, this will was made well after the time when one's standing in life was enhanced by the importance of the witnesses to one's will (and also when the standing of the witnesses could be similarly enhanced if the testator was important), but two locally important figures being used, rather than, as today, the draftsman of the will and a member of his staff, does tend to highlight that Jacob was still of some consequence and connection in local society.

Under the terms of Jacob the elder's will, his wife Margaret received a life interest in his estate. This meant that she would be entitled to receive all the income from his estate during the remainder of her lifetime, but she would not have had access to the capital. The capital would have been held in trust until her death and managed during this period by herself and her son John, the trustees appointed in the will. After Margaret his widow's death, the capital was to be distributed to his two children, John Banks the elder and Margaret Banks the younger.

On his widow Margaret's death, the will directed that the personal estate (that is to say, the non-land assets) was to be divided equally between his daughter, Margaret and his son, John, after payment of a legacy of £200 to Jacob Banks the younger. The will then made further detailed provision as to how Jacob the elder's land was to be divided between John and Margaret by specific gifts of designated properties. The listed properties appear to be numerous shops, houses and workshops in Keswick. John Banks the elder's share of the properties is later described during the litigation over the will as being 'some cottage property' in Keswick, but despite this slightly disparaging description, in Keswick terms it was more significant and they were not merely cottages.[5]

In view of John Banks the elder's mental health (discussed in detail in Chapter Two) it is also significant that his father appointed him to be one of the executors and trustees of his will. John and his mother, Margaret, would have been supported in their trusteeship by the advice and guidance of a local solicitor, but notwithstanding this legal advice, the appointment of John does point to his father having some faith in his son's mental abilities. It was also a public gesture of that faith in John's abilities as the contents of the will would have been known to the public once it was admitted to probate, as at that point the will is a publicly accessible document. Curiously, John was only twelve when this will was drawn up and just eighteen when his father died. Given the uncertainty of life in early nineteenth-century England it was expecting quite a lot for Jacob to live long enough for John to attain the age of twenty-one before he died. As it was, John did not reach twenty-one until approximately three years after his father's death, when he would then have been able to take up his role as trustee.

Margaret, Jacob's widow, died on 29th January 1848 in Keswick and was buried in Crosthwaite churchyard. She was sixty-nine years old and her death was registered by her son-in-law Thomas Goodfellow as a person who was present at her death. It is assumed that John would still have been living with his mother at this time, and therefore also present at her death, but that Thomas was thought more suitable to arrange the registration.

From this it can be seen that John Banks the elder was born into a middle-class provincial family of some local distinction and modest wealth in Keswick. The family money should have given him the chance of an advantageous marriage within his class and the chance to make his own way with this financial advantage in life. That he did not do so was down to being cursed by an illness that nineteenth-century medicine was powerless to understand properly or treat effectively – madness.

CHAPTER TWO

John Banks the Elder: His Life, Illness and Death

From the evidence given at the first trial of his will, at Cumberland Assizes in 1869, it is clear that John Banks the elder's life was always lived under the shadow of his mental illness. This mental illness was not related to, or made worse by, alcohol abuse, as such evidence as is available points to him having been teetotal throughout his life. The evidence of Mary Usher at the first trial of his will was that he was 'a sober man and did not take intoxicating drinks'. There is no evidence that he had any additional physical handicap, or at least not one that restricted his mobility, until towards the end of his life with the apparent onset of epilepsy and a probable stroke.

There are reports of him, when an adult, walking in the Lake District and around the various lodgings he rented. Walking would have been the primary means of getting about in his life – there is no reference to him owning a horse or riding one. His nephew, John Banks the younger, recounted that in 1860 or 1861, when his uncle was nearly fifty, they walked up Skiddaw together – not a walk for the infirm as it is the sixth highest peak in England, at 931m. The return trip to Skiddaw summit from Keswick is approximately ten miles, rising over 2,700ft, but possibly a slightly shorter distance if they started and finished on the Bassenthwaite side. It is worth noting that John died aged fifty-three; an age that was comfortably in excess of what was then average life expectancy for a man, even for one born in the year that he died, and this argues for a man in generally good physical condition for most of his life.

John's Childhood

During the trial at Cumberland Assizes, evidence was given by Joseph Usher of Harryman Field, Keswick (in whose house John Banks lodged in 1851–52) that John Banks had been 'simple' as a child. This word does not tell us much, if anything, about his mental health, but it does indicate that he was regarded by others as being different from other children. The word was used then, and for some time afterwards, to indicate that a person had sub-normal intelligence or was slow to learn. It may have been that in John's case, because of his incipient mental illness, he was less engaged with his surroundings than other children and that he generally related less well to others around him. If this was the case he would have been different in his behaviour from other children, rather than necessarily having an impaired intellect.

That John was regarded as being different from other children seems a reasonable assumption today. His mental illness as an adult tends to suggest that he might well have had, in modern terms, a schizoid personality in his childhood. This would have been before his probable psychosis developed when he was a teenager or a young adult[1] (see towards the end of this chapter for more detail on a modern view of his mental illness as an adult). Such a view is speculative at this distance in time, but a schizoid personality in childhood could have resulted in solitariness, secrecy, emotional coldness towards others, apparent apathy or lack of interest (or ability) in forming normal social relationships. A schizoid personality can be associated with a lack of social skills and a lack of desire for sexual experience. Thus, as an adolescent or young adult, there would often be few friendships, little or no sexual experience and little inclination to marry. This also fits in with what we know about John's adult life. A schizoid personality would have set John apart from other children and adolescents in terms of behaviour and this could well have been interpreted by others, particularly those who did not know better, as showing that John lacked intelligence. It would certainly mean that John would be perceived as not being like 'normal' children, and the label 'simple' is then easily, but erroneously and cruelly, applied.

John was capable of learning, as we know that he became literate, numerate and had, at least to some degree, an enquiring mind.[2] Not only did he learn to write, but one witness even drew attention to the neatness of his handwriting – something that was valued in the nineteenth century and which schoolmasters would spend time teaching. At the first trial of the will, two documents were produced, annexed to an affidavit, that were in the handwriting of John Banks.[3] Joseph Tolson, who produced them, added that at the time of John's death there were:

many other letters and papers ... which were in [his] handwriting and would have afforded strong evidence of his sanity, but as I saw no reason to suppose that any attempt would be made to question his sanity or the validity of his will I had no reasons for keeping them and I have mislaid or destroyed [them].

These papers could have helped the court considerably.

John also had enough basic arithmetic to enable him to keep his own cash accounts as an adult, and these included accounts of income and expenditure relating to his properties in Keswick after he inherited them from his father. John was sufficiently widely read to be able to conduct a rational conversation about Martin Luther and the Reformation with a local schoolmaster. At the first trial of the will, evidence on this was given by Mr Edward Highton, a schoolmaster at Brigham School in Keswick[4] who knew John well (although there is no evidence that he ever taught him). Mr Highton related that, in 1864 (the year following the making of the disputed will and the year preceding John's death), he met John in Joseph Tolson's grocery shop in Keswick. John noticed that Mr Highton was carrying a book entitled *Luther and his Times* and they then had a rational conversation about the subject of the book. This left the schoolmaster with the firm impression that John understood the subject of the book. This would indicate some reading, or education, on the subject of the Reformation and that he had the intellectual curiosity to understand it. John is also reported to have some knowledge of Latin, as William Thirlwall said, in giving evidence in the will dispute, 'sometimes I could get a little sensible conversation from [him] particularly about Latin'.

It is not known if John's education came from attending school or from private tuition. We can only guess how it was acquired, but quite probably it was the latter given his father's means and the extra assistance that John might well have required. If John was regarded as simple by other children, then education privately, away from ridicule and bullying by other children, would have made sense to his parents. There is no other information about John as a child apart from the, unfortunate, single word 'simple'.

A reporter, when reporting on the first trial for *The Times* of 20th February 1869, summarised the evidence given as to John's character, writing that:

> It appeared that the testator was peculiar in his habits, of a shy and reserved temperament, a book worm, and a very well-informed and learned person on some subjects; but had indifferent health and suffered from indigestion, ...

This is at some variance with the later appeal judgment, which contained the remark, based on the affidavits of the witnesses at the first trial, that:

> ... we must take it, for the present purposes, as a fact, that the testator, though generally of weak intellect, was able to manage his affairs.

A weak intellect, although it sounds less positive than *The Times*' view of 'well-informed and learned', does not of itself indicate any bar to having sufficient understanding to make a will.

John as an Adult

There are no medical records for John Banks that survive (or at least that can now be traced) and thus it is not known when John's mental health significantly worsened with the onset of his psychosis. The significant parts of his condition that we know of were delusions of persecution, and his hallucinations that made his persecutors visible to him. This worsening of his mental state occurred, in all probability, in his late teens or early twenties. One witness, William Robinson, gave evidence that he knew John Banks well and that he was 'always peculiar' but that the first time he saw him 'outrageous' was an incident in the Methodist Church that caused John's committal to Dunston Asylum early in 1841, when John was twenty-nine. The evidence is rather slender, but it is conceivable that this was around the start of his psychosis.

John appears to have always lived with his parents, and after his father's death he continued to live with his mother until her death in January 1848. His sister Margaret also lived with them until her marriage in March 1846. There is a reference to a John Banks living in Keswick in the 1841 census, and it must be that this is John Banks the elder of this history. This census entry shows a widow, Margaret Banks, and two adult children, John and Margaret Banks, living at the same address – all the correct names for this family. The apparent slight problem with this census entry is that the two children are both shown as then being aged twenty-five – thereby implying that they were twins born in 1816. This entry for their ages is incorrect as John was then twenty-nine and Margaret twenty-six. It appears that the census taker will have rounded both ages downwards to the nearest five years – this was the then official instruction to the census takers, although it was not followed in all cases.[5] In all other respects the census entry is correct. Their residence in the census entry is recorded as Showley Crow in Keswick. Showley Crow is probably a property that still exists and is today known as

Shorley Croft. It is on the Penrith Road in Keswick[6] (see more on the inheritance of property later, in Chapter Four).

Ann Hindmoor also gave evidence at the trial. She said that when her daughter was a servant for Mrs Banks, John was often violent 'and bad to manage' and that he would dance and shout about for most of the day before rushing into town and back 'as if someone was after him'. She stated that his disturbed behaviour was such that 'one would think he would almost have killed himself sometimes'. His disturbed behaviour was in the form of agitation, shouting, smashing objects and occasionally actual violence towards his own person (usually reported as banging his head against furniture). There is no record of any attempted suicide nor of harm, or threatened harm, to others.

There is no mention of John Banks ever being employed, but this is not surprising given what we now know about his mental health. At the first trial one witness referred to John as having spent some time 'working' in his mother's draper's shop in Keswick shortly before he was confined in Dunston Asylum (he was twenty-nine when he went to Dunston in 1841). After John's return from Dunston the business was given up. Ann Robinson, a tenant of Jacob Banks the elder, and later of John Banks, gave evidence at the first trial that John 'was always very peculiar and when in the shop would scarcely speak or do anything'. This appears to indicate more that his mother had John with her in her shop in order to keep an eye on him, rather than that John worked there, or participated in any meaningful way in running the business.

Shortly before John's short spell in Dunston Asylum, and again for a time after his release, John's mother engaged watchers 'to go about with him and take care of him'.[7] A man called Cartmel is known to have watched over John before he went to Dunston. After his release one of the watchers was a man called McBridee, but he is said to have become frightened of John and gave the job up.[8] There is no implication from the evidence at trial that John was ever a danger to others. Instead, the evidence points much more towards the watchers being there to prevent him being a danger to himself. There is also another possibility to consider and that is that the watchers were also intended to protect him from others who might abuse him, make fun of him or try to take advantage of him because of his illness. There is also some indication, which is considered later, in Chapter Eight, that John could be susceptible to persuasion over matters of money and that some in Keswick might have taken advantage of him.

John was a patient at Dunstan Asylum between 19th January and 6th April 1841. This was presumably a voluntary committal, arranged by his family, perhaps on medical advice and out of concern for his welfare. Even so, a voluntary committal of an adult to an asylum then required an independent assessment by two doctors who were required by statute[9] to sign the appropriate medical certificate. The appeal judgment makes no reference to this having been a compulsory committal, i.e. one ordered by a court, and this confirms, at least to a degree, that it would have been at John's family's instigation. The two local doctors who certified John for confinement in an asylum were John Stoddart and John Scott, both practising surgeons in Keswick at that time.[10] Both were dead by the time of the will dispute and therefore no evidence from them was available at trial concerning John's illness in 1841.

Despite their decision to have John committed to an asylum, his mother and sister clearly retained a degree of trust in John's abilities when he was not in a disturbed state. Comment was made in Chapter One about John's father's will and his appointment as an executor and trustee. In addition, his sister's marriage and his brother-in-law's will, both dealt with in Chapter Four, have a bearing on their trust in him.

The incident that brought on the decision to have John committed to Dunstan Asylum occurred one Sunday in late 1840 or early 1841 at the Methodist Chapel in Keswick. William Robinson, a miner, and member of the Congregation, gave evidence that John's mother and sister were members of that Congregation. He relates that John:

> … broke out and shouted and knocked about and frightened all the congregation.[11]

The words 'knocked about' should not suggest that he assaulted any of the congregation, but that, as with his behaviour later in life, he was prone to kicking over furniture, throwing objects to the floor and deliberately banging his head against walls or furniture. He later said of banging his head that 'it was the devil in his head that was striking it not he'. Interestingly, evidence from Shepley Watson Watson, clerk curate of Plumbland parish, was that towards the end of John's life 'he was unable to receive religious comfort or consolation', yet, around the same time, we also know that he was able to have a rational discussion with an acquaintance about Martin Luther and the Reformation. Clearly John was able to consider religious issues, but was it the church or chapel that brought on his delusion – or could it have been the language of prayer and the service that had that effect?

In 1841, when John was confined, there was not yet a county lunatic asylum for Cumberland. The later Cumberland and Westmoreland Asylum, near Carlisle (also known as Garlands Hospital) was not opened until 1862. Dunston Lodge, Whickham, in County Durham[12] was opened c 1830[13] and, as already mentioned, was a purpose-built lunatic asylum – as opposed to the more usual conversion of existing premises that were not necessarily suitable for the function (and this was too often the case). Despite being in a different county, Dunston Lodge seems to have regularly taken patients from Cumberland. Later, around 1846, a formal contract for this was put in place between the Cumberland and Westmorland Magistrates and the asylum. This agreement was to cover commitment to an asylum by process of law by the Cumberland courts.

The Treatment of the Mentally Ill in Mid-nineteenth-century England

The term 'psychiatry' had been coined in 1808 by the German physician JC Reil. The word was derived from the Greek words for the medical treatment of the soul. This word did not appear in the evidence in the trial of John Banks' will, nor in the Queen's Bench judgment. The forerunner in England of Royal College of Psychiatrists was founded in 1841. The science of psychiatry was not then far advanced, particularly in the area of treatment of disorders. But some first steps had been taken in the law concerning lunacy and control of asylums.

The general issue of the treatment of pauper mental patients in England was the subject of the 1844 Report of the Metropolitan Commissioners in Lunacy ('The Metropolitan Report'). It described the county of Durham as then being one of the centres in England 'of the trade in lunacy'.[14] Durham, as a county, had sufficient facilities to take into care patients from other counties that had insufficient provision – such as Cumberland. The Metropolitan Report was mainly concerned with the question of care of pauper lunatics and the control of asylums. The Report was quite clear and damning in some of its conclusions about the treatment of paupers. Some of these findings help us to understand how mental illness was approached at that time.

A number of asylums, including two in Durham, were found in the Metropolitan Report to 'deserve almost unqualified censure'.[15] Dunston Asylum, on the other hand, was commended in the Report as being among the best conducted of the asylums that took in pauper patients. The patients' diet at Dunston was noted as being good. This may seem an odd remark in the twenty-first century, but almost by definition paupers would generally have had a more meagre diet than those in work. Therefore, providing a pauper lunatic with a better diet when in the asylum would help to develop better physical well-being and remove the anxiety and ill health produced by semi-starvation. Dunston was further commended because it had a farm, on which some patients worked (and which contributed to the better food available in the asylum). Constructive work was also thought to be beneficial to patients, not only in terms of physical well-being, but also because it occupied the mind and hands. The 1846 Report by the Cumberland Commissioners in Lunacy[16] ('The Cumberland Report') on Dunston Asylum draws attention to the use of employment to beneficial effect for the patients. As well as the farm, patients such as joiners, shoemakers and a tailor had worked there. The patients were also employed in general cleaning, bed-making, laundry and washhouse work and cooking, as well as gardening. The Cumberland Report notes than no patients were injured by the tools or sharp instruments that might have been used.

The Metropolitan Report sheds light on the general treatment of patients in asylums at that time. The Commissioners considered that patients were treated better (and were more likely to be cured or capable of safe release) when they were housed in adequately constructed buildings and where the institution was adequately resourced in terms of food and trained staff. These are matters that might appear to be self-evident now, but were clearly worthy of note in the nineteenth century. The Commissioners' comments drew attention to the fact that many other asylums kept patients inadequately housed and fed. Given that today we would consider the nature of Victorian housing generally to be well below today's standard, the accommodation offered by the worst asylums would have been barely fit for human habitation (and certainly would have been unfit by today's standards). The Commissioners also found there to be a correlation between inadequate asylum resources and the use of physical restraints for the patients. In addition to the criticism of unsuitable accommodation and excessive restraint there were general criticisms in the Report of the lack of occupational work and training, poor diet, inadequate clothing and the absence of amusement and exercise. The Cumberland Report shows that Dunston offered better than average accommodation that was suitable for purpose, as well as constructive work.

The Metropolitan Report contrasts the conditions of various asylums in the 1840s and in doing so highlights the qualities of Dunston Lodge. The Commissioners' Report complained that:

> The asylums in which the lunatic poor are received, have however been the subject of our most especial enquiries. These places (even such of them as are upon the most extended scale) are, we regret to say, filled with incurable patients, and are thus rendered incapable of receiving those whose malady might still admit of cure. It has been the practice, in numerous instances, to detain the insane pauper at the workhouse or elsewhere, until he becomes dangerous or unmanageable; and then when his disease is beyond all medical relief, to send him to a lunatic asylum where he may remain during the rest of his life, a pensioner on the public.[17]

And:

> For years past, we have endeavoured, within the metropolitan district, to diminish this evil practice; but it still prevails; and we doubt whether it will be altogether suppressed, unless some plan be adopted and enforced, for removing, from time to time, each Lunatic as he becomes incurable from the asylum to which he has been sent, and supplying his place by another whose case, from the recent nature of the attack, may still admit of cure; and unless, also, there be a strict and frequent supervision, not only of asylums, but of all workhouses, and other places in which the lunatic poor are detained.[18]

It should be noted that a workhouse was a local (often parish-based) institution to house the poor and destitute. Conditions were deliberately harsh to deter those capable of working from remaining there any longer than necessary (and thereby ensuring that they ceased to be a financial burden on the parish any longer). As the nineteenth century went on, workhouses increasingly provided shelter mainly for the sick and elderly. Charles Dickens' *Oliver Twist* is a novel of the 1830s, but its depiction of a workhouse resonated with the public throughout the century and fuelled the public horror of ending their days in such a place. Workhouses were abolished by the Local Government Act 1929. The author can recall his great-aunt, who was born at the end of the nineteenth century, still expressing a fear of such institutions late in her life.

According to the Metropolitan Report, 'the professed and indeed the main object of a county asylum is, or ought to be, the cure of insanity'.[19] Despite this, there was evidence of conditions in many asylums that were not conducive of any cure at all. Two asylums in County Durham were the subject of very direct criticism:

- At West Auckland Asylum on 5th December 1842 there were thirteen male and sixteen female pauper patients, but:

    each sex had only one small sitting room, with windows that did not admit of any prospect from them, and the violent and quiet, and the dirty and clean were shut up together. There was only one small walled yard, and when the one sex was in it, the other was locked up.[20]

- At Wreckenton Asylum, Gateshead, on 2nd December 1842 the day rooms (three for each sex) were 'confined and gloomy'.

In addition, both of these institutions were criticised for an 'excessive and highly censurable degree of restraint':[21]

- At West Auckland the Commissioners noted that:

    In the small, cheerless day-room of the males, with only one unglazed window, five men were restrained, by leg-locks, called hobbles, and two were wearing, in addition, iron-handcuffs and fetters from the wrist to the ankle: they were all tranquil. The reason assigned for this coercion was, that without it they would escape.[22]

- While at Wreckenton:

    it was the practice to chain patients by the leg, upon their first admission, in order to see what they would do.[23]

This comment seems quite inhuman – what would have been an acceptable reaction of a patient to being placed in irons?

While restraint chains clearly were used routinely in some areas of England at this time, this practice ignored advances in patient treatment on the Continent. In France, it was almost fifty years earlier that chains had been banned in two major French hospitals. Jean-Baptiste Pussin[24] was appointed superintendent of the mental ward at the Bicêtre hospital[25] in Paris in 1784. Assisted by his wife Marguerite, he developed a more humane regime for mental patients that was non-violent and non-medical. This approach led to the use of chains, as restraints, being banned in 1797. Philippe Pinel,[26] who had worked alongside Pussin for a short time, built on this approach. After his appointment to the Salpêtrière hospital, also in Paris, Pinel invited Pussin to work with him and chains were also banished there as a result. Pinel is widely credited with being the sole reformer in this area, but Pinel always gave Pussin the credit for his part in this reform. The approach that these two reformers used has been referred to as moral treatment. It involved observation, conversation and the creation of a detailed record of a patient's disease and behaviour, while at the same time eschewing forms of treatment that had an element of punishment such as fetters. Both reformers argued that this approach was more in sympathy with a patient's needs and allowed those treating the patient to have a greater understanding of each individual's psychiatric disorder. In England, Willian Tuke in York also pioneered the moral treatment approach. Lincoln Asylum led the way in banishing restraints by 1838 and this practice was then introduced in Hanwell Asylum, which was then the largest asylum in England.

The approach used at Dunston tried to follow these ideas. Although the Cumberland Report admits that restraints were still used at Dunston on occasion, it makes it clear that these occasions were exceptional. The Cumberland Report writes of a pauper lunatic being brought to Dunston in November 1845 'his arms and legs fettered', the irons connected to 'a massive chain'. His knee-joints were so contracted he could neither stand nor walk – 'his mental powers were entirely destroyed'. His two sisters had kept him in this way in an outhouse with his chain stapled to the floor. He remained semi-naked with no bed and forced to crouch constantly for twelve years before what his sisters had done was discovered and the magistrates ordered him to be taken to Dunston. Dunston removed the irons and tried surgery to return movement to his legs. In a footnote to this section of the report there is a sharp rant against the criminal law:

> We read of the miserable outcast whose want drives to the commission of theft, sentenced to years of banishment and toil; we see the law legalizing at Cambridge the murder of her whose first fault was 'that she loved too well', her second that poverty and her fall left her only street-walking to supply her daily food; must we add as our third illustration of England's laws, that two fiends, in woman's form, guilty of atrocities such as the above detailed, remain unpunished?

The Report's authors obviously felt deeply about this patient's inhuman treatment.

Pinel also dispensed with the general use of bleeding, blisters and setons as treatments for the insane. The Metropolitan Report noted that at West Auckland Asylum the medical attendant considered that:

bleedings, blisters, and setons were the *principal resources of medicine* for relieving maniacal excitement.[27] (author's added emphasis)

These are treatments that have long since banished from psychiatric treatment.

Bleeding a person has an ancient medical history. It was based on the idea of draining the body of bad blood and with it the ill humours[28] that caused the illness in the body. It is recorded as being used in Egypt about 1000 BC and in due course the practice was taken up by the Greeks and the Romans. Bloodletting was usually carried out in the nineteenth century by deliberately opening a vein to draw off the patient's blood, although leeches were still used by some practitioners to the same effect.[29] The letting of blood would often lead to the patient fainting from the rapid blood loss – this was regarded by physicians as a positive sign.

Blisters were applications of a caustic substance to the skin, often using mustard compounds, in order to irritate and burn the skin causing it to blister. It was thought that the subsequent discharge of fluid from the site of the blistering would be beneficial to a patient's health by relieving his symptoms and drawing from him the source of his illness. It seems from this type of treatment that knowledge had not progressed from the Tudor belief that eating whole a roast mouse would cure madness.

Setons were fabric strips inserted under the skin of a patient and left there with the ends protruding in order to drain fluid from the site of the insertion (again to draw from the patient the source of his illness). A seton was also thought to act as a counter-irritant to the pain or irritation of the original illness which would distract the patient from the pain of the main illness by creating further pain around the seton.

The modern view would be that all three of the above treatments are not only very unlikely to be of any benefit at all to a psychiatric patient, but they could have been positively harmful to a patient by introducing further infection into his system, through the wounds, or by lowering his resistance to any existing physical disease. For example, in late 1799, George Washington's throat infection caused him difficulty in both swallowing and breathing. The bloodletting to cure his condition almost certainly hastened his death – if it did not actually cause it. It is estimated that the doctors involved drew off half of his blood in just a few hours.[30]

While all three of the above practices were not approved in the Metropolitan Report, twenty years on from the Report, in the later stages of John Banks' life, his local doctor still treated him with mustard blisters, applied to his head, in an attempt to relieve his pain from epileptic fits.

Needless to say, this treatment could not cure the epilepsy which was shown as a cause of his death in 1865 (see later in this chapter on the causes of his death).

The Cumberland Report is a little more equivocal on these three (and other similar) treatments. It describes the use of opiates 'in very large doses' to address sleeplessness (warm baths and cold shower baths were also thought to work). Emetics at bedtime could be another treatment. (An emetic is a medicine intended solely to produce vomiting and today it is regarded as patently of no material benefit in the treatment of mental illness.) For the 'paroxysms of acute mania' 'local' bloodletting could help, as could 'very large doses of antimonials'. Antimonials were pills made from metallic antimony. The pill was used to purge the bowels. The pill passed through the system and could then be recovered and re-used many times – earning it the nickname of the everlasting pill. The *Medico-Pharmaceutical Critic and Guide* of 1907 cites a Dr Paris as writing that this pill 'was economy in right earnest, for a single pill would serve a whole family during their lives and might be transmitted as an heirloom to posterity' (in the author's long career of administering estates he was pleased not to have encountered such a family heirloom). The Cumberland Report also writes of 'nervous irritability and excitement', yielding to the use of stimulants such as brandy or ether. 'Melancholy forebodings of unknown danger' had been on one occasion dispelled by an emetic and 'brisk' cathartic. The Report also claims success for the sole occasion that year that a seton was used as a counter-irritant.

The Cumberland Report touches on the use of cold showers, but they were not always what they might seem to the modern reader. On 17th June 1856, *The Times* carried a report of a hearing in Bow Street Magistrates' Court. The Metropolitan Commissioners in Lunacy had brought proceedings against Charles Snape, the resident surgeon at the Surrey County Lunatic Asylum, for the unlawful killing of Daniel Dolley, a 65-year-old patient there. Dolley, who was described as 'an excitable patient', was ordered by Snape to be given a cold shower bath followed by an emetic. Dolley had been given such a shower the week previously and therefore he knew what to expect. In the light no doubt of this previous experience, he objected to the treatment and punched Snape on the head. The surgeon then ordered his assistants to strip Dolley and put him in the shower bath. The shower bath was an upright box, with drainage at the bottom, in which the standing patient was confined with no light. Over 600 gallons of cold water were poured through a hole in the top of the box, and thus over him, during the next twenty-eight minutes of his confinement. Fifteen minutes after being released from the box, Dolley died. Mr Snape wanted the cause of death to be certified as heart disease, but the surgeon who carried out the autopsy disagreed. In defence of Snape it was said that cold showers were a common practice in asylums for excited or agitated mental patients. Snape's evidence was that he had often used this treatment and opined that it was of great advantage to patients. A grand jury at the Central Criminal Court refused to indict him on the charge of unlawful killing. In an editorial on 18th September 1856, *The Times* acknowledged that 'shower-baths and emetics when used in moderation are of advantage in the treatment of mad persons'. However, it also called for moderation in their use.[31] Cold showers seem to have been no more than a brutal physical sedative, and in Dolley's case a lethal one. In 1848 the Lunacy Commissioners had been denied access to Bethlem Hospital, London. When it was discovered that routinely female patients slept naked in straw and were washed by being hosed down with cold water, the governors of the hospital maintained that this was common practice in England.

From all of the above it is clear that John Banks was fortunate that his only spell in an asylum was at Dunston Lodge. It was, as the Metropolitan and Cumberland Reports made clear, definitely operating in a more beneficial way than many contemporary institutions. The fiftieth annual report of the Friends' Retreat, York[32] (1846) noted that 'The name of Dunston, indeed, is not unworthy of notice in the history of early efforts to improve the condition of the insane' – public acknowledgement of the worthy and progressive steps taken at Dunston. Perhaps knowledge, on the part of those close to John, led them to choose Dunston because of its reputation, but thereafter to encourage local care rather than confinement in any other asylum.

It might be tempting to assume that private institutions run for upper- and middle-class families at this time would have presented a more humane picture than those asylums for paupers or working-class patients. That would be a false assumption. The treatment could be better, but equally it could be as cruel. The ability to abuse the certification of individuals, often for financial gain, or simply to hide an embarrassing or eccentric family member in an asylum, were long-running issues in the nineteenth century. Some patients who were certified for admission to asylums were not insane, merely inconvenient to spouses or family.[33] The medical practitioners who treated them, like the rest of the profession, at that time understood little about the true nature of mental illness.

While John was at Dunston he would have been under the care of John Etridge Wilkinson,[34] who ran the Lodge from its opening until 1852. In 1841 there were eighty-four residents at Dunston Lodge. By 1844 there were seventy-seven pauper patients and twenty-three private patients. A weekly charge was made for paupers of 8/- and this included clothing.[35] John would not have been a pauper patient when he was there, given the financial resources available to his mother. Therefore, as a private patient he would have been maintained in a little more comfort.

Despite the reputation of Dunston in the 1840s, there was a setback later in 1851 when John Etridge Wilkinson the proprietor was found guilty 'of the most flagrant cruelty' by the visiting magistrates of Cumberland and Westmoreland. The matter was then referred to the Lunacy Commission and the renewal of his licence was denied.[36] This all came about after a male patient had bitten Wilkinson's arm. Wilkinson then punished him by flogging, isolation and the removal of his upper two incisors.[37] A few years after a change of management, the local press carried[38] a report of an inspection of Dunston by representatives of Carlisle Council on 28th December 1857:

> … we today visited the Asylum at Dunston, and are glad to be able to state that we found the establishment in a most satisfactory condition as to cleanliness and order and altogether most creditable to Mr Garbutt. Considerable alterations and additions have been made to the buildings, which have added to the comfort of the patients, particularly in a new laundry and work-room for the women and an enlarged dining room for the men. The dinner for the day consisted of suet-pudding with treacle sauce, of which each patient is allowed an unlimited quantity. We examined the pudding and beer, half a pint of which is allowed to each and found them of excellent quality. All were well clothed and during our inspection there was an excitement amongst the patients which was most satisfactory. The present number under charge belonging to [Cumberland and Westmoreland] is 114; of whom 65 are males and 49 females. We regret to observe the great and increasing number of chronic and almost hopeless cases [which will account for] our not being able to sign any discharge on our present visit.

The change of management had restored standards. Beer was given to the patients as it was generally far safer than drinking water in the mid-nineteenth century. Robert Koch's work, first published in 1883, eventually convinced the world that the bacterium *vibrio cholera* was responsible for cholera and that it was spread through contaminated water, but until then water supplies were often heavily contaminated by today's standards.

John Banks at Dunston

The Times report of the first trial says of John's confinement that:

> he was subject to delusions and to violent conduct, and while labouring under one of these paroxysms he had been sent to Dunstan Lunatic Asylum, near Gateshead, 1840, but was discharged cured in 11 weeks[39]

(The date in this report is one year earlier than the actual year given in the appeal judgment.)

The reference to John being discharged from Dunston having been 'cured' in all probability meant no more than that, after eleven weeks of improving behaviour, he was then deemed to be sufficiently calm, and able to manage day-to-day life, with help, that he could return to living with his mother and sister. Nothing in John's subsequent history suggests that he was ever free of mental illness, in the sense that a cure would normally imply, but his release does suggest that, at the time of his discharge, he could cope, with appropriate help from others. Understanding of his mental condition and available treatments could not, in 1841, have brought about a permanent cure for John's mental illness. It is significant, however, that his behaviour at Dunston was sufficiently calm and rational to permit him to be released. This tends to bear out the evidence at the trial, from those who gave evidence for his will, that John could be rational if given time and approached sympathetically.

During his time at Dunston, it is unlikely that John would have been treated with any drugs. There were few, if any, that were in use then for the treatment of psychiatric conditions and those there were would have been of little or no effect. Sedatives, which calmed the symptoms rather than treating the underlying disorder, were in use. A near-contemporary *Manual of Psychological Medicine*[40] noted that active medicinal treatment was of no value, particularly in chronic cases, and that it was generally more likely to do harm than good. Paraldehyde, which had been first synthesised in Germany in 1848, had some uses as a sedative and anti-convulsant, but it was not introduced in Britain until much later, in 1882.[41]

The more likely treatment at Dunston, as noted earlier, would simply have been a regime based around a good diet, fresh air and exercise. This calmer environment would also have provided a steady routine that would have been sympathetic to the patients' illnesses. But, taken altogether, this treatment for mental illness, while it was a sensible and humane approach that could calm some patients, could not treat the psychiatric condition and control symptoms in the sense of treatment today.

True cures might have been intended by the Dunston regime, but they were probably not common and most recorded cures were probably more a calming of the patient than a cure. Mental illness at this time was something that simply had to be endured, often with far less sympathy than John received and more usually in far worse conditions. Too often the treatment offered by Victorian 'mad doctors' (as doctors then claiming to treat mental illness were known) seems now to be more akin to punishment inflicted on the patient – punishment that was aimed at forcing a patient to see the error of his ways and stop being mad: much along the lines of 'I will keep hurting you until you snap out of this and stop being so daft'.

Against the view that John was cured after his stay at Dunston is the evidence given against the will at the first trial, by William Robinson. He maintained that John returned from the asylum:

> rather better and attended the chapel as before but he was not long in being as bad as ever and he used to be so unruly at the chapel and disturbed the congregation so much that his sister had often to take him out and afterwards kept him away altogether.

This view was supported by Ann Hindmoor in that she maintained that soon after returning:

> he was as bad as before but perhaps not quite so violent.

Notwithstanding these views on John returning to the same behaviour as before his asylum admission, John was never returned to an asylum. His family seemed to have decided that their own care was sufficient (and almost certainly preferable). The Cumberland Report referred to earlier cites a Dr Browne who wrote:[42]

> I have seen a lunatic who, bound and galled, and cut by his bonds, had been crushed and confined in a small hole beneath a stair, where, altogether deprived of every means to inflict injury, and dependent upon those who had shorn him of his former powers and privileges, he was shunned by his relatives as the plague-stricken were formerly shunned. It is known that lunatics are immured in cellars, closets and

lofts; that they are allowed to wander nearly nude in the pitiless storm; that they are ill-fed, neglected and cast out.

John was fortunate in the care of his family and help of those around Keswick who took him in as lodger; he was never subject to the abuse that Dr Browne described.

When John was lodging with Isaac Thwaites at Bassenthwaite (between October 1860 and January 1862), Isaac by his own account sometimes threatened to get John sent back to an asylum if John's behaviour was extreme and this 'made him rather better for a time'. Later, in November 1863, when John was lodging at Arkleby, his landlady, Elizabeth Routledge, claimed that that there was a meeting of her family to decide if John would continue to stay with them 'as we thought it best for him to be sent to a lunatic asylum and it did not pay us to keep him any longer'. The evidence of Joseph Tolson and George Ansell, John's solicitor (see Chapter 3 for their dealings with John Banks), was that there was no such discussion. If there was a discussion, its timing would suggest that it was merely a negotiating ploy to extract more rent. Elizabeth Routledge did negotiate an increased rent personally with John at the first meeting about the will in December 1863, despite later declaring under oath that he was an 'imbecile' incapable of transacting business, at this time. The evidence of Joseph Tolson was that he and George Ansell suggested that 17/- per week was a good sum, but that Mrs Routledge wanted £1. The evidence of Mr Ansell was that he did not contribute to the conversation, but that John Banks did. Tolson further stated that Mrs Routledge had then said that John himself would be the best judge of what should be paid and proceeded to agree £1 with him. A higher rent having been obtained, the question of the asylum did not progress and John was not examined with a view to committal to an asylum. In the light of events, it seems clear that the second part of Mrs Routledge's evidence quoted above was more important to her than the first. The appeal court's finding was that there was:

> a conversation … as to the amount which he should pay her weekly for his board and lodging combined, which if truly reported, tended to shew strongly that he was then capable of managing his own affairs.

John's stay at Dunston would also have removed John from the risk, outside the asylum, of his illness not being taken seriously or being openly ridiculed. Both of these reactions to his condition would be capable of heightening John's frustration with both his perceived persecution and the failure of others to understand that what he believed he saw was real to him. John said to Mary Thwaites in 1860/61, when she could not see the spirits of Featherstone Alexander and Thomas Goodfellow, 'You are a strange woman not to see them'. Jane Clark also told of him '*getting quite vexed*' at her because she could not see Featherstone Alexander.

Being away from ridicule or scorn would have helped to calm him sufficiently to allow him to be discharged from Dunstan. Ridicule was experienced by John, even later in life, when at Arkleby 'his imbecility was so notorious that the children used to run after him on the roads'.[43] The evidence at the first trial shows that those who knew John well, and who were patient with him, had a higher opinion of his mental abilities and conduct when he was not afflicted by his delusions. These were usually people who were acquainted with John from his younger days. Those who knew him less well (or perhaps had less patience with him) tended to give less sympathetic evidence at the trial. This may well be accounted for by the degree of trust that John could develop over time and the manner in which he was treated in return.

John's Later Life

After the death of his mother in 1848, John was supported financially by the rents of what were described at the first trial of the will as '15 cottages in Keswick'. These properties were more accurately described in the Bill of Complaint, initiating the action regarding the will, as fifteen 'dwelling houses shops and premises'.[44] The properties came to him from his father's estate, after the death of his mother, when her life interest in them ceased. During the first trial of his will, the properties were reported, without much exactness, as being worth somewhere between £1,000 and £2,000. Whatever the value, it is clear that for the remainder of his life John could support himself from these rents. He could manage his own finances, but he needed help in terms of looking after himself, that is, in his day-to-day care.

The death of John's mother, in 1848, came almost exactly a year after the death of his sister. His mother's death brought to an end his life within his own family. It is not at all stretching the bounds of credibility to suggest that these two deaths must have been very stressful events for John that could reasonably be expected to have worsened his psychotic condition and his loneliness. After the death of his mother, John went to stay with his brother-in-law, Thomas Goodfellow, in Keswick. But, two months later, in March 1848, Thomas married his second wife, Sarah (see Chapter Four for more on Thomas Goodfellow and the death of his first wife, John's sister Margaret). Life in the Goodfellow household eventually became too difficult for John to stay. John's strange behaviour is alleged to have frightened Sarah so much that Thomas had, on occasions, knocked him down in order to stop him behaving so extremely. Ann Hindmoor's affidavit refers to Thomas Goodfellow visiting John when he lodged with her to:

> smoke a pipe with my husband. He has told me that he had knocked [John Banks] down many a time and when I asked him why he said 'Because he frightens Sarah'.

It is possible, to explain, but not necessarily excuse, Thomas's behaviour, in that by 1851 when John left this house, Sarah now had one-year-old child – Edward Barron Goodfellow, who eventually inherited John's estate – and was pregnant with their second child, a daughter Mary.

After leaving Thomas's household, John remained for most of his life in the immediate area of Keswick and coped with life by taking paid lodgings with various local families. In the 1851 census, three years after his mother's death and shortly after leaving Thomas's household, John was recorded as a 'visitor' at Harryman Field, Keswick, in the home of Joseph Usher who, with his wife, kept a grocery shop.[45] John was shown as aged thirty-eight, and described as unmarried and a 'proprietor of houses'. Evidence was given at the first trial, at Cumberland Spring Assizes, which showed that John stayed at this property for some time and was not therefore correctly recorded as being merely a visitor. Joseph Usher's evidence about the arrangement, as reported in the press, was:

> My wife knew how to drive a bargain. What she said you might depend she would stick to. (Laughter) She agreed with John Banks for 10s a-week for board, washing, and lodgings. John Banks was very greedy for money. He kept books and referred to them when I reminded him of forgetting to pay me for work done to his property.

This evidence, while given for the plaintiff challenging John's competence to make a will, helps to illustrate that John was not only capable of negotiating for his board and lodging, but also that he understood the value of money and how to keep a record of it. He also understood something of the necessities of property management in ordering repairs when needed. Mary

Usher, Joseph Usher's wife, gave evidence that John lodged with them for about twelve months after he left his brother-in-law's house. She also said that Thomas Goodfellow used to visit John 'and be friends again with him'. This remark carries the implication that while Thomas was alive John did not fear him when he was present, and that his later delusion of persecution by Thomas may only have occurred when Thomas was absent.

In a relatively small community such as Keswick, those who took John in as lodger would have known of his illness and have understood what they were taking on. In exchange for rent, John received his laundry, board and lodging and, no doubt, some basic home-nursing during any crises in his health. The lack of physical restraint, when compared to chains and locks in asylums, and the relative normality of some family life within lodgings in a familiar locality, should have provided a beneficial environment for him. In a strange role reversal, while John was with the Ushers, he was not locked in at night, but Mary Usher locked her servant girl in her room at night 'in case he might suddenly take it into his head to do some mischief'. But there is no record of John ever being violent towards another, nor is there evidence of any wrongful behaviour on his part towards a woman. The lock was probably more for the peace of mind of the maid than anything else. Mary Usher usefully added that John 'did not show any disposition to hurt anyone'.

It is clear from evidence at the first trial that John remained a challenge to those he lodged with. Being of independent means gave him the choice to walk away from any lodgings where he might have been ill treated, but there is no evidence that he ever had occasion to leave for this reason, apart from when he was with his brother-in-law. There is evidence that he had to move sometimes simply because his hosts grew tired of his behaviour.

Later, John lodged for a time with Superintendent[46] and Mrs Bird (see later for evidence from Mrs Bird). He left them and lodged elsewhere during part of the 1850s. He then returned for a second period with them in 1859. This period covered the death of Featherstone Alexander (who was the subject of one of John's delusions – see later in this chapter) in 1860, but John was no longer with the Birds by the 1861 census. At the 1861 census he was lodging with the farmer Isaac Thwaites at Slack Houses, North Row, Bassenthwaite.[47] After this, in February 1862, he moved to Gill Foot Cottage,[48] Arkleby. Arkleby was further north and more remote from where John had previously lived. He lodged in Arkleby with James Routledge, a grocer, and his family, until his death. Members of the Routledge family registered both John's death, and, later, that of his niece Margaret (more of her in Chapter Four).

Lodgings provided for John Banks the Elder

Margaret Banks the elder (mother)	Up to January 1848
Thomas Goodfellow	February 1848 to 1851
Joseph and Mary Usher	1851 to 1852(?)
Not known	1852 to April 1853
Isaac and Margaret Bird	May 1853 to March 1854
Not known	March 1854 to August 1859
Isaac Bird and Margaret Bird	September 1859 to October 1860
Isaac Thwaites	October 1860 to January 1862
James and Elizabeth Routledge	February 1862 to July 1865

NB While it is simple speculation, the gaps in this list could be because the landlords would not give evidence against the will. All of those listed, with the exception of Thomas Goodfellow who was dead, opposed the will and their evidence still exists.

Care in the Community

A supplement to the Metropolitan Report made reference to a practice in Wales known as 'farming out' the mentally ill. It was apparently the practice of local councils there to look to provide care for 'idiots and lunatics'[49] by lodging them with a relative. If no willing relative could be found, then lodgings would be sought with anyone else (usually a farm labourer, or small farmer) who was prepared to take charge of the individual for money. This was, apparently, a well-established method in Wales of providing a form of care in the community.

A weekly rate was paid to the person taking the patient into their house. The weekly payment was negotiated between the local Poor Law Guardians[50] and those who took charge of the lunatic. There does not appear to have been a standard rate for this payment; much depended upon the amount of care required. Examples were given in the Report of 7/- a week being paid to Edward Grey, a farmer, for the care of Catherine Williams because she was 'dangerous to others' and 'of dirty habits'. Ellen Davies, 'a harmless idiot', was also lodged with Edward Grey, but only 2/9d a week was paid. The average fee in Wales appeared to be between 1/6d and 2/6d a week, and in cases where the lunatic, or idiot, could be put to useful labour, in the house or around the farm, it went much lower (in one case as low as 4d a week). This system was not without its abuses. Ann Abney from near Bangor:

> had been kept chained in the house of a married daughter, and, from having been long kept down in a crouching posture, her knees were forced up to her chin, and she sat wholly upon her hips and her heels, and much excoriation was caused upon her chest and stomach by her knees when she moved. She could move about with velocity, and was almost always maniacal. When she died [in Hereford Lunatic Asylum on 30th January 1844], it required very considerable dissection to get her pressed into a coffin.[51]

This Welsh system, without its abuses, appears to be little different in principle to that which was privately negotiated by John Banks for his various lodgings around Keswick. He was doing this for over twenty years after the above report was written. He paid more for lodging than the rates that were paid in Wales, but he certainly appeared to obtain better care than would have been available in many asylums.

John's Income

The appeal judgment shows that, when John made his last will in 1863, the cottages in Keswick produced a combined rent of £80pa. This was more than enough to support him in his way of life, at that time. In 1851, for example, the evidence was that he negotiated to pay 10/- per week (£26pa) for laundry, board and lodging (the evidence of Joseph Usher quoted earlier in this chapter indicates that he thought his wife had struck a good bargain at this price). Later, in 1865 at the end of John's life, the weekly wage of an agricultural labourer in England was only 11/3d, on which he supported himself and his family (probably in tied accommodation). Therefore, the additional weekly income from John's rent would have been useful to any household that took him in, even though all of them had better household incomes than that of an agricultural labourer.[52] The strain of coping with John probably eventually outweighed the extra income, as he changed lodgings several times before his final lodgings at Arkleby – although in fairness to his hosts, at least one, Mrs Bird, accepted him for a second stay.

At Arkleby, after John's health began to decline, the cost of his lodging went up to £1 per week. The evidence of Mrs Routledge was that, prior to this increase, she was charging '6/- pw for his lodging and charged him for his board whatever he got'. Given the additional care he needed an increase was probably not unreasonable, but the jump is rather large. This increase, as noted earlier, was negotiated by Mrs Routledge directly with John Banks at the same time that the disputed will was made. She apparently saw no contradiction in negotiating to double the weekly payment, at a time when she was later to claimed, under oath, than he was insane. She later gave evidence that John 'was in an imbecile condition which was usual ... his mental imbecility was so apparent that no one of ordinary intelligence could be in his company without seeing it'. This entire episode must have undermined the value of any evidence she gave.

In the last years of John's life, the rents from the Keswick properties were collected on his behalf by Joseph Tolson, a grocer in Keswick. He seems to have been trusted by John, as he appointed him to be one of his executors in the later disputed will. There was also a connection between Thomas Goodfellow, John's brother-in-law and Joseph, most probably as cousins. It may be that Joseph only took on the collection of rents after John moved further away from Keswick and was less able to make a regular collection. Until John moved to lodgings in Bassenthwaite (around 1860) he certainly dealt with payment of the local rates[53] on these properties himself. Mr Gibson was the assistant overseer for Keswick with responsibility for Keswick rate collection and he had being dealing with John for a number of years over the local rates on John's properties. He gave evidence at the first trial that when he saw John 'he frequently had these beatings in the head', but Mr Gibson waited 'until he calmed, and they went on to business'. Mr Gibson was definite in his view that John was mentally capable of conducting such business.

John's Illness

The most helpful contemporary evidence of the severity of John's illness is that which was given at the first trial of the will. However, this evidence needs to be viewed with some care today. None of the evidence was given in medical terms as we would recognise today (including that from John's doctor). Also, evidence given on behalf of contending parties at any trial will be partisan to their cause. Evidence is called by either side to support their own position, not to undermine it. This practice tends to present two different pictures to the court. The usefulness of the evidence to the point at issue in the trial is dealt with later in Chapter Five.

As an adult, John suffered from delusions that he was being pursued and persecuted by the devil, assisted by various demons, and the evil spirits of two dead grocers. These delusions would make John extremely agitated. On occasions, he believed these persecutors, particularly the devil, were visibly present and the hallucinations added to his agitation. Whether or not these delusions existed before John went to lodge with Mr and Mrs Usher is not wholly clear. Evidence before this period is mainly of strange behaviour, shouting, withdrawing from company, running into town and back again, and so forth. This behaviour was sufficiently erratic that men were employed, as noted earlier in this chapter, to watch him to see that he came to no harm, but none of the witnesses expressly mentions delusions until after he lodged outside the family. The incident in chapel, also mentioned earlier in this chapter, could be evidence of his delusions of persecution by the devil, but the evidence is by far from conclusive.

It is worth bearing in mind what happened to John around this time when considering his excitability and agitation. In 1846 his sister married and left home; his sister died in 1847; his mother died a year later, and this last event saw the end of John's own life within his own family and surroundings, structured around a routine that had been familiar to him from a young age. When he was subsequently lodging with Thomas, his brother-in-law, Thomas's focus would have been on his new wife and children, and by 1851 John had left that household. Thereafter John lost his family life and lodged with strangers (most of whom considered him to be insane and probably at times said so to his face). The loss of his sister and mother would probably have affected John heavily, as these were the two people who had been closest to him and cared for him for the first thirty-six years of his life. The loss of family security and their care for him in the future must have added to the strain of the bereavement. This break with his past family life, and his consequent isolation and insecurity, would have been a dramatic contrast to what had gone before, and in turn this change in his life could quite well have exacerbated his illness.

Along with the delusions of persecution by the Devil and his demons went a violent antipathy towards a local grocer, Featherstone Alexander. The name of this man is given as 'Featherstone Alexander' in the judgment, as 'Fetherstone Alexander' in a press report and as 'Featherstonehaugh Alexander' in a census. If the latter is correct, it raises the question of pronunciation – was it pronounced 'Fanshaw'? That the shorter 'Featherstone' (pronounced as spelt) was used tends to point against Fanshaw/Fanshawe. Curiously, a newspaper report of the appeal judgment gives the name as 'Featherstonehaugh', although that is not how the judgment sets it out.

John believed that Alexander was also persecuting him, and the mere mention of his name would induce violent and irrational excitement in John.

A Victorian Tragedy: The Extraordinary Case of Banks v Goodfellow

The Featherstone Alexander who so troubled John Banks did exist and he is thought to have been, like Thomas Goodfellow John's brother-in-law, a grocer and tea dealer, who appears in the 1851 census at 62 Main Street Keswick. Mr Alexander is also listed as a grocer later in an 1855 guide which covered Keswick.[54] Featherstone Alexander, who had married Susanna Hopper on 28th March 1842, died in Keswick on 24th June 1860. John Banks attended his funeral, which given his known antipathy towards the deceased must have caused some consternation among the mourners, and we must assume that it was unlikely that he was invited to join the family at the funeral tea afterwards. John returned to his lodgings in Isaac Bird's house, remarking that 'he had got quit of him at last'. Isaac Bird's evidence was that it was 'not more than a couple of days or so till [John] was again troubled by him'. Jane Clark quotes John as saying of Alexander 'Don't you know he is a very bad man'. At the first trial, Joseph Tolson said in his evidence that John was frightened that Alexander would 'fash' him. 'Fash' then had a meaning of to worry, to bother or to annoy.

Jane Clark provided evidence for the claimant that John:

> would sometimes ask me if I did not see [Featherstone Alexander] and point him out to me when there was nothing and would often stamp about and get quite vexed at me because I did not see him.

She said John 'frequently saw imps and would dart his head about and ask if we did not see them and he would curse and swear at them'. Her evidence confirms the frustration and disturbance caused, unsurprisingly, by those who denied seeing what John knew that he saw.

There is little in the personal details that we know of Featherstone Alexander's life that would account for John Banks the elder's aversion to him. Given that they were near contemporaries it is possible that the animosity went back to childhood or school. Thomas Goodfellow, John's brother-in-law, was also a tea dealer and grocer resident in Main Street, but whether or not there is anything significant (a business rivalry with Alexander?) in this or it is merely coincidence is impossible to tell. One possible clue comes from a witness, Mrs Margaret Bird, who gave evidence about John's belief in persecution. When John was 'wrestling with the devils' sometimes he would get up and say 'Now my man I have done for you'. She had heard him talking, as she thought, to Alexander, saying, 'You are a devil, you are a damned devil, you've been tormenting me for years, you shall never have her'. Margaret Bird thought that this was a reference to John's sister Margaret. She took this to mean that John imagined that Alexander at one time wished to marry his sister, and it is possible that Featherstone was at one time her suitor. Whether or not there was any basis for John's belief is unknown. But if Alexander, during his life, had behaved badly towards John, or his sister, then the possibility of acquiring him as brother-in-law must have been rather terrifying to him. If Mrs Bird is correct in her interpretation of 'you shall never have her', John's remark also carries the implication that he thought that Margaret was still alive. The belief that Featherstone Alexander was pursuing him continued throughout John's life.

It was also represented by Margaret Bird that John also believed that his brother-in-law Thomas Goodfellow was pursuing him, again both before and after Thomas's death in 1858. If this evidence is correct, this delusion seems to have started before his brother-in-law died but after John had left his household. As there is, as mentioned earlier in this chapter, reason to believe that Thomas did hit John when John lodged with him, this would not necessarily be a delusion on John's part while Thomas lived. However, it is a little more difficult to deal with for the period after Thomas's death. Was the belief that Thomas was then pursuing him a delusion or simply John reliving an unpleasant past experience?

John's delusions about specific individuals, who had done him harm in life and were then then persecuting him after death, are not untypical of persecutory delusions in that they may have had some grounding in reality. Religious persecution at this time and earlier was often encountered, perhaps because of the central role that organised religion played in life, with a heavy emphasis on regular sermons and preaching against sin and its consequences.

Evidence at the first trial also revealed that John had a further delusion concerning a man named as 'Dudlow'. It was said that John claimed that Dudlow was a good man who gave him good advice. There is no indication in the evidence as to whether Mr Dudlow was alive, how frequent this delusion was, or even whether or not there was a real Mr Dudlow. However, it seems likely that this name was either misreported in the press or those giving evidence did not associate the name with someone that John actually knew. The Reverend Joseph Dallow was a non-conformist minister living in Harryman's Field, Keswick. The Reverend Dallow's time at Harryman's Field would have overlapped with John's time lodging there and he may well have given John good advice and treated him sympathetically during that time. Further, there is a strong connection between the Reverend Dallow and Thomas Goodfellow (see Chapter Four for more on this point), and John may well have had further contact with the Reverend Dallow while he lodged with his brother-in-law. Mrs Routledge in her affidavit correctly identified 'a Mr Dallow an independent minister' and she added that John believed that

Dallow, like Featherstone Alexander and Thomas Goodfellow, was following him. She does not specify that the spirit of Dallow was malign.

This delusion about the Reverend Dallow, if indeed it was a delusion, seems to have been non-persecutory, but this does not mean that it could not have been a paranoid delusion. 'Paranoid' in the context of delusions does not equate with persecution. Paranoid delusions are often thought of as solely persecutory, but they also can be, for example, delusions of grandeur (belief of having special status or skills) or of a relationship with another (a delusion that someone, quite improbably or irrationally, is in love with the person). Whether the Reverend Dallow did give John good advice or John merely believed that he did cannot be ascertained. The Reverend Dallow died shortly before John in 1862. Given that John may not have been treated well by everyone he met, his view of the Reverend Dallow may just be that John was speaking highly of someone whose kindness he remembered fondly, and he was not being delusional.

John had other visual hallucinations, according to evidence given about his behaviour. John Banks the younger in his affidavit for the trial of the will recounted that on their way down from a walk to the summit of Skiddaw in 1860 or 1861, his uncle stopped to hit out at the air around him as he claimed that there were spirits following him.

In the early 1860s William Robinson encountered John walking from Bassenthwaite to Keswick. This journey takes the walker along the western side of Skiddaw and around the south side of the mountain. William Robinson gave evidence that described how John stopped on this walk and exclaimed 'Don't talk to me there is a regiment of soldiers before me'. This would appear to be an unusual hallucination, if it was a hallucination, in that it involved something outside persecution by the devil and local people that John knew. However, it is possible that there could be a more rational basis for his comment.

Not far to the east of Skiddaw is Blencathra and at the eastern end of that fell is Souther Fell. In 1735 and 1745 there were reports (later published) of a ghostly march of soldiers and carriages across the fell over terrain known to be impassable for carriages. The army left no footprints. Over twenty people gave evidence of seeing this in 1745. There are no reported later sightings. The Spectral Army of Souther Fell then entered local folklore. This is the type of local story that would have been told and retold down generations in the area. The local children, including John, will have heard this story from their older relatives. John's vision of soldiers is more likely to have been prompted by his imagination, and the stories he had heard as a child, than by his schizophrenia.[55]

Further evidence against John's mental capacity was given by Grenip and Mary Cartmel, tenants of John. In their opinion, John 'could not keep his mind on anything for more than a few minutes together' and that they 'could have persuaded him anything (sic) he was like a child not a man. He could not be depended upon in transacting business affairs unless watched'. None of this is about an inability to understand what a will is, the property he owned and those members of the family that were deserving of his bounty, and today we would have given limited weight to such evidence when compared to expert medical opinion.

There was mention in the appeal judgment of medical evidence being given at the first trial that spoke of John's 'general insanity'. This was from a doctor who treated him at various times between 1856 and the end of 1862. There was further evidence from a local clergyman to similar effect for the period up to John's death in 1865.

At the first trial of the will, the evidence given by Mrs Margaret Bird was highlighted in the press reports. Her evidence, vividly reported, gave a more detailed picture of John's behaviour and is worth quoting at greater length. John had lodged with her initially in 1853/54. Her husband Isaac Bird was clearly known to the Banks and Goodfellow families as he was a witness to the will of Thomas Goodfellow very shortly before Thomas died. According to a press report of Margaret Bird's evidence:

> He [Banks] was very unruly, one night he pulled the grate out, observing that he was going up the chimney to catch the devil. (Laughter) Had frequently to go to the door to stop him. He used to promise to be quiet, but as soon as they went away he began again. Never knew him sensible for more than a few minutes. While Banks was living with witness the second time, Fetherstone Alexander died. Banks said it was a good job Alexander was gone, as he would not be tortured again. He had a delusion about Goodfellow. Banks two or three times thought that he had killed the devil. (Laughter) Once he said he had killed the devil with a cream jug. (Laughter) Saw him once struggling on the floor, and on witness asking what he was doing, he replied, 'I am choking the devil'. (More Laughter) He further observed 'I have done for the devil at last'. He forgetting, went out naked. Once she (witness) caught him dancing on the flower bed, and he said – 'I have got Alexander here, and I am pushing him down a little further'. After witness and her husband removed to Wigton, Banks came to their house one very stormy night, and said that the devils drove him along the road from Bassenthwaite to Wigton. He was then very cold.[56]

The walk from Bassenthwaite to Wigton would be between twelve and thirteen miles. Clearly John still had the physical ability and endurance to complete that walk, over country roads, at night, when almost fifty years old. In her affidavit Margaret Bird gave further detail by explaining that on the night in question there was frost and snow and that John arrived exhausted.

Similar evidence to Mrs Bird's was given by Mrs Routledge, John's landlady in Arkleby. Again, acccording to press reports:

> He was very unruly at times, knocking and shouting. And saying the devil was in his head. Once he asked her to bring a gun and blow his brains out. He used to often speak of Alexander, who was dead. He used to talk about imps, and say the devil was in his head. In his bedroom he used to pull off the bedclothes, and break the chamber ware. He used to say the devil was in his room, and would not let him lie in his bed. He used sometimes to strike his head against doors. He said it was the devil who was in his head. He once jumped out of a window in 1864, and they nailed it down. He shouted 'I am dead' after he had jumped out. Had known him run through Parsonby with his trousers down; and sometimes he had got into another house and fancied it was hers. Has seen him open the oven door, thinking that was the way out. Once when she made a batch of currant cakes, he ate them all – six of them. He was fond of sugar; she had seen him eat a basinful.[57]

John's appetite was erratic, as this suggests. Mrs Routledge gave further evidence 'that we had to set a certain portion of food before him or he would gorge himself ... at other times he would almost starve himself'.

The striking of his head appears several times in the evidence for the claimant:

- Mrs Usher said he used to be 'continually striking his head against things violently ... He once cut his eye and frequently black them'. Mrs Usher also made it clear that he struck only himself and did not strike others, despite what she or others might sometimes fear.
- The evidence of Isaac Bird also refers to John hitting himself 'sometimes his brow was quite black with hitting it'.
- Jane Clark (housekeeper to William Thirlwall, and Mrs Routledge's sister-in-law) stated that John 'would often shout wildly and strike his head with some degree of violence against the wall and also strike his head with his fist'.

The Times report on the first trial summarised the evidence as:

> He was possessed occasionally with a delusion that a person to whom he had taken a great dislike – Featherstone Alexander – followed him about, and became violent whenever his name was mentioned, and this continued for six or seven years after Alexander's death. He used sometimes to think that devils followed him, and took the poker to protect himself from them, and on such occasions he would thump his own head with his doubled fists; but when these fits of violence passed away he became perfectly rational on every other subject.[58]

There was evidence that, at least later in his life, John's language was extreme when affected by his delusions and he would curse his persecutors – Mary Thwaites in her affidavit said he 'used terrible language'. He used to say that that those who persecuted him used shocking language to him.

John's physical health worsened in 1863 with the onset of epilepsy. John is reported to have suffered from epileptic fits from September that year until the end of his life in 1865. During these fits Dr William Jones of Aspatria, who gave evidence at the first trial, considered that John was unable to transact business. This doctor was first acquainted with John in May 1863[59] and he claimed he 'used to see him and speak with him frequently'. Dr Jones' affidavit is, however, regrettably brief, and disturbingly vague about John's illness and treatment:

1. The doctor said he treated John first for an epileptic fit on 5th September 1863 and he added that 'on referring to my books I find I attended him down to the 24th September for the same illness'. It is not clear if this is for different fits during this period or for continuing treatment after the first fit. It also gives no detail of how often during this period he treated John, or even how he treated him.
2. Further visits were made by the doctor on 24th October and 17th December 1863. His prescription on the first date was 'soothing drafts' (sic) and on the second occasion 'soothing drafts most probably against a threatening attack' (sic). But his affidavit gives no detail of exactly why he was called.
3. On 22nd December 1863 the doctor 'blistered his head to relieve the pain', but no reason was given as to what was causing the pain he was treating (by inflicting more pain).
4. Further visits were made on 24th and 27th December 1863, but again the doctor gives no reason for his visits or what the

treatment was. This is somewhat incredible to the modern mind as the 27th December is the day before the second will was to be signed, yet the doctor's statement, made less than five years after the event, gives no particulars of the medical reason for the visit, the treatment given, nor any detail of the physical or mental state of the patient. This is of some consequence given the evidence given by some witnesses that at this time John was in a poor state and unfit to make a will. That the doctor thought his condition was not worthy of comment even to note the reason for his visit cannot have helped the case against the will.

5. Three non-medically qualified witnesses stated that in September 1863 John suffered a stroke that resulted in left-sided paralysis. The doctor's evidence makes no mention at all of this. The natural implication of this would be that he observed no symptoms of a stroke nor did he did treat a stroke. The lack of comment from John's doctor about the occurrence of a stroke, and the complete absence of any evidence from him as to how this affected John afterwards, seriously undermines the claims of others that John was incapacitated by stroke. Alternatively, if some credence is given to the evidence of others about the stroke and its effects then that substantially undermines any value that Dr Jones' rather vague evidence might have had.

The doctor continued to visit John at various other times until John died. He described John as follows:

> When the fits came on [John] was quite insensible and very violent and difficult to manage for days together and then gradually subsided down and became stupid and harmless but still labouring under delusions. After the attacks he was generally in a quiet pliable mood. [John] was insane from the time that I first knew him till his death and always exhibited insanity when I saw him and from my experience of him I am of the opinion he had no lucid intervals. I could have got him to sign anything. I only had to ask him.[60]

Even trying to ascribe any credibility to this evidence is difficult. Was the 'fit' referred to an epileptic fit or an example of John's extreme mental agitation? Who would be expected to be capable to transact business during a fit (epileptic or a fit of insanity)? The doctor only saw John during or immediately after epileptic attacks when it would not be surprising that he might not be capable of much. It is a bit of leap to state from this that 'he had no lucid intervals', particularly when Edward Highton, the Keswick schoolmaster, gave evidence of a rational discussion with John about Martin Luther in 1864. The doctor's general statement 'insane from the time that I first knew him' seems too sweeping to have much value. All in all, Dr Jones cuts a poor figure in this story.

It also seems rather odd that if Mrs Routledge really did have concerns at the time about the ability of John to make a will (discussed in Chapter Three), the issue was not raised with the doctor during some of the December visits, but there is nothing in her evidence, or his, to indicate that the matter was raised by her at the time. This may well have gone against the value of her evidence and helped the jury in finding for the will. Mrs Routledge, in giving evidence against the will, stated that:

> when in his fits he was insensible and had to be watched continually and when he was coming out of a fit he would strike and kick and was very violent and dangerous and took sometimes two or three people to hold him and when he was in his fits he was very low and stupid.

In reality, nothing about this evidence is surprising. The modern analysis of the characteristics of types of epileptic seizures includes confusion, an inability to respond to questions, on occasions a loss of consciousness, and physical spasms. Following fits there is typically a period of confusion before normal consciousness returns. Other post-seizure symptoms can include tiredness, headache, speech difficulty and abnormal behaviours. Mrs Routledge's evidence, in this light, does not necessarily tell us much.

Mrs Routledge's evidence is rather general in terms and in fact says little about John's ability between fits. However, she and her daughter Hannah both also stated that John:

> ... was an imbecile and insane and incapable of understanding business or ordinary affairs *during the whole time he lodged with us.* We consider that he had no lucid intervals though he was sometimes quieter and more sensible than at others but he always laboured under delusions. (author's added emphasis)

There is a clear divergence between this evidence from Mrs Routledge and that from the solicitor and Joseph Tolson about John's capacity at the time the will was made (and the schoolmaster Mr Highton's evidence of his meeting with John). Her evidence that John was incapable of conducting business is strange in the light of her decision to negotiate a higher weekly rent directly with John at the time the will was made. At best this undermines her testimony; at worst it argues that she financially exploited John when she knew he was incapable. Neither position puts her in a good light. At both trials other evidence was preferred to hers.

One medically qualified person who did give evidence in favour of John having capacity was Dr John Tweddle of Keswick, who knew John well for much of his life and 'had seen him hundreds of times'. While his views might have helped to counteract some of the views about John's limited capabilities while he was in Keswick, there is no indication that Dr Tweddle had seen John after he moved away from Keswick and therefore he could not be useful as to John's mental state during the time at Arkleby. While admitting that the name of Featherstone Alexander put John into an excited state, Dr Tweddle considered that John could talk rationally and would be able to conduct his own business as long as no one mentioned Featherstone Alexander's name. He added the further view that he would not have signed a certificate for John's removal to a lunatic asylum. The ability of John to deal with his own business was also supported by one Mary Murray, a cousin of the defendant Edward Goodfellow (although the press reports give no details of her evidence). John's business capabilities were also supported by Joseph Usher's evidence (set out earlier in this chapter) which, although it was evidence given against the will, showed John to be capable of handling money and keeping a record of it.

After John went to Arkleby and the epileptic fits began, Margaret Bird, who had twice had John lodging with her, claimed that he was scarcely able to recognise her for more than a minute when she visited him. She also refers to his paralysed shoulder. This paralysis was also commented on by Elizabeth Routledge who referred to John having had a stroke. This, she said:

> paralyzed his left side and he became so helpless in a general way he had to be taken to his bedroom and put into bed and covered up and in the morning we had to wash and dress him. He even had to be fed like a child.

This is confirmed by the evidence of Jane Clark, Mrs Routledge's sister-in-law '… in September 1863 … had a stroke which deprived him of the use of his left side'.

As noted above, Dr William Jones who gave evidence about John's epilepsy made no reference in his affidavit to John having had a stroke or that he had treated John for one. Mrs Routledge's evidence of his condition is strongly suggestive of him having had a stroke. However, Mrs Routledge's evidence was essentially about John's physical condition and not his mental capacity. Her evidence is also plainly exaggerated, if she was trying to suggest that this was his state always after his stroke. Her own evidence of the events surrounding the wills in December 1863 makes it clear that John was mobile and capable of feeding himself. None of the contemporaneous evidence from the day when the will instructions were taken (or when it was executed) deals with any continuing effects of a stroke being exhibited at that time.

The evidence of some left arm paralysis suggests that if it was caused by a stroke, then the stroke was in the right side of the brain. This can produce various symptoms (although not all patients will show all of them) that can include:

- the sufferer having little insight into his own behaviour, problems and limitations (anosognosia);
- reduced understanding of social situations;
- poor recognition of faces (prosopagnosia);
- lack of understanding of how one should dress or in what order (apraxia);
- fast, impulsive behaviour, and sometimes inappropriate behaviour;
- sometimes little consideration for others; and
- reduced self-control.[61]

Some of these can plausibly be thought to have contributed to John's behaviour post-stroke but none are necessarily indicative of a loss of capacity to make a will. The extent to which any of these symptoms might have been present is rather unclear given that John's existing psychiatric condition affected behaviour in some similar ways.

There was an incident during this time that was dealt with in the evidence of Jane Tolson, the daughter of Joseph Tolson. She recounts a market day in July 1864 when Mr and Mrs Routledge and John Banks visited Joseph Tolson's house in Keswick for the day. She viewed John Banks' manner favourably and averred that nothing led her to consider him to be insane. This is several months after the other evidence of the onset of epilepsy and his stroke. It was a long and tiring day out when travel is taken into account. John cannot have been as physically restricted as the other evidence suggests if he could undertake such a day out. Mrs Routledge said nothing about this day in her evidence.

Several witnesses, when offering the opinion that John was insane, said that he was easily led and could be persuaded to sign anything that was put in front of him. That John was gullible, or trusting to excess, does not mean he was unable to make a will or that he was insane. But there is possibly a more sinister side to these traits which is explored later in Chapter Eight.

At times, with regard to what was said of John's capabilities, one is forced to consider that too often John was simply dismissed as being a madman and therefore not capable of making a will (or doing anything significant for himself). That is, those giving evidence considered his actions and appearance and concluded from this that he was mad, as opposed to making an objective assessment of what he was mentally capable of despite his illness. Although it might be tempting to put this down to the difference between nineteenth-century and twenty-first-century thinking, the five judges involved in the two trials did not approach it that way and clearly focused on what John was capable of, not how he behaved.

How would John's Mental History be Viewed Today?

John Banks' mental disorder as an adult was characterised by delusions and by hallucinations – he talked of being pursued by the Devil and his demons and by the spirits of Featherstone Alexander and Thomas Goodfellow. At what stage the hallucinations and the delusional belief of persecution began is unclear, but there is no evidence that this was before adulthood, although as discussed at the start of this chapter there is the suggestion of a schizoid personality disorder being apparent in childhood.

A modern diagnosis of his adult condition would most probably be that it was one of paranoid schizophrenia.[62] Unknown at the time of John Banks, paranoid schizophrenia is today considered to be the most common type of schizophrenia. Paranoid schizophrenia is a chronic mental illness in which a person loses touch with reality (psychosis[63]). The dominant effects of the illness are delusions (most commonly of persecution) with accompanying hallucinations, both visible and auditory – and these features closely match John Banks' reported condition. Today, a normal way of life is quite possible with this illness, but only with constant medical treatment. As the illness could not be identified for what it was in John Banks' time, there was no effective treatment or control, or even understanding of its nature, hence the general description applied to him by many that he was simply 'insane'.

A second possible diagnosis could be bi-polar disorder, formerly known as manic depression. While this should not be completely ruled out, it is probably less likely than paranoid schizophrenia. John was morose at times and wished he was dead (consistent with depression). At other times he was disinhibited and disturbed at night (consistent with manic behaviour).

However, persistent delusions, which were a very significant feature of John's illness, would not be a typical symptom of bi-polar disorder.

A third possible diagnosis to at least consider is tertiary syphilis. This is the last of the four stages of syphilis (the four stages being primary, secondary, latent and tertiary), and was much more common in the mid-nineteenth century, before the discovery of penicillin and its subsequent application as a treatment for syphilis. Syphilis is not solely transmissible through sexual activity and it can be transmitted from mother to unborn child (congenital syphilis). Tertiary syphilis could cause psychosis, epileptic fits and dementia. However, infection from parent to child can be ruled out in John's case as he was not born with the recognised stigmata of the disease, nor did he develop them, as far as we know, in his early years. Further, there is no evidence of transmission of this disease to his younger sister at birth. The stigmata of the disease were well known in the nineteenth century as, given the lack of treatment for syphilis and the lack of general use of prophylactics, it was commonly encountered, and therefore one would expect its symptoms or stigmata to be identified by witnesses if they had been present. Tertiary syphilis was then often referred to as 'general paralysis of the insane' (now 'general paresis of the insane') and prior to the availability of penicillin it was inevitably fatal.

A fourth, and probably the least likely, possible diagnosis would be a hydatid cyst in the brain. Hydatid disease is caused by a type of tapeworm – *echinococcus granulosus*. It is a disease that is rare now in the UK because hygiene is now much better than it was in the mid-nineteenth century. This disease is commonly caught from sheep via dogs. One has to recall that Cumberland has always been sheep country, so this would not be a totally unreasonable diagnosis.

If it is correctly reported that John's epilepsy came on years after the onset of schizophrenia, when he was fifty-two or fifty-three, and twenty-one months before his death, then it was probably unrelated to the existing mental disorder. A likely cause of the epileptic fits would then be a space-occupying lesion in the brain, such as a brain tumour or cerebrovascular lesion. This could have been due to a head injury, but there is no known history of head trauma, other than self-inflicted banging of his head, which often would cause bruising, but probably nothing more serious. The evidence of Mary Usher was that:

> ... while he lived with me used to be continually striking his head against things violently and stamping with his feet. He once cut his eye and frequently blackened them. Once a woman friend of mine

was sitting in our kitchen where he was and he suddenly jumped up and struck his head and she ran screaming out of the house and nearly fainted.

It is possible that the epilepsy came on before the mental disorder, although the evidence is against it, but if the fits were what are known as simple partial seizures, others could well have been unaware of them. If that were the case the mental disorder might be connected to the epilepsy. Early onset epilepsy is likely to be idiopathic, meaning that there is no known cause. It is now recognised that longstanding idiopathic epilepsy can be associated with all sorts of mental disorders, one of which is schizophrenia. Although idiopathic epilepsy usually comes on before the age of fifty, it can begin at a later age.

The epilepsy, which could not then be controlled effectively, would have weakened John's physical health, particularly if it was caused by a space-occupying lesion, as suggested above. The evidence that John suffered a stroke towards the end of his life is not conclusive, but such evidence as there is makes it likely that it occurred, and again this would have weakened John's physical health and thereby contributed to an earlier death. Whether or not the stroke was a further side effect of the same space-occupying lesion that was the likely cause of the epilepsy is unclear but it could well have been connected. The evidence of Jane Clark is that both the stroke and the start of the epileptic seizures occurred in September 1863, increasing the likelihood that the two were connected. The combined effect of these two new ailments could have been to weaken John's physical condition and also curtail his physical exercise. Some of the witnesses' evidence also points to John being seen outside much less frequently after the stroke, although Jane Tolson, as noted earlier, recounts a visit from John to Keswick in July 1864.

John Banks the Elder's Death

Causes of Death

John died on 28th July 1865 aged fifty-three. The causes of John's death are recorded on his death certificate as 'Epilepsy, Insanity and Coma'. It is not known which doctor certified the death, but it is likely that it was Dr Jones. Inaccuracies in the causes of death recorded on Victorian death certificates are not at all uncommon, as often all the doctor attending could do was observe conditions rather than understand the actual causes of the conditions. However, if it was Dr Jones who certified the death, it is all the more strange that no connection was made to the earlier stroke.

Two of the recorded diagnoses, insanity and coma, are not strictly speaking feasible causes of death. Insanity, of itself, cannot be a direct cause of death; it is instead related to causes of death through inducing, for example, suicide or inanition (exhaustion from not eating). Before the days of antidepressants and electroconvulsive therapy, some patients would be so depressed that they could literally starve themselves and went into a state of stupor (mental inaccessibility). Sometimes, in the process of starving themselves to death, patients might develop a fatal pneumonia, due to their weakened physical state. Similarly, coma is a state of unconsciousness that could be caused by a very large number of underlying physical diseases, any one of which could have been the real cause of John's death.

So, what then is likely to have been the real cause of John Banks' death? Insanity and coma, as shown on the death certificate, can be ignored for the reasons given above. There is a possibility that a space-occupying lesion, suspected as having been the cause of his epilepsy and also as having caused the first stroke, may have eventually produced a second, and fatal, stroke. This conclusion must be speculative, but given what we know of John's history, it is probably a far more likely explanation than what was recorded on the death certificate.

Registration and Announcement of Death

John Banks the elder's death was registered by Isaac Bird Routledge,[64] the fifteen-year-old son of James and Elizabeth Routledge. His qualification to register is shown as 'present at the death'. It is a little odd that the Routledge's youngest child is given this task, although it could be that he was more literate than others in the family. He also registered his father's death only seven months later.

John's death notice in the *Westmorland and Kendal Advertiser* of 12th August read:

> On 28th ult, at Arkleby, at the house of James Routledge, wherein he had long been an inmate, Mr John Banks, youngest son of the late Jacob Banks, pencil manufacturer, aged 53.

This is a most odd death announcement, almost bordering on the bizarre.

One the main functions of a death notice in the press is to allow time for readers to attend the funeral, or to send their condolences if unable to attend. This notice makes no reference to the date or location of the funeral and burial, presumably because the notice was not published until two weeks after the funeral and interment had taken place. That almost seems to suggest that it was thought that no one would want to attend the funeral of a mad man – or that the notice was overlooked initially.

The word 'inmate' in this announcement stands out. As used today, the word would suggest someone who was confined in some way, usually in an institution, rather than merely being a voluntary lodger. The word does have a less common, and older, meaning of one who lives with others in the same house. It is more likely that it was used in this sense in the announcement. The irrelevant 'had long been' is not very accurate. John was not resident in Arkleby until 1862.

It is also rather odd that James Routledge's name comes first in the notice, ahead of that of John Banks, who was, after all, the subject of the announcement. Beginning the announcement with the deceased's surname, as is usual, means that anyone scanning the column will pick up the deceased's name quickly. Hiding the name of the deceased towards the end of the notice almost looks like a deliberate concealment. James Routledge's name is irrelevant in John Banks' death notice and its inclusion smacks more than a little of self-importance – he was, after all, only the deceased's landlord. That James Routledge was responsible for the notice is not necessarily unusual, as John's nearest relative, his niece Margaret, would probably have had no experience in such worldly tasks. Nonetheless, it is odd that James Routledge included his own name in the notice but omitted hers. She was John's closest relative and sole heiress and should have been the chief mourner at the funeral. Her omission seems more than a little disrespectful. Whether this attitude was on account of her age or sex can only be guessed at. All in all, it appears to be a death notice that is rather lacking in respect for the deceased and his family.

Burial

John Banks was buried in Crosthwaite Parish Church, Keswick on 31st July 1865,[65] shortly after a funeral service held at Parsonby Church adjacent to Arkleby. The Crosthwaite parish register entry for his burial gives his place of residence as Keswick, a place he had not lived at for some years. Keswick is probably written there because of his family's connection with the town and with Crosthwaite Church, rather than implying residence at death. What the arrangements for any Crosthwaite service and burial were, and who the mourners were is not known. It is hoped that his niece Margaret was well enough to attend the funeral service at Parsonby Church, if not the interment in Crosthwaite as well. George Ansell, the solicitor who prepared the disputed will for John, is known to have attended the service at Parsonby.

There is no marker for John's grave that can be identified today in Crosthwaite churchyard. There is a strong suspicion that John's body may well have been brought back to Crosthwaite to be buried in his parents' grave. As Jacob the elder was a man of substance locally, it is unlikely that he would have been buried without some sort of memorial in the churchyard. John's mother would normally have shared her husband's grave after her death. John's sister Margaret, who died in Crosthwaite in 1847, does not share a grave with her husband or her daughter, and this tends to point to her being buried with her parents as well.[66] Any memorial for Jacob the elder would originally have been inscribed not far short of 200 years ago, and the chances are that it would be among the older graves near to the church, where many of the gravestones no longer have legible inscriptions. Even if there was a later inscription added for John or Margaret, and that is far from certain, the climate of the Lake District is against enduring inscriptions in its churchyards.

CHAPTER THREE

The Wills of John Banks the Elder

The 1838 Will

John Banks the elder made his first known will in 1838. This will was referred to in the appeal court judgment. It was described by John's solicitor Mr George Ansell as having been entirely in John's own handwriting (usually referred to as a holograph will) and this was confirmed by Mr Highton, the schoolmaster, who was familiar with John's handwriting, at the trial. It was also said to have been, on the face of it, validly executed and witnessed. That this will was written out by John tells us something of his mental capabilities when he was in his mid-twenties and at a time when his mental illness had deteriorated significantly. Even if he was copying the format from a precedent book, or from the wording used in another will, it was something that is unlikely to have been achieved by someone as lacking in any significant mental ability as the plaintiff's witnesses often claimed: to write it out correctly would have required concentration and care. It is of course possible that he was helped by someone else dictating what was required. This might sound unlikely, but even if it did happen this way it would still have required care and concentration on John's part. That John was capable of writing a will also confirms that his standard of literacy was above a basic level.

In a similar vein, the understanding required to complete the formalities required for valid execution of a will would have required a level of organisational ability. Valid execution of a will (signature by the testator in the presence of two witnesses who both sign in the testator's presence[1]) needs a degree of understanding that frequently defeats would-be testators today, unless they have professional guidance. In 1838 the requirements for valid execution of a will could be found in the, then newly enacted, Wills Act 1837.[2] This Act was a major reform of the law of wills and it would be surprising if John did not receive some advice on it, or was at least provided with an example of how execution of the will should be carried out. Either way, John showed that he was capable of understanding what was needed. It is also worth adding, generally, that John appears to have been capable of understanding that it was the new requirements of the 1837 Act that had to be followed and that the multiplicity of ways to make a valid will before that Act were no longer available to him. Neither the original 1838 will nor a copy has survived, but we do know of its terms from the evidence of John's attorney[3] at the first trial of the will. John produced this will for the attorney's inspection during his 1863 visit to take instructions for a new will.

There is no evidence of John having made a will before 1838, but as John was aged twenty-six when he made this will, it is more than likely to have been his first will. The earliest he could have made a valid will would have been immediately after his twenty-first birthday, in 1833. It was clearly necessary that once he was over the age of twenty-one he should make a will, given the property that he would inherit from his father's estate after his mother's death. His interest in that property was such that it would pass into his ownership if he survived his father and had reached his majority – which at this time was twenty-one. As he did attain his majority and survive his father, he became entitled to his share of the properties, but could not take possession of them until after his mother had died and her life interest ceased. A will was therefore both desirable and sensible to deal with his interest in the trust property.

By the terms of the 1838 will John left his entire estate to his sister Margaret, who died before him in 1847 (see Chapter Four). The decision to leave his estate to his sister at this time was quite rational. Apart from his mother, his sister Margaret was John's only other close relative. The only asset of significance that John owned was his interest in the distribution of his father's will trust after his mother's death. There would, of course, have been no point in bequeathing that interest to his mother – his sister Margaret was the logical choice.

The 1863 Visit for Instructions for a New Will

John Banks decided upon a new will in 1863 and, for reasons explained later, two wills in identical terms were prepared and executed on different dates in December of that year (these are referred to in this chapter as the draft will and the engrossed will). It is the latter will that was the subject of the challenge after his death. But, in reality, the plaintiff had to attack both 1863 wills during the trial. Merely showing that the engrossed will was invalid would leave the draft will, on identical terms, still valid until shown to be otherwise. Showing both wills to be invalid still might not have been enough to achieve the claimant's objective, as defeating both the 1863 wills would then have left the 1838 will still valid: the revocation provisions in the 1863 wills would have been of no effect if the wills themselves were invalid. The potential significance of this point is discussed later in this chapter.

What prompted a new will at this stage in John's life is not clear. Concern for his health after the probable stroke and onset of epilepsy around September 1863 could have been the reason and, if it was, that would show something of John's mental capacity at the time in that he could understand his declining health and the need to review his will. An allegation about his reasons for a new will was put forward at the first trial and this is discussed towards the end of this chapter. According to the evidence of Joseph Tolson, John Banks had decided upon a new will 'sometime before the 1st December 1863'.[4] John Banks asked Tolson to call on him at Arkleby to account for the rents he had collected on John's behalf since Tolson's last accounting for them. John further asked that Tolson bring John's attorney to the same meeting in order that he could give instructions for a new will.

John's attorney, Mr George Ansell, had practised in Keswick as an attorney since 1826 – he was therefore a practitioner of thirty-seven years' standing at the time that he prepared the 1863 wills. His evidence was that he had been acquainted with John 'for upwards of twenty years'. However, having lived in Keswick for so long he would also have known of Jacob Banks the elder (who died in 1829) and his family's circumstances. George Ansell, by his own account, had previously acted for John in his legal affairs, presumably in connection with his properties in Keswick or possibly the estates of his father and mother. That he had acted previously for John also makes the point that John cannot have always been as lacking in mental capacity as was claimed. The length of time that he knew John is quite important as it made him the only person who had known John for business purposes since around the time of John's discharge from Dunston Asylum. He had seen John on 'several occasions' while John was living in Arkleby.

Joseph Tolson, who arranged this visit, was a grocer in Crosthwaite. He had been helping John for some time by collecting the rents from John's Keswick properties for him (he was also, at one time, one of John's tenants). There is other evidence that indicates that he had been friendly with John for many years and that he was trusted by John. He was described by the plaintiff,

John Banks the younger, as being a cousin or other near-relation to the defendant Edward Barron Goodfellow. The arrangement for the rent collection came about because Bassenthwaite, where John was living in 1860, was six miles away from Keswick and John was reluctant to make the journey. He thought that the spirits of Featherstone Alexander and Thomas Goodfellow would follow him on the journey and, to avoid them, he would not use the road. Instead, he crossed the fields and then crept along the hedgerows to try to hide from view. Tolson was aged fifty-eight by the time of the first trial in 1869. Having been born in 1811 he was almost an exact contemporary of John Banks. As he had lived in Keswick all his life, he would have known of John for most of this time. His evidence at the trial is reported as:

> He knew the late John Banks perfectly well from a boy upwards … John Banks … was rather excited at times, but anyone speaking to him would get a sensible answer.

The exact timing of this visit to John might have been determined by William Thirlwall, the brother of John's landlady Elizabeth Routledge. William Thirlwall was a farmer at Parsonby, a hamlet next to Arkleby. He lived within a short walking distance of his sister's home.[5] He had written to Tolson and informed him that John Banks was now seriously ill. He advised Tolson to visit John without delay if he had any business with John. That John Banks was known by others to be ill is supported by the other evidence at trial of the onset of his epilepsy in this year and also his probable stroke. The degree to which he was ill was disputed in the evidence given by both Ansell and Tolson, about both this first visit and the subsequent one. The letter from Thirlwall to Tolson could not be found at the time of Tolson's affidavit before the trial, but Tolson denied in his evidence at the trial that the letter had said anything of John's mental incapacity. Tolson stated that the letter was received around the end of November and, despite its absence, he recollected that it was to the effect only that John Banks was dangerously ill:

> I have sufficiently clear recollection of its contents to be able to deny positively that it contained anything which could be construed as an allusion to any mental illness weakness or incapacity …

The only possible explanation for this is that the illness referred to must have been the stroke and that no comment was made in the letter that this had impaired John's mental ability. Thirlwall was not called to give evidence on the contents of his letter, or had refused to do so.

It would be unusual for an attorney to bring someone else with him to a will instruction meeting with a client. Given the private nature of the business, a testator would usually not want a third party present (and, for possible reasons of undue influence on a testator, most professionals today would try to avoid others being present). But, as Tolson had to see John at the same time, a joint visit made sense (and it provided company for a lengthy journey). John knew and, it is believed, trusted Tolson, so his presence could have been of use to Ansell in talking with John. Mr Ansell's evidence at the first trial was that he was aware of John's earlier sojourn in a lunatic asylum and that John had been 'discharged therefrom quite cured'. Ansell also 'frequently saw him and conversed with him whilst he lived in Keswick …'. He was therefore aware of John's character, behaviour and, at least to some extent, his capabilities, before he agreed to visit him.

The Journey to Arkleby

The two travelled from Keswick to Arkleby on Wednesday 2nd December 1863. It would have been an unpleasant journey on poor, unmade roads, over rugged countryside, in winter weather with the usual seasonal shortage of daylight. The amount of daylight in this area would have been around seven hours and thirty-seven minutes at the start of December, decreasing to seven hours and sixteen minutes by the end of the month.[6] Winter in the Lake District usually involves significant amounts of wind and rain,[7] if not some sleet and snow as well, particularly on the fells. Seven years before these events, in 1856, there had been a great flood in the whole Vale of Keswick, which was caused by a heavy snowfall and then a sudden thaw accompanied by heavy rain. It had inundated many roads and cut off Keswick from Cockermouth.

It was recorded in the appeal trial judgment that 'The distance between Keswick and Arkleby is about 20 miles and the road was said to be bad'.[8] A forty-mile round trip in these conditions would have been quite arduous with horse-drawn transport, even for Cumbrians used to their own roads and weather. On behalf of the claimant against the will it was alleged that the journey was thirty miles and on behalf of the defendant that it was eighteen miles. Twenty miles looks about right on a modern map, although it is difficult to be precise as to the route that they would have taken in 1863.[9] It is difficult to understand why the claimant made an issue of this point when there were two witnesses giving evidence who had undertaken the journey.

The comment in the appeal judgment that 'the road was bad' needs to be understood not against the bad state of a modern road, but against the relatively unmade country roads of nineteenth-century England. These would have been long-established routes, but not purpose-built roads finished with tarmac we are familiar with today.[10] Main roads were, in general, better built and maintained, but this journey was not on those roads, but instead on country lanes. The latter would often not have received much repair work, leaving a rough uneven surface that was dusty and stony in dry weather and soft, muddy and rutted in wet weather. The problems of road maintenance would have been worse in sparsely populated upland areas, which had less important roads (in terms of priority for expenditure).

Their journey was undertaken in a hired gig. A gig was a light two-wheeled carriage pulled by one horse. Usually, it would have had seating for two on a bench seat raised up above the level of the gig's shafts. Some gigs had a closed back behind the passengers, which would have offered some protection from the rain and wind, but none from the cold. However, many gigs would have no overhead cover or closed back to protect against the weather. Joseph Tolson would presumably have driven, and the cost of the hire was treated as a disbursement by Mr Ansell. John Banks paid the cost in cash during his meeting with them.

It would have taken them a long time to travel the twenty miles each way. A horse's normal walking pace is around four miles per hour, which would indicate a journey of five hours each way or ten hours for the round trip. But this pace does not allow for the tiring of the horse during the journey and slowing effect of the load being pulled, the bad weather, poor roads or difficult gradients – all factors that would have increased the tiring effect on men and beast. In a light carriage, as they were, the total travelling time for the one-way trip would have been in excess of the five hours indicated above, before considering any stops for refreshment. The evidence of Mrs Routledge is that they arrived at her house at three o'clock in the afternoon, which would have (just) been within daylight hours. To then attempt the return journey on the same day would have meant travelling after dark on the same bad roads that were then, like all country roads, unlit. This would have been a too long and tiring day for both men and their horse, and the round trip was therefore broken, both men staying overnight with Mrs Routledge. The horse and gig were stabled overnight at William Thirlwall's farm in Parsonby. This trip was a far cry from the modern out-of-office visit to take will instructions.

On the second visit when Joseph Tolson returned with the will on 27th/28th December he was described as having travelled to Arkleby by pony and cart. He perhaps opted for cheaper travel as he was not accompanied by the attorney this time, although he was accompanied by his own teenage daughter.

The Evidence about John Banks' Condition and the Two Wills

The evidence about the wills came mainly from Mrs Routledge and her brother William Thirlwall (for the plaintiff and against the validity of the will), and from Mr Ansell and Mr Tolson (for the defendant and for the validity of the will). The versions of events from the two sides paint two very different pictures of John and the conduct of the meeting. Much of the evidence of Mrs Routledge and William Thirlwal, is flatly denied by Ansell and Tolson – Ansell described Mrs Routledge's evidence as 'a very incorrect account of what took place'. No evidence could be given by Mr Routledge, as he died on 5th March 1866 (when Margaret Banks Goodfellow, John's heiress, was still alive, and therefore before the will dispute started).

That each side's evidence was so diametrically opposed to the other is quite striking. This conflict posed a simple question for the jury at the first trial: which side was to be believed? Whose evidence was the more credible? Mr Justice Brett and the jury at the first trial had the great advantage of hearing the witnesses give evidence and then seeing their manner when that evidence was tested by cross-examination in court. This process allows both judge and jury the chance not only to hear what is actually said but to assess the demeanour of the witnesses and their reactions under questioning. The later appeal hearing in Queen's Bench only examined the written evidence, Mr Justice Brett's summing up to the jury and then heard argument from counsel. Both hearings appeared to have given little credence to Mrs Routledge.

The First Will, of Wednesday 2nd December 1863

Elizabeth Routledge's affidavit of 20th April 1868 sets out her evidence of the visit on 2nd December. She places the date precisely by saying it was the second day of Bridekirk coursing, when both her husband James and her brother William Thirlwall had left early that morning for Bridekirk and did not return until seven o'clock at night – hence their absence from the will meeting itself. Bridekirk is a village just over five miles south west of Arkleby. Hare coursing was a form of hunting for hares, usually with greyhounds, and usually as a competition between different hounds. These competitions were a regular feature of the rural sporting calendar, attracting spectators and gamblers alike. While popular as a rural sport for centuries, hare coursing has been illegal in England since 2005 (Hunting Act 2004). In 1863 such an event would be a notable occasion; hence the way Mrs Routledge could precisely identify the date.

She described John as being on that day 'in a low moping and imbecile condition' and that he was unable to understand what was being done in the meeting. Elizabeth Routledge's second affidavit, of 14th July 1868,[11] also declares that on 2nd December John Banks was in 'an imbecile state'. She stated that this imbecile condition 'was usual to him when he was not in his fits and his mental imbecility was so apparent that no one of ordinary intelligence could be in his company without seeing it'. This is consistent with her first affidavit, but expressed in rather stronger terms. One of the unanswerable questions about this evidence is the extent to which Mrs Routledge's affidavits are her own words or statements that have been polished by the plaintiff's attorney who would have prepared them. They do seem to be too polished for the wife of a farm labourer (as her husband was when she first married him).

Mrs Routledge's evidence was that, on the visitors' unexpected arrival around three o'clock in the afternoon, Mr Ansell announced that he was there to make a will for John Banks. Mrs Routledge made her visitors some tea, but John, she stated, took his tea by himself as he 'did not get on with them'. The suggestion that she thought that John did not get on with both his solicitor and his rent collector is somewhat surprising. Her affidavit does not explain the comment nor is there any detail of cross-examination on this point in the press reports. While not plainly stating that this meeting was not requested by John, Mrs Routledge's evidence that the meeting was unexpected and that John did not appear to know what was going on seems to suggest that she believed it to be the case (although her brother had written to Joseph Tolson to suggest that they should call for this purpose). Her view that John did not get on with Ansell and Tolson carried the implication that John would not have invited them to deal with such a personal matter as a will. The statement is so at odds with fact of the visit and the absence of any evidence from others to support her contention that John did not get on with them that one is left with the impression that this statement must have damaged her credibility in court. She also stated that John was 'not fit to take his meals in company at all'. This remark is not particularly helpful as it appears to be more about table manners than being competent to make a will.

Mrs Routledge claimed that later, after tea, John was asked to come into the sitting room to join the visitors. John came in but, in her account, there was no discussion of the terms of a new will. She did say that Tolson suggested that he should be one executor and that William Thirlwall 'would do' for the other executor. This was strongly denied by both Ansell and Tolson, who said that the choice was John's alone.

She further claimed that after Ansell had finished writing he asked John to sign the paper. When John asked what the paper was, she said that his question was ignored by Ansell, and John was asked again to sign his name where Ansell pointed to and John duly obliged. Others gave evidence that John was easily led and would sign anything that was put in front of him. This part of her affidavit is connecting with that claim. The implications of this claim that John could easily be persuaded to sign anything are considered in Chapter Eight.

Mrs Routledge said that she was then asked to sign as a witness to John's signature on the will. She complied, but claimed that she protested that she ought not do so as John was not in a fit state to make a will. This does prompt the question of what she knew about the capacity to make a will. Her objection, she said, was brushed aside by Ansell with the comment that without the will Margaret Banks Goodfellow would inherit anyway as she 'was the nearest to him', i.e. the person who would inherit if John died intestate. This comment about Margaret was also supported in the affidavit of 20th April 1868 by William Thirlwall, who stated that on the following morning Ansell and Tolson called at his house to collect their horse and gig. Before they set off Mr Ansell and William Thirlwall 'took a glass or two of spirits', and the solicitor told him of the will and his appointment as executor. Thirlwall stated that:

> I thought it rather strange but Mr Ansell told me the will was for the benefit of Miss Goodfellow who was the right heir so it would make no difference.

Thirlwall's doubt about the will's validity sits rather ill alongside the oath that he later swore as an executor of the last and true will in order to obtain probate to that will. However, he addressed this point in the same affidavit by saying that he proved the will as:

> I had no interest of my own to serve but thought I was acting for the benefit of the said Margaret Banks Goodfellow who I then believed was the heir of [John Banks] and had a right to succeed to his property and it was never suggested to me and I had no idea that the said alleged will would make any difference to anyone else or would if valid change the course of succession …

The comment about 'change the course of succession' does seem to suggest that the essence of this dispute was that the will was acceptable as long as Margaret inherited, but unacceptable once it would lead to Edward Goodfellow being the heir. Margaret Banks Goodfellow was at this time lodging with William Thirlwall. She later lodged, until her death, with Mrs Routledge.

Mrs Routledge summarised what happened at the meeting as:

> Mr Ansell did not read over the will to ... John Banks ... or tell him anything about it. Mr Ansell, and Joseph Tolson and Margaret Banks Goodfellow and John Banks and myself were all that were present when the said will was made and signed.

Mrs Routledge further states that the other witness to will was her husband James and that he added his signature after his return from Bridekirk, but not in the presence of John Banks or Mrs Routledge – an invalid attestation to a testator's signature which would render the will itself invalid (section 9 of the Wills Act 1837 requires the testator to sign in the presence of both witnesses and for each witness to sign in the presence of the testator). If Mrs Routledge's evidence had been accepted as the true version of events, she would have made out a matter of serious malpractice by Mr Ansell (this is discussed further in Chapter Five).

Not surprisingly, George Ansell's affidavit of 26th June 1868 sets out a very different version of events. He describes Elizabeth Routledge's evidence as giving 'a very incorrect account of what took place'. He starts with the request from Tolson to accompany him to Arkleby as John Banks had requested that Ansell prepare a new will for him. Soon after Ansell and Tolson arrived at Mrs Routledge's house they met John. There was, Ansell stated:

> no truth in the statement of [Mrs Routledge's affidavit] that [John] was then in an imbecile condition if that expression is intended to mean mental imbecility or that he did not understand what was being done.

After Ansell had had some preliminary discussion with John about his affairs, John proceeded:

> to give me instructions for his will in a perfectly rational manner and he appeared fully to understand the nature of the disposition which he proposed to make of his property.

Ansell also confirmed that John produced his old will, which John had written out in 1838. (This will still existed at the time of the trial and was attached as an exhibit to Ansell's affidavit.) Ansell drafted a will based on the instructions and read it through to John 'who appeared to understand it thoroughly'. Unfortunately, a copy is not attached to the copy of the affidavit held in the National Archives.

While Ansell was doing this, his evidence was that Margaret Banks Goodfellow and Elizabeth Routledge were present 'all or nearly all the time'. Margaret Banks Goodfellow asked John to appoint Tolson as an executor, and then John also asked for Thirlwall to be the second executor. Ansell's affidavit goes on to specifically deny:

1. that Elizabeth Routledge said anything to him to the effect that John was not in a fit condition to make a will; or
2. that he said that a will would make no difference, as Margaret would inherit anyway.

But he added that Mrs Routledge seemed glad that Margaret was being made John's heir and said words to the effect that 'Now he has made you all right'. Although Mrs Routledge's second affidavit denies that she said this, it is an expression that fits well with a non-lawyer's description of what had been done and it carries the ring of authenticity. Tolson remembered her words as being 'Now Margaret my lass he has made you alright'.

Ansell's account goes on to state that, after staying the night at Mrs Routledge's house, he and Tolson walked to Thirlwall's farm, accompanied by John who wished to see them off on their journey back to Keswick. His account of the visit ends with a denial that any discussion occurred at any time during the visit about John being sent to a lunatic asylum. He further denied that there was any reference at all made to John's mental condition. He added that he saw 'nothing in [John Banks] to lead me to suppose that he was of unsound mind'. Further, in his judgment 'he was then and also on the 28th December … of sound mind, memory and understanding and quite capable of making a will'. While his views are quite clear, it is a little odd that he was attempting to give evidence as to John's mental capacity at the signing of the engrossed will on 28th December, which was an occasion when he was not present.

The document that was signed at this meeting on 2nd December was a draft will written out by Ansell during the meeting. It would have been more usual for Ansell to have returned to his office with his notes of John's instructions for the will and then to have the will prepared in a more usual form for execution (called an 'engrossment'). An engrossed document was at this time one that was written out in a style known as court-hand. An engrossed will would have been written out in this way with all dates, words and amounts written out in full. This was not essential for the will to be valid, but it was at this time more a question of the professional appearance of a document.[12] To prepare the will in this traditional form would have meant Ansell returning to his office, having one of his clerks prepare the engrossment and then later returning to Arkleby to get it executed. Instead of following this traditional approach, Ansell took the decision that, on this visit, he should simply write out the new will in his own handwriting and have it executed at John Banks' lodgings at the end of their meeting. The reason for Mr Ansell doing things in this way was that the handwritten will, prepared and executed at the meeting, would be valid and would give immediate effect to John's wishes, should anything happen to John before the formally engrossed will could be brought back and executed. Ansell, quite rightly, was concerned that there could be delays, occasioned by the weather, illness or business matters, which could delay execution of the engrossed will. He said in evidence that this was his usual practice.[13] Ansell was clearly conscientious and realistic about the difficulties of travel in the winter possibly delaying execution of the will. There could also have been some concern at the state of John Banks' physical health. Despite the above being Ansell's normal practice because of travel difficulties in the area, the care he took over John's will does seem to indicate that he regarded John Banks as a client who should receive full attention.

Ansell's evidence about this meeting, given personally at the first trial, described John Banks as being neither 'cracked' nor 'crazed'.[14] He conceded that John was eccentric, but described him as being held in great esteem and respect by his neighbours, notwithstanding his eccentric behaviour. As Ansell was giving evidence on oath, this declaration of John's character and the witness's opinion of how John was regarded will have carried weight with judge and jury, particularly given his standing in the local community as a professional man.[15] Today a court will place great value on evidence of testamentary capacity given by an experienced and independent solicitor who has carried out his work properly.

Joseph Tolson's affidavit of 25th January 1868 also dealt with this meeting and John Banks' mental health. He stated that John was:

> for two or three years before and at the time of making the will subject to nervous affection [sic, but should be 'affliction'] of the head which came upon him at intervals but immediately passed away and did not

in any manner affect his mind memory or understanding ... and he was in good health and of sound and disposing mind at the time of the date of execution of his said will.

While Tolson seems to have been a credible witness, it is curious that his evidence implied that John had only suffered from mental health issues for two or three years before the will. He did not definitely state that John's illness was of such short duration, but that is the implication in restricting his remarks to 'two or three years before the will'. The other evidence was wholly against his illness being of such recent development. But the question before the court was not how long John had been ill, but how ill he was when he signed his wills. Tolson added that John was 'not to my knowledge or belief in the month of September 1863 or at any time seized with epileptic [sic] nor save as aforesaid any other attack'. This is consistent with his earlier evidence that no mention of epilepsy was made in the letter from Thirlwall. Unless anyone had told Ansell and Tolson about epileptic attacks and a stroke they would have no knowledge of this, unless there was a recurrence while they were at Arkleby.

What was said about this meeting was not directly relevant as to the validity of the later will signed at the second meeting: the validity of that will would depend upon John's mental capacity on that occasion and whether or not the formalities of execution were complied with. The main purpose of Mrs Routledge's evidence therefore appears to have been an unsuccessful attempt to discredit the evidence of the attorney and rent collector.

The Second Will, of Monday 28th December 1863

Back in Keswick, Mr Ansell had the engrossment of John's will prepared and Joseph Tolson returned to Arkleby with this on Sunday 27th December for John to sign it the following day. This time Joseph was accompanied by his daughter, Jane Tolson. Jane Tolson was to stay overnight with Margaret Banks Goodfellow (then almost eighteen), who was then lodging with William Thirlwell in Parsonby, while her father would stay overnight at Mrs Routledge's house. Jane was then to stay on for the remainder of the week to provide some company for Margaret.

Jane Tolson was aged fifteen at the time of this visit. At the time of her evidence she was twenty and had, for almost two years, been a teacher at the National School at Brigholm in Crosthwaite under the direction of the Reverend Battersby of St John's Church, Keswick. A National School was a school in England or Wales established by the National Society for Promoting Religious Education. These schools provided elementary education for the poor, and the teaching given conformed to the doctrine of Church of England. The National Society, as it was more simply known, was a Church of England organisation. Employment in such a school required a person to be of sound moral character and because of this Jane's evidence would be likely to carry greater weight than that of the average twenty-year-old recalling events of five years before.

Jane gave evidence that she knew John Banks as:

> he was frequently at our house before he went to Arcleby [sic] ...I saw him on more than one occasion after he went to live at Arcleby he was shy and reserved in his manner it always appeared to me that his understanding was correct and that he was of sound mind and fully capable of managing his own affairs.

Her visit to Arkleby lasted until the following Saturday (2nd January 1864). She said she was in John Banks' company:

> every day and I had plenty of opportunity of observing his manner and behaviour and although he was reserved at times (as in fact he had always been as far as I could recollect) I observed nothing in him to shew he was of unsound mind.

She also told of a visit that John Banks and Mr and Mrs Routledge paid to Keswick one market day in July 1864, when they spent part of the day at Joseph Tolson's house before returning to Arkleby in the evening:

> upon that occasion Mr Banks appeared quite the same as he had been while I was staying at Parsonby ... I had always been accustomed to his peculiar manner.

She added that 'he was sensible and exact in all he said and he did nothing to lead me to suppose that he did not understand what he was about or that he was of unsound mind'.

However, Jane Tolson's evidence was roundly attacked in the affidavit of Jane Clark (housekeeper to William Thirlwall and Mrs Routledge's sister-in-law), who denied that Jane saw John Banks every day she stayed there. Instead she claims that both Jane and Margaret Banks Goodfellow only saw him once as they 'were afraid of [him] and avoided his company as much as they could'. This paragraph in her affidavit ends by disparaging Jane, saying she 'was so young and childish as to be a very unfit and incompetent person to make an affidavit as to the state of mind of John Banks'. The choice of words seems to reveal a degree of the animosity that underpinned this dispute. Referring to a local Church of England schoolteacher as 'a very unfit and incompetent person' was perhaps not the wisest tactic without fairly good corroborating evidence. Mrs Routledge gave evidence that Jane stayed with Margaret Banks Goodfellow at William Thirlwall's 'and did not stay with us at all'. However, that throws no light on the girls' meetings with John, as all the evidence agrees that they stayed at Parsonby.

That George Ansell did not accompany Tolson to supervise the execution of the will is a little unusual as normally the person preparing the will would have supervised the execution of it to ensure that the formalities of the Wills Act 1837 were complied with and that the testator knew and understood the contents of the will. Strict compliance with these formalities is required by the court. The reason for this strict approach to the formalities in the 1837 Act was more recently, and colourfully, explained:

> Darkness and suspicion are common features in will cases: the trust too often is the secret of the dead or the dishonest. Because it is often difficult, and sometimes impossible, to discover the truth, the law insists on two types of safeguard in will cases. The first type of safeguard is part of the substantive law – the requirements of proper form and due execution. Such requirements ... are no mere technicalities. They are the first line of defence against fraud upon the dead. The second type of safeguard is the second line of defence. It is invoked where there are circumstances which give rise to suspicion; it is the safeguard of strict proof. In cases where no suspicion reasonably arises the court will allow inferences – presumptions as they are sometimes called – to be drawn from the regularity of a testamentary instrument upon its face, or the fact of due execution. But if there are circumstances, whatever be their nature, which reasonably give rise to suspicion, the court must be on its guard.[16]

No doubt Mr Ansell would have carefully explained to Tolson what was required for valid execution by John.

There is a further reason why the attorney would normally have supervised the execution of the will and that is to help establish that the testator had the necessary mental capacity to make the will when it was executed. In terms of the validity of the will this is when the court tests the testator's capacity. The fact the Ansell did not attend could be taken as indicating that he had no real concern as to John's capacity. There is nothing in the press reports of the first trial to show that the attorney was cross-examined on this point. Today, it would be suggested that for a testator with a known history of some mental illness it would be prudent for the solicitor to attend the execution of a will.[17]

Mrs Routledge's evidence was that, on the second visit, no will was brought to John other than a copy of the will from the previous visit (an engrossed copy prepared for signature could have looked to a lay person like a copy as it contained exactly the same information). Her evidence, and that of her brother, was that no will was signed on this occasion. The will that was admitted to probate is dated 28th December 1863 and bears the signatures of Elizabeth Routledge and her husband James as witnesses. No evidence could be taken from James as he died on 5th March 1866. Elizabeth Routledge's statements do not deal with the issue of how her signature, and her husband's, came to be on the later will if no will was signed on that occasion. The Bill of Complaint of 11th November 1867 that initiated this action does not clarify this point at all (and clearly shows some confusion between the events of 2nd and 28th December). Cross-examination of Elizabeth at the first trial would make for interesting reading on this point, but there does not appear to be any record of her explanation as to how her signature came to be on the engrossed will. Mrs Routledge does not allege in her affidavits that the second will is a forgery – although that is a possible inference from her claim, this allegation was unlikely to have been made at trial. Indeed, she admitted in evidence that the will did bear her signature. Alleging a local attorney was party to a forged will without firm evidence would have made headlines in the local press had she been believed.

Not being able to account for her signature on the second will would greatly undermine her evidence. Implying that Ansell and Tolson were parties to a forgery was a serious matter that, without evidence of forgery, must have damaged her credibility. Mrs Routledge's view that there was no second will is simply not credible without some account of how the signatures of herself and her husband came to be on the second will. She must have been questioned on this point, but no press report covers this. It also did little for her brother's credibility, in that his sworn statement that the will of 28th December was the last and true will of John Banks to obtain probate sits most uneasily against his later view that no will was ever signed on that day.

This denial that a will was signed, but no denial of the witnesses' signatures, is one of the curiosities of this case. Another is the apparent confusion on the part of the plaintiff's legal team to focus so much on the first will. It was essential to prove the second will was invalid before moving to attack the earlier executed draft will. It must be said that it appears throughout the matter to be a much less exact focus on each of the two wills than we would expect in a modern court.

The Lease for John's Properties

When the engrossed will was brought over to Arkleby by Joseph Tolson on 28th December 1863, and was duly executed and witnessed, John also signed the engrossed lease of his Keswick properties. This had been another important aspect of the first meeting, which was not directly concerned with the will but which had significant implications when considering John's mental capacity. The appeal court thought that it was sufficiently significant to be set out in some detail in the judgment.

After the draft will had been dealt with on 2nd December, John offered a business proposition to Joseph Tolson. John had calculated, apparently correctly, that the rents from his properties amounted to £80 per year. He offered to lease the properties to Tolson for seven years at £76pa, thereby effectively offering Tolson a £4 annual commission (a 5% fee) for the collection of the rent from the existing tenants and accounting to John for amounts due. Tolson agreed to the proposal and Ansell took notes of what was required in order that the lease could be prepared and signed at the meeting later that month. There was also an accounting for the rents to date (£40.7s.4d), and Tolson offered £29 in cash and his cheque for the balance. John refused the cheque (there was no bank near to him) and asked for it to be paid instead into his existing account at a bank in Keswick.

Mrs Routledge's evidence was that at the first meeting 'I heard nothing about a lease and was with [Mr Ansell and Mr Tolson] all the time except perhaps going out a few times and waiting on them'. Mrs Routledge also gave evidence that when the lease was signed on 28th December, it was not explained to John Banks, he was merely told to sign it, 'and the said John Banks to the best of my remembrance and belief made two or three attempts before he got his name written and [Joseph Tolson] perfected the signature'. The evidence of William Thirlwall, her brother, who was also present, agrees that there were two or three attempts, but says nothing of Joseph Tolson perfecting the signature. Despite this, Mrs Routledge's brother and husband then witnessed the signature without apparent protest, although she claimed that Tolson added afterwards, 'I don't care how soon Mr Banks dies I'm secured for seven years' – a point flatly denied by Tolson. The lease was executed by John and dated 28th December. It was produced at the trial, bearing the signatures of William Thirlwall and James Routledge as witnesses.

That Joseph Tolson came to this meeting holding £40 in rent indicates that John was not relying from day to day on the rent to meet his immediate expenses. This sum was over half a year's rent that had been accumulating while John had been able to pay his way during that time from his cash in hand. The existence of a bank account adds to the suggestion that the income from the properties was more than adequate to finance John's way of life. But there are some mysteries surrounding John Banks' estate and where his money went to, both during his life and after his death, and these are dealt with later in Chapter Eight.

The relevance of the court hearing about of these transactions was that they illustrated how much John was able to understand of his own business affairs and his ability to conduct business for himself. Of the negotiation over his rent monies, the appeal court remarked that this, 'if truly reported, tended strongly to shew that he was then capable of managing his affairs'. What exactly took place regarding the lease and the rent is strongly disputed in the evidence on behalf of the plaintiff, but the above is based on the appeal judgment's finding of fact.

The Dispute over the Will

One of the curiosities of these events is that no dispute about the validity of the last will arose on John Banks' death. It was only after Margaret Banks Goodfellow died that the argument began. Quite why this was so is not wholly clear. Margaret Banks Goodfellow would inherit on John's death either by will or on his intestacy. It was only when she died before attaining twenty-one that the possibility of two different heirs came to the fore. If John lacked a valid will and therefore died intestate and Margaret was dead before twenty-one, then John Banks the younger would have been John Banks the elder's heir. If John died leaving a will on the terms that he did, then Edward Banks Goodfellow, Margaret's half-brother, would be her heir on her death. Edward was related to Margaret only through their father and thus he had no 'Banks blood' in him. It looks at this point as though the argument begins about why a Goodfellow should get Banks money – such arguments are still encountered today. However, there are some other factors that may need to be explored in this case.

The *Cumberland Pacquet* in July 1870 carried a report of the appeal court judgment. In it reference is made to Margaret Banks Goodfellow being the heir at law (i.e. the person who would inherit if John died intestate) with the additional observation that 'it seems to have escaped all parties that the niece would have taken without the will'. This appears to reflect what Mrs Routledge claims that she was told. This remark was based, presumably, on the point that if the two wills made in December 1863 were invalid, Margaret Banks Goodfellow would still have been the heir at law on John Banks' intestacy (being a niece of the whole blood as opposed to the plaintiff's being a nephew of the half-blood[18]). But Margaret Banks Goodfellow's inheritance on John's intestacy would have then failed through her not attaining her majority, and in the absence of her leaving any spouse or issue (as was the case), then John Banks the younger (the half-nephew and plaintiff) would be the heir at law of his half-uncle, John Banks the elder, and he would receive the entire estate. The possibility of Margaret not marrying before twenty-one and not surviving to that age does not appear to have occurred to Mr Ansell, the attorney. It would today be quite common practice to draft a will for someone in John's circumstances which covered this point and made it clear who would inherit in default of Margaret attaining twenty-one without leaving issue. While Margaret was not known to be ill when the will was made, the higher mortality rates in the nineteenth century made this possibility much greater, and not covering the point does seem to have been a lapse on the part of Mr Ansell. 'This possible consequence of Margaret Goodfellow dying without issue and intestate, does not however, appear to have presented its self to the mind of any of the parties at the time of making the will'[19] – nor did the possibility of a young lady, possibly known to have consumption, dying while a minor appeared to have occurred to anyone.

A point that does not appear to have been commented on is that John Banks' first will from 1838 (described at the start of this chapter) was in favour of his sister Margaret. This will obviously had not been revoked by destruction (with *animus revocandi* – the intention to revoke), given that it was produced at the trial. Nor was there any subsequent revoking document until the executed draft will in 1863. But the 1838 will could not have been revoked by either of the two 1863 wills if they were both shown at trial to be invalid for want of testamentary capacity. Therefore, showing that those two wills were invalid either by reason of John's lack of testamentary capacity or conceivably that the execution was invalid, does not look likely to have achieved the plaintiff's aim. If they had been invalid, John's estate would have passed under the 1838 will, which remained valid as the 1863 wills could not have revoked it.

If the 1838 will was drafted in the usual early nineteenth-century manner in favour of his sister Margaret and 'her heirs or assigns', then John's estate would appear, at least at first glance, to have then passed on his death to Margaret's heir at law. As Margaret had died in 1847, her interest in John's estate would then appear to pass to Thomas Goodfellow, her husband, as her heir, and in turn, as he died a widower (twice over, as both his wives, Margaret and Sarah, predeceased him) in 1858, his heirs would be his three surviving children (which included Margaret Banks Goodfellow). However, this line of reason is fallacious, as despite the provision regarding heirs and assigns in the 1838 will, Margaret's death defeated the provision for her entirely.[20] This then raises the question as to whether not the 1838 will contained any alternate provisions in the event that Margaret did predecease John. The lack of judicial comment on alternate provisions in the 1838 will suggests that the will did not contain such provisions.

Both trial judgments tell us something of the 1838 will, as it was described as having been produced at the will meeting by John Banks in 1863. What happened to the will, after the first trial when Mr Ansell produced it for the court's examination, is not known. But if the argument that John lacked testamentary capacity at the time of the 1863 wills was successful, then the revocation provisions in those wills could not possibly have revoked the 1838 will. Further, John Banks would not have had the capacity to necessary to revoke the 1838 will by destruction then or afterwards (but he had in fact not done so). The 1838 will would have remained unrevoked, albeit probably not containing any effective dispositive provisions.

It seems therefore that the plaintiff's case could only have succeeded in producing an inheritance for him if the two 1863 wills were invalid, and the 1838 will was either shown to be invalid because of lack of capacity as well[21] or because it contained no effective dispositive provisions. No attempt was made at the trial of the will to attack the 1838 will specifically by maintaining that John lacked the capacity to make it. It would have been helpful if either the summing up at the first trial or the written judgment at the appeal had stated clearly that the 1838 will contained no disposition of his wealth that was valid once Margaret had predeceased him.

Quite why John Banks the elder determined to make a new will in 1863 is not wholly clear. There is usually some event or consideration that prompts a testator to make a new will. It is often a change in wealth, in family circumstances or in the testator's personal circumstances, such as his health, that provides the impetus for a new will, but none of these reasons are apparent here, unless John understood that his stroke and the onset of epilepsy could well presage his death. It could be thought that Margaret Banks Goodfellow's health might have been a reason to prompt a new will if her consumption was apparent. There is no evidence that it was, but it would have been more likely if she was known to be ill at this time that John would have been asked to decide on who should benefit in default of Margaret not surviving and attaining twenty-one. Those wishes would then have been recited as alternative provisions in the will.

In *The Times* of 20th February 1869, the report of the first trial provides a possible reason for the new will. It was stated in court, on behalf of John

Banks the younger, the plaintiff, that John Banks the elder had taken a strong dislike to him:

> It was suggested on the other side that he had taken a strong dislike to the plaintiff, who had, he had heard, been making inquiries whether or not he was his heir, should his niece die; and to satisfy him, the testator was allowed to make his will in favour of his niece, as she was heiress to him, it was thought it could do no harm.

This report contains two elements, first the possibility that John Banks the elder resented the enquiries, and secondly that there was then collusion in making a will when he had not the power to make one. It is, however, implicit in the point being made in court, ostensibly against the will, that John Banks the elder could understand well enough what the enquiries were and why he did not want was his nephew to benefit.

John Gill, the Keswick letter carrier, offered some thoughts on this point in his evidence:

> …I believe that on the 1st day of December 1863 and for long before [Joseph Tolson and Mr Ansell] well knew that John Banks [the younger] was not the heir of John Banks [the elder] in preference to Margaret Banks Goodfellow and I make it out from the fact that I was informed by Mr Dallow (one of the trustees of the will of Thomas Goodfellow) in about the year 1860 that Mr Ansell had taken counsel's opinion on behalf of Margaret Banks Goodfellow and that counsel's opinion was that the heir to the property of John Banks the elder would be Margaret Banks Goodfellow and failing her John Banks [the younger].

While this paragraph certainly continues the common belief that village postmen will always know everyone else's business, it not particularly helpful. The first reference to John Banks the younger not being the heir in preference to Margaret seems to be clear and no one really suggested that this could or would be the case. With or without the will, Margaret would have inherited. It is interesting that counsel's opinion is said to have been taken at Margaret's expense, as this is the only evidence that raises this possibility. That counsel is said to have advised that, if John Banks the elder died intestate, John Banks the younger would be the heir in default of Margaret reaching twenty-one again is not surprising as that is the premise behind the challenge to the will (if one ignores the 1838 will). George Ansell's evidence was that no counsel's opinion on this point had been taken.

The Times report does not suggest that there was anything delusional in John Banks the elder having this belief – it was based on him having heard, and resented, his nephew John Banks the younger making enquiries to find out if he was his uncle's heir. John Banks the younger admitted to seeing Mr Ansell in the spring of 1860 to ask him who his uncle's heir would be. He was told that Margaret would be, and John Banks the younger maintains that this was only enquiry he made. One can see why the nephew made the enquiries, particularly if he had any concerns about Margaret's health (although that is unlikely in 1860). On the other hand, it is not unreasonable for a testator to resent relatives being openly inquisitive about the terms of his will – this is regularly encountered today. Also, it is far from unknown, where curiosity is pushed too far, for that resentment to lead to the testator making a new will which either prevents the person who made the enquiries from inheriting or curtails their benefit. Joseph Tolson's affidavit of 25th January 1868 acknowledges that John Banks had told him sometime prior to the meeting that he had heard that John Banks the younger had been making enquiries as to whether he would be his uncle's heir instead of Margaret.

But the plaintiff in this case was attempting to fight back and challenge both wills on the grounds that John Banks the elder lacked testamentary capacity when he had taken against his nephew and had a new will prepared. If the nephew was correct in this contention, it would mean that John Banks could not have validly made a new will. In framing his claim in this way, the nephew would have been alleging that the attorney, Mr Ansell, effectively conspired with Joseph Tolson to let John Banks the elder make a new will, even though he lacked the mental capacity to do so, solely in order to make a new will that made it clear that the nephew could not inherit. It did this by naming Margaret to be the sole heir, with descent in default of her surviving then being by operation of law to her heir at law, the defendant Edward Goodfellow.

Several things arise from this claim. First, it again attacks the professionalism, indeed honesty, of Mr Ansell, the attorney. That is not a claim that should have been made lightly in court as, without at least some credible evidence to support it, it was likely to have little persuasive effect on the judge or jury. Indeed, it may well have had the opposite effect, for the plaintiff may have lost credibility in the eyes of the jury if they resented seeing the honesty and reputation of a local professional of long standing being attacked in this way. When put alongside the evidence of Mrs Routledge, the core of the claim very easily looks like an attack simply based on Mr Ansell's lack of integrity.

Secondly, even if this claim was successful, it does not seem to get the plaintiff further forward unless he could also show that the 1838 will was ineffective (as discussed above).

Thirdly, although we know little about the closeness or otherwise, of John Banks the elder to his half-brother's children, we do know that John Banks the elder had once talked in the early 1860s of going to see his nephew in America. This was said, apparently not in the context of any particular affection for John Banks the younger, but in the context of John Banks the elder trying to escape the evil spirits that tormented him. He had said the evil spirits could not follow him to America as they could not swim.[22] John Banks the younger claimed in his affidavit that his uncle 'was much attached to me', but that is not corroborated by other witnesses, and indeed seems a little unlikely as John Banks the younger spent the greater part of his time in North America (see Chapter Six). Mrs Routledge in her evidence gives some support to the idea that John Banks the elder might have wanted his estate to pass to his nephew as he 'had a great dislike to all the Goodfellow family' except for his niece Margaret. There is no evidence at all as to John's views on Thomas Goodfellow's children, other than Margaret. There is some evidence of John's delusion about persecution by the spirit of the dead Thomas Goodfellow. But Thomas Goodfellow's own will demonstrates his continued trust in John. John had been charged with looking after Margaret Banks Goodfellow in her father's will. She now lodged with him. It therefore became reasonable on his part to want to look after her.

CHAPTER FOUR

Margaret Banks Goodfellow: The Niece and Beneficiary of the Last Will

Margaret Banks Goodfellow, who was mentioned in the previous chapter as John Banks the elder's heir, was his sister Margaret's only child. Margaret Banks Goodfellow was the sole beneficiary under the terms of her uncle John's disputed wills. To us today, Margaret Banks Goodfellow is an even more shadowy figure than her uncle. We know a lot less about her, much shorter, life than we do about his. She outlived her uncle by a little less than two years, dying of consumption (on the death certificate recorded as *phthisis* – an alternative name then for consumption – but today known as pulmonary tuberculosis), aged only twenty, on 6th May 1867. It is understandable that not much is now known of her life, given that it was by, nineteenth-century standards, fairly unremarkable, despite its brevity and family tragedies.

Margaret Goodfellow (née Banks)

Margaret Goodfellow, the mother of Margaret Banks Goodfellow, was slightly younger than her brother John Banks the elder, having been born three years after him in 1815. She lived with her mother and brother until 1846. On 16th March 1846, she was married to Thomas Goodfellow, in Crosthwaite Parish Church, Keswick. Although Margaret attended a non-conformist chapel in Keswick, it is thought that the meeting house used as a chapel was not then licensed for marriages (or funerals), hence the use of the Anglican Church.

A Victorian Tragedy: The Extraordinary Case of Banks v Goodfellow

John Banks the elder was one of the three witnesses to his sister's marriage. His attendance, and his involvement in the ceremony, attests to a degree of closeness between Margaret and John. They had been together, with their mother, from birth until Margaret married, apart from the few weeks John spent away in Dunston Asylum. Clearly, Margaret was not one to embarrass or insult her brother by excluding him from her wedding – nor was she one to deny him some important part in the formalities. His eccentricities might well have caused a degree of nervousness ahead of the service, but obviously this was not sufficient to deter her from involving him. Having three witnesses, as she did, when two would have sufficed, could well have been planned as a precaution in the event that John's illness prevented him from attending or that he had to be removed from the church because of some misbehaviour during the service. Did John perhaps also give Margaret away and walk her down the aisle in place of their dead father? It is likely that he did, and that would have been even more to Margaret's credit.

It is also relevant to our view of John that Margaret's request that he act as a witness gives us some hint as to his family's view of his understanding and his capability of acting reasonably in public when it was necessary for him to do so. Bearing in mind that John had caused disruptions previously in chapel, there could have been some concern as to how he might react in church this time. At this service, John signed his name as a witness, rather than making a mark, confirming, at least in part, other evidence of his ability to read and write.

No ages for either bride or groom are shown on their marriage certificate; both are simply shown as being 'of full age'. This might have been done in deference to the disparity in their ages. Margaret was in fact thirty years and six months old when she married. She was four years older than her husband. While it is only speculation, it does seem a little unusual that a woman, from a local family of some standing, who stood to inherit property on her mother's death, had to wait until she was over thirty to marry. While not old enough to then be thought of as an old maid, most young women then would have been married before they passed thirty. Was the knowledge of her brother's illness something that had deterred suitors – perhaps thinking that such a condition might be capable of being passed to their children? At this time, it was often assumed, and indeed asserted in some areas of the medical profession, that madness could be an inherited condition. As the cause of John's illness was not then known, far less understood, the idea that his condition was the result of bad blood, or some strain of madness in the family pedigree, could easily have taken root. It is all too easy for such suppositions to become accepted, in the absence of a science-based understanding of mental illness. Any local gossip to this effect could have later been seen as justified, in that Margaret Banks Goodfellow, Margaret's daughter, was described, shortly before her death, as being of 'weak although not unsound mind'. Of course, it could just be that men were not attracted to Margaret, or she was not attracted to her suitors, or even that she was reluctant to leave her mother to look after John alone, but being an heiress, in a minor way at least, would usually have had significant attractions in itself in the nineteenth century.

On the marriage certificate, Margaret is simply shown as being a spinster of no occupation. The lack of occupation in her case is not indicative of idleness but indicates more that her family was of sufficient independent means that she was not required by their financial circumstances to earn a living. Thomas Goodfellow is shown on the certificate as a bachelor, with his rank or profession shown as 'Grocer'. Their marriage announcement in the *Carlisle Journal* of 22nd March 1846 reads:

> At Crosthwaite Church, Keswick, on Tuesday last, by the Rev. Edward Wilson, Mr Thomas Goodfellow, shopman to Mr Robinson, grocer, to Margaret, only daughter of the late Jacob Banks, pencil manufacturer, of Keswick.

Here we again see the local standing of the bride's father's occupation being publicly noted, despite his death some sixteen years earlier.

Thomas Goodfellow

Thomas's parentage was omitted from this press notice of the wedding. Quite why this was done is unclear. He was the son of Archibald and Mary Goodfellow and was born at Bolton Fell End in the parish of Stapleton[1] on 6th September 1819. The 1841 census shows his parents as living by themselves in Bolton Fell End, both aged fifty-five. No occupation is given in the census for either of them; they are shown as being of independent means. Archibald is thought to have lived until 1857, approximately a year before Thomas died. If either parent attended Thomas's wedding, neither was asked to act as a witness for their son. William Robinson, Thomas's employer at the time of the wedding, was Thomas's witness at the marriage. That Thomas's employer acted so, rather a member of Thomas's family, would usually indicate a lack of surviving close family, but it may in Thomas's case be evidence of a family estrangement.

A Victorian Tragedy: The Extraordinary Case of Banks v Goodfellow

In the 1841 census Thomas was recorded as lodging with a Christopher Woodall, a marble mason, in Barwises Court, English Street, Carlisle. Fellow lodgers there were David and Thomas Blain. David Blain was a plumber and glazier, and Thomas Blain was a tea dealer. Thomas Goodfellow was recorded in the census as an apprentice tea dealer – presumably starting his career apprenticed to Thomas Blain in Carlisle. On 11th June the following year, the *Carlisle Journal* carried a report of a young boy being rescued from drowning in the River Eden 'a little below where the Pettril runs into it'.[2] Some boys, who could not help their friend, raised the alarm and:

> Mr Thomas Goodfellow, tea dealer, and two friends … at once ran to the spot to render assistance. Mr Goodfellow jumped into the river, with his clothes on, and fortunately succeeded in seizing the drowning boy and dragging him to land.

The boy was saved and 'the humane promptitude of Mr Goodfellow is deserving of the greatest praise'. If this was the same Thomas Goodfellow, and there must be every likelihood that it was, he would have been twenty-two at the time (and clearly preferred being called a tea dealer rather than an apprentice).

Thomas's description of 'grocer' on the marriage certificate (the certificate of course being a less public document than a newspaper notice) appears grander than the lesser-sounding, but probably more accurate, term 'shopman' in the public notice. A shopman was then a member of staff in a shop, more likely to be described today as a shop or sales assistant. Thomas uses the description of 'grocer' on all later registration documents and in his will. His son John's death certificate describes Thomas as being a 'Master Grocer' – a term that in this area merely indicates that he employed staff in his shop. Also, from later advertisements in the local press, it is clear that he regarded himself as both a grocer and tea merchant. Tea merchant sounds grander to the modern ear, but then it meant no more than being a vendor of tea. At that time, being a seller of tea would not necessarily have followed from being a grocer. In 1855 the *Carlisle Patriot* carried a series of advertisements for the teas and coffees of Smith Abbot & Co. The advertisements list the local grocers carrying their products, and Thomas Goodfellow appears as their stockist in Keswick.

Thomas's additional description as tea merchant was obviously important to him, but it was also indicative of the central role that tea had then taken in British life. Tea had been subject to excessive taxation in the eighteenth century and this restricted its use to better-off households.[3] The reduction of the tax on tea in 1784 not only reduced the smuggling of tea into Britain but it also meant that tea would no longer be a luxury item. In 1841, seeds of the tea bush had been brought from China to Darjeeling, in north east India, and this was the beginning of the break-up of the Chinese monopoly on the supply of tea.[4] In the nineteenth century, tea sales increased hugely and tea became part of the staple diet of all classes in Britain. Tea shops serving food and tea began to appear in the 1860s[5] and soon became very popular. The growth of tea drinking in the middle of the century also became associated with the rise in Britain of the Temperance movement. A background event to the times of this book caused by the boom in tea drinking was the importance of the new season's tea harvest reaching the domestic market. The end of the East India Company's monopoly in 1834 and the repeal of the Navigation laws had opened up the tea trade. Higher prices for the first of each year's new crop gave rise to the famous Clipper races, culminating in the 1866 race when ten clippers[6] left China on the same day and *Taeping* and *Ariel* docked first in London within twenty minutes of each other after ninety-nine days' sailing. Tea was now fully established in the British way of life.

After his marriage to Margaret, Thomas was able to take a step up from working for someone else to running his own grocery and tea business. Whether or not it was his marriage to Margaret that enabled him to do this is not clear, but the marriage cannot have harmed his financial position: indeed, it should have transformed it. Even if his mother-in-law did not help him financially at the time of the marriage, less than two years later she was dead and, through being Margaret's heir, Thomas would have gained Margaret's share of her father's will trust. Thomas had then become what most Victorian men aspired to be – a man of property.

The Birth of Margaret Banks Goodfellow

Unfortunately, Margaret and Thomas's marriage did not last long. Margaret died in childbirth on 12th January 1847; not quite ten months after their wedding (the *Kendal Mercury* of 16th January 1847 records her death as 'in child-bed'). The child, Margaret Banks Goodfellow, was born on 8th January 1847.

The death of a woman in childbirth was far more common in Victorian England than it is today. Being such a harsh fact of life, death in childbirth had become a regular theme in Victorian fiction. Dickens described it in *Oliver Twist* for Oliver's birth in the workhouse, Little Paul's birth in *Dombey and Son*, and Scrooge's younger sister in *A Christmas Carol*; Emily Brontë used it for the death of Catherine Earnshaw in *Wuthering Heights*; Thomas Hardy used it twice, once for the death of Fanny Robin in *Far From the Madding Crowd* and again for the death of Lucetta Farfrae[7] in *The Mayor of Casterbridge*; in *War and Peace*, Tolstoy wrote of Lise Bolonskaya's death in giving birth to the young Prince Nikolai.[8] The child orphan was even more commonly encountered. Being orphaned was a reality of the times, as Margaret Banks Goodfellow and her later siblings would discover.[9] Orphaned, unwanted and destitute children could have limited life expectancy, particularly if they fell into the system of pauper asylums for children – the infamous baby farms, homes of malnutrition, disease and abuse.[10] One of the worst examples was Drouet's Pauper Asylum for Children in Tooting which, in early 1849, contained 1,400 gaunt, semi-starved, ill children, some bearing marks of violence. The scandal that followed shook society. Drouet was charged with manslaughter but was acquitted.

Death in childbirth always appears to be so wasteful, but particularly so in the nineteenth century when fit and able mothers were also at high risk of dying, from causes that are now avoidable, leaving motherless children. Maternal death rates in childbirth for 1850 were approximately fifty-five per thousand births.[11] The causes were mainly puerperal fever, haemorrhage, convulsions and illegal abortion – 'The Four Horsemen of Death'[12] – but of these four, puerperal fever is the most likely cause of Margaret's death.

It has been estimated that in both the eighteenth and nineteenth centuries in England and Wales puerperal fever infections occurred in between six and nine per thousand deliveries, and deaths between two to three per thousand deliveries.[13] Although this estimate at first glance makes puerperal fever look uncommon, births were very frequent (it was an age of much larger families than today) and if a woman went into labour ten times there was clearly a greater risk of death. In terms of maternal mortality, puerperal fever accounted for approximately half of all deaths.[14] Between the mid-nineteenth century and the late 1930s maternal mortality was second only to tuberculosis as the main cause of death. It is estimated that this fever might have accounted for between 250,000 and 500,000 deaths in England and Wales in the eighteenth and nineteenth centuries.[15] It is therefore no surprise to see that the wording of the Anglican Book of Common Prayer referred to the churching of women after safe delivery as a 'thanksgiving'. The prayers commence, 'Forasmuch as it hath pleased Almighty God of his goodness to give you safe deliverance, and hath preserved you in the great danger of child-birth …', and conclude, '… we give thee humble thanks for that thou hast vouchsafed to deliver this woman thy servant from the great pain and peril of child-birth …'.

These words would have been more heartfelt in Margaret Goodfellow's time, given that the risk to the mother was so much greater then.

Margaret Goodfellow's Death

The death certificate for Margaret Goodfellow records only two causes of death, but this certificate, like her brother's, reflects the usual Victorian failing of recording observable conditions not the underlying illnesses (often, of course, because the medical science of the time was not capable of identifying the underlying condition). The first cause of Margaret's death is given as 'Diarrhea' (sic) existing for two weeks preceding death. The second recorded cause is 'Child Birth 5 days' – meaning death five days after childbirth. Neither of these two would be considered to be causes of death for a modern death certificate.

The events surrounding this birth are worth considering in a little more detail. There was in the mid-nineteenth century a realistic acceptance of the considerable risk inherent in childbirth. The risk of the mother's death was then regarded as being unavoidable – whereas today childbirth is regarded as normally carrying far less risk to the mother. We can now identify much of the nineteenth-century risk as being avoidable with today's medical knowledge.

Labour, without any medical assistance or interventions, such as are available today, would have been a trying experience for any mother in 1847. Margaret's labour and death took place in her mother's house where, no doubt, her mother would have assisted the local doctor with the nursing. Home birth was far more routine then, particularly in country areas that lacked easy access to hospitals. But, as commented on below, nineteenth-century hospitals were not necessarily safer environments for childbirth. Neither the home nor the hospital would have matched today's sterile conditions – as no one then understood the significance of asepsis.

Margaret's husband was present when she died, but would almost certainly not have assisted with the birth of their child. The father's involvement in, or presence at, the birth was not then, and for a considerable time afterwards, considered helpful (or indeed even proper).

A major risk at this child's birth will have been the severe weakening in Margaret's physical condition on account of the diarrhoea she suffered from for the nine days that preceded the birth. The duration of this illness, coupled with the doctor viewing it as severe enough to be a cause of death, points to something of much more consequence than a minor gastric infection. It is more probable that there was some significant underlying disease, probably bacterial, that produced severe diarrhoea as a symptom. But, in the absence of effective fluid replacement for the mother, typically given today by intravenous drip, there would have been the near-certainty of Margaret being dehydrated by the time that she went into labour. Dehydration would have caused headaches, light-headedness, even disorientation and confusion, as well as tiredness and lack of stamina. The lack of stamina would in turn have led to increased levels of exhaustion, that were reached more quickly than usual in labour if it was anything other than a straightforward birth. The diarrhoea would also have diminished Margaret's appetite and prevented her taking much, if any, benefit from any food or liquid that she did manage to ingest before her labour started. This lack of effective sustenance would have added to her general physical weakening through exhaustion. Margaret's declining physical condition after eight or nine days of diarrhoea could even have brought on her labour prematurely – although not too prematurely, as post-natal care for premature babies at this time bears no comparison to today's care, and therefore Victorian survival rates for premature births were generally low.

Whether or not the process of Margaret's labour was difficult is not known, but however easy or difficult it was, Margaret would have had no effective pain control, or relief, and this would have introduced another debilitating factor for her health (and her chances of survival). Chloroform's anaesthetic properties were only discovered in 1847,[16] and its use in childbirth in England spread only after 1853 when it was used to assist Queen Victoria with the birth of Prince Leopold.[17] However, this form of anaesthesia was not without its risks given the toxic nature of chloroform, and it could lead to fatalities in the hands of insufficiently trained doctors. In 1847, labour for a woman such as Margaret would have been endured without effective pain relief. The then position favoured for childbirth was usually with the mother lying on her left-hand side with her legs drawn up towards the abdomen. The use of this position meant that mother and doctor had no face-to-face view of each other and this was intended to save any embarrassment to either party.

Today, a difficult labour might be shortened and made safer by medical intervention such as a Caesarean section.[18] Although this surgical procedure was known, and used, from very early times it was not used regularly in Great Britain in the mid-nineteenth century, as it would, in the overwhelming majority of cases, result in the death of the mother. Hence, the procedure was then used more as a matter of last resort to save a child, rather than to assist a mother. In 1865, the death rate of mothers in Great Britain from attempted Caesarean interventions has been estimated at 85%.[19] It is most unlikely therefore that surgical intervention could have been used by a country physician in Keswick in 1848 unless as a last resort entailing the near-certainty of the mother's death.

There is a potentially greater significance in the 'diarrhoea' entry on the death certificate. Quite what caused this illness cannot, at this remove, be established. It could have been produced by a range of factors common in Victorian England from food poisoning to personal hygiene (especially unwashed hands) to contaminated water supply or to poor domestic sanitation. Margaret's mother died in the same house barely a year after her. Her death is recorded as being through influenza (five weeks) and dysentery (eight days). Dysentery is a condition typically with diarrhoea, fever and abdominal pain. It is a type of gastroenteritis caused by a variety of bacteria, viruses, etc. It is tempting to wonder if this was from the same source as Margaret's diarrhoea, for example faulty drains or sewers, or a contaminated water source.

The lack of knowledge of bacterial infection would have meant that the doctor[20] attending a birth would have been wearing his everyday clothes (worn to attend other patients with a variety of injuries and diseases). No gloves, gowns, hair covering or masks that we would expect today, would have been used but perhaps, if matters became particularly bloody, an apron might be used to save the doctor's suit and shirt – if they were not already too stained by blood and other matter from earlier patients (a reason for the customary dark suits worn then by doctors). Sterilised cleaning of clothing was not available (or understood) nor was scrubbing of hands. With this lack of understanding of the need for sterile barriers, doctors themselves could then be the source of potentially lethal infections to their patients. They could also worsen existing infections by introducing new sources of infection.

It is possible that the cause of Margaret's diarrhoea could have been a more serious, but undiagnosed, physical illness affecting the digestive system. But, of course, if it was the latter, then her chances of survival are likely to have decreased. Whatever its origin, the likely bacterial infection from the diarrhoea discharge itself carried the high risk of bacterial contamination of other parts of the body, including Margaret's genital area. The risk was also present of diarrhoea contamination on the hands of those who nursed her thereby reinforcing the same infection in Margaret by contact or feeding. Given the lack of understanding of bacterial infection, and the consequential need for hygiene for both patient and those attending her, this meant that simple acts of nursing could further endanger the lives of both mother and child.

The threat to the mother increased significantly if internal examinations by the doctor were made before, during or after the labour. This would easily carry additional bacterial contamination deeper inwards towards the mother's uterus. Similarly, any attempt to assist the birth manually, or with instruments, would increase the chances of infection. Any tearing, scratching or abrasion by the hands or instruments would have helped to introduce infection from faecal matter (or any other bacteria on the doctor's hands or instruments) into the bloodstream through the raw areas in the reproductive tract. Infections of the reproductive tract generally led to what was then known as puerperal fever, and is usually referred to today as post-partum infection.

All of this made for a grim prospect as Margaret endured her labour. But, in the same year, the work of Dr Ignaz Semmelweiss, in the Vienna General Hospital, was leading him to understand that the origin of puerperal fever lay in germ infection from poor hygiene during childbirth. He was concerned that in the two maternity wards at the hospital there was a noticeable variation in puerperal fever rates (and consequential death rates from puerperal fever). The lower rate was in the ward used for training midwives and the higher rate was in the ward used for training doctors. This variation was known to expectant mothers in Vienna, who would often go to great lengths to avoid being admitted to the ward used by the doctors.

Semmelweiss suspected that, in most cases, poor hygiene on the part of the doctors was involved. Simple washing of hands, in a chlorinated lime solution, after doctors and students had performed autopsies, but before they examined patients in the maternity ward, was found to be effective in lowering the incidence of puerperal fever in that ward. Medical staff assisting in childbirth, or the examination of expectant mothers, with unwashed hands is quite repugnant to us today, but it was not then. That the examination of the patients took place after the trainee doctors' human autopsy classes (practical not theoretical) is even more disturbing. Indeed, it was the accidental death of a colleague following blood poisoning contracted during an autopsy that led Semmelweiss to consider a connection between the two infections. Semmelweiss's work was pioneering work in the understanding of germ infection, but sadly, like many innovative ideas, his theory of bacterial infection was flatly rejected by most of Vienna's medical establishment. As a direct consequence of this rejection, his position at the Vienna General Hospital was not renewed in 1849.

The humiliation of the public rejection of his ideas and termination of his professional position may well have contributed to Semmelweiss's subsequent mental decline, but it was clear by 1865 that his mental state had deteriorated to such an extent that he should be taken to a mental institution. His mental condition has been the subject of modern analysis:

It is impossible to appraise the nature of Semmelweis's disorder. It may have been learned helplessness, which is known to cause chronic and severe depression. It may have been Alzheimer's disease, a type of dementia, which is associated with rapid cognitive decline and mood changes. It may have been third-stage syphilis, a then-common disease of obstetricians who examined thousands of women at gratis institutions, or it may have been emotional exhaustion from overwork and stress.[21]

Two weeks after being admitted to the mental institution, Semmelweiss died from – irony of ironies – blood poisoning, which almost certainly arose from an infection in the injuries he sustained after severe maltreatment by the institution's attendants when Semmelweiss objected to being confined there. Ignaz Semmelweiss died on 13th August 1865. His death occurred barely three weeks after that of John Banks the elder.

There had been some other voices preaching in the wilderness on this issue. Alexander Gordon, an Aberdeen physician, had suspected that he was the agent that carried infection from patient to patient in the 1790s. Like Semmelweiss, he was driven out by the medical establishment for his heresy. In the USA, Oliver Wendell Holmes Senior, polymath and ardent unionist, published an essay in 1843, 'The Contagiousness of puerperal fever', in the *New England Quarterly Journal of Medicine and Surgery*, arguing that puerperal fever was carried between mothers by their physicians. He was attacked for this view, but stood by it and republished the essay twelve years later as a pamphlet entitled *Puerperal Fever as a Private Pestilence.*

Puerperal fever is now established as being caused by a bacterial infection of the reproductive tract following childbirth or miscarriage. The process of birth leaves this area vulnerable to infection at a time when the mother's resistance to infection can be lowered by the strain placed on her body by labour (and any greater than normal loss of blood after the child's birth). An infection can invade the mother's system in this area and, as noted earlier, through any abrasions, cuts or punctures made by instruments or rough hands. The severity of any infection will depend upon the type of bacteria, the extent to which it can invade the system, and the physical health of the mother. The symptoms of puerperal fever can include a fever, temperature, possibly alternating with chills, severe pain in the lower abdomen and foul-smelling discharge from the source of the infection. Symptoms appear usually appear between one and ten days after delivery. Where, as in 1847, there is no antibiotic treatment, the infection will frequently be fatal, particularly if septicaemia occurs. For Margaret Goodfellow, her weakened physical state will have lowered her resistance and, if puerperal fever was indeed the cause of death, the bacterial infection could have been worsened by being re-infected from several different sources. The presence of existing infection and the time lag between birth of the child and the mother's death make puerperal fever the likely cause of death. We cannot be certain that this was the cause of Margaret's death, but it is more likely than the other possibilities. The other frequent causes of death in childbirth would have been poor blood clotting, leading to uncontrolled bleeding and death and retained placenta causing fatal bleeding. If Margaret Goodfellow had post-partum haemorrhage it would have been much more likely to have been given as a cause of death, and for death to have been sooner after birth.

A social effect of the high rate of deaths from puerperal fever was the increased number of motherless children: not only the child whose birth caused the death but also any older siblings. A side effect of this was the greater pressure on the father to marry again in order to provide a mother for the children. There were occasions where the deceased wife's sister might come to look after the children, and intentions of marriage of convenience (or love) might be formed. But in the nineteenth century such a marriage was void in England and Wales, and this later had consequences for one of the half-brothers of Margaret's child, Margaret Banks Goodfellow.

That Margaret Banks Goodfellow was both born alive and survived is rather against the odds given her mother's difficulties – although the human body can often act to protect the child during birth at the expense of the mother. The ill health of a mother before and during labour is today recognised as a risk factor for any unborn child. In this instance, the child survived but there is every likelihood that at birth Margaret Banks Goodfellow was both undernourished and to a degree underdeveloped. The child's condition would have been made worse by distress if the labour was prolonged. Being born in such a condition could well have led to a sickly and uncertain start to childhood.

Margaret Banks Goodfellow would have required nursing after her mother's death. This may well have been organised and supervised by her grandmother Margaret. The first months of the child's life would therefore have been spent at a house in the company of her grandmother, and her uncle, with whom she would later spend some of the last years of her life as well. A wet nurse could well have been hired to breastfeed the baby. The use of wet nurses is said to have declined as the nineteenth century progressed, with a corresponding rise in dry nursing, which was the use of an infant milk substitute based on animal milk, with additives. Commercially manufactured baby formulas – milk substitutes – were not available until 1867 onwards.[22] In rural Britain, wet nursing, the traditional way of nursing an orphaned child, would probably have been the choice and would have been provided by a local mother hired for that purpose.

Thomas Goodfellow's Second Marriage

Margaret Goodfellow was just over thirty-one years old when she died, while Margaret's widower, Thomas, was twenty-seven. It is not surprising, at that age and with an infant daughter, that he remarried a little over a year later. This marriage, to Sarah Barron, took place on 7th March 1848 – for propriety's sake it would have been planned to take place after, rather than before, the anniversary of Margaret's death. The marriage was announced in the *Carlisle Patriot* of 14th March 1848:

> At Crosthwaite Church, Keswick, on Tuesday last, by the Rev. Edward Wilson, Mr Thomas Goodfellow, grocer, to Sarah, daughter of Mr Edward Barron, assistant overseer, both of Keswick.

Sarah Goodfellow was again a wife who was older than Thomas, by eighteen months, and again potentially stood to inherit some property on her father's death.

There is evidence that Thomas took on a more prominent role in Keswick during this second marriage. He stood for election as surveyor of highways in the parish (but lost by five votes). He was clerk to the Keswick Board of Health.[23] The rise of the Temperance movement in the nineteenth century was noted earlier in this chapter, and in 1851 Thomas was involved as a speaker at the first annual soirée of the Keswick Total Abstinence Society.[24] Over two hundred people attended. There was a parade through the town, and tea was served afterwards at the Oddfellows Hall. A purveyor of tea speaking on the advantages of abstinence from alcohol, while over two hundred people listened and drank tea cannot have been bad for the business of a local tea merchant. Also in 1851, the census shows Thomas as living in Main Street, Keswick. As well as his wife and two children there was also present Sarah Jackson, a general servant, Daniel Waite, a grocer's shopman and Joseph Gaites, a grocer's apprentice. That Thomas could support a household of four plus three employees suggests that at that time his business was prospering to a reasonable degree. But prosperity and family life were to prove short-lived.

Sarah Goodfellow died on 6th April 1857, aged forty, after less than ten years of marriage. The announcement in the *Carlisle Journal* of 10th April 1857[25] described her death as sudden and also described Sarah as 'much respected'. Her death certificate gives the cause of death as apoplexy, with the first attack coming two days before death. Today the cause of death would most likely have been recorded as a stroke.

This second marriage had produced two half-brothers for Margaret Banks Goodfellow – Edward Barron Goodfellow (b 1850) and John Tolson[26] Goodfellow (b 1853) – as well as a half-sister, Mary Mitchinson Goodfellow (b 1851). Edward's Christian names came from his maternal grandfather, John's second Christian name was his maternal grandmother's maiden name and Mary's second Christian name was her paternal grandmother's maiden name.

John Tolson Goodfellow has no real part in this story as he died on 21st March 1865,[27] shortly before John Banks the elder died. Mary Mitchinson Goodfellow also played no part in the will dispute or, so far as is known, Edward Goodfellow's later life, although she was one of the witnesses to his first marriage. There is much more to say about Edward in Chapter Seven. After Sarah's death, Thomas Goodfellow was left a widower, with four children aged nine, seven, six and four. In the upbringing of these children he appears to have been assisted to some degree by his housekeeper, Elizabeth Birkett. Thomas later left her a legacy of £10 in his will, 'for her kindness towards my dear departed wife and also she has been kind to my children'.

Thomas Goodfellow's Death and Burial

Margaret's time with her step-mother was quite short and we have no clues as to how well, or badly, they got on with one another. But her time with just her father and half siblings was much shorter, as Thomas Goodfellow died on 6th April 1858, aged thirty-eight years and six months. His death was from pulmonary tuberculosis (shown on his death certificate as 'Phthesis pulmonalis 5 months', indicating that he was diagnosed with the disease five months prior to death, i.e. sometime in October 1857). With a coincidence worthy of a Victorian novel, he died on the first anniversary of his wife Sarah's death. His death notice in the *Westmorland Gazette* of 10th April 1858 was rather terse, 'On 6th inst, at Keswick, Mr Thomas Goodfellow, grocer, aged 38 years'. It would be difficult to have a shorter notice, or one that says less about him – more information appeared in John Banks' death notice and that was placed by someone who was not a relative (see Chapter Two). Who placed Thomas's notice is not known.

Thomas was buried in the churchyard of Crosthwaite Parish Church. His grave is close to the church on the north side.[28] There are no personal details engraved on the headstone other than his name, date of death and age – very much like the death notice for its absence of personal or family information. A curiosity, however, is the opening inscription placed at the top of the stone, which reads, 'Erected by a friend to the memory of …'. It is not known who the anonymous friend was who valued Thomas's friendship sufficiently to bear the costs of the headstone when no one else could, apparently, even be bothered to mark the grave. When this marker was put there is also not known.

Why was this done by an anonymous friend? One would normally expect the interment and headstone to have been paid for out of Thomas's estate. One would also expect his family to have been involved in the arrangements as a mark of respect to Thomas. He had a brother-in-law (John Banks the elder) from his first marriage and at least one sister-in-law from his second marriage. But it would have been, perhaps, too much to expect of John to have organised this on behalf of the family. It would normally be the case today that the cost of a suitable marker would be paid out of the estate by the executors. Although the estate could pay for a suitable headstone it would be unusual for the executors to take the initiative without some direction in the will. There were no funeral or interment instructions in Thomas's will. Whoever the anonymous friend was he undertook the work at no little expense to himself.

Whether or not Thomas had any living siblings is not known, but it seems unlikely from what little we know of his life. If there were any, they would normally have dealt with the funeral and burial, in the absence of a wife or adult children, unless there had been some severe rupture in family relations. Thomas's will argues against a family rupture as there was a £20 legacy to a nephew, John Murray.[29]

Thomas's death was not, apparently, registered by someone identifiable as a member of his family, but by John Scambler, a farmer of Millbeck Underskiddaw who was qualified to register it by being present at death. John Scambler was close enough to Thomas for Thomas to have appointed him one of his two executors. The other executor was a Joseph Dallow, 'Minister of the Gospel' (the Reverend Dallow is mentioned in Chapter Two in connection with John Banks the elder's delusions). That no member of the family was appointed his executor also suggests that either there were no close relatives in the Goodfellow family or that there had been a break in relations for whatever reason.

Joseph Dallow was described in the 1861 census as a 'Minister of the Christn Brethen' (sic). He was a member of the Christian Brethren, also called the Open Brethren. This church derived from the split in the Plymouth Brethren into the Exclusive and Open Brethren.[30] Joseph Dallow was not a native of Cumberland, having been born in 1820 in Hereford, but he had moved to Keswick by 1847, when his eldest child was born there. Between 1851 and 1861 he lived in Harryman Field, Keswick. He would have known John Banks the elder as, in 1851, John lodged with Joseph Usher at Harryman's Field as well. Dallow might seem an unusual choice as executor given that Thomas was buried at Crosthwaite Parish Church. But Thomas's first wife and mother-in-law were attenders at a chapel rather than the parish church, and it may well have been that at the time of his death the chapel did not have consecrated ground available for burials. Dallow was described in 1850 by the Reverend Hartford-Battersby,[31] an Anglican curate in Keswick, as 'an admirable minister'.[32] His qualities seem to make it less likely that John Banks the elder had a delusion of persecution by Dallow, and that it is likely that the comment that he thought Dallow gave him good advice is more accurate.

The inscription on Thomas's gravestone 'Erected by a friend', while touching as tribute by a friend, does also seem to be rather pointed, as it draws attention, whether deliberately or not, to the absence of family involvement. Further, the headstone makes no reference to Thomas's immediate family, and this is very curious for someone who had had two wives and four children. The terms of his will make it clear that he was not estranged from his children, or his brother-in-law, which makes the lack of reference to the wives and children all the more unusual. Thomas did not share the graves of either of his wives, nor were any of his children later buried with him. The latter point is again unusual in that Margaret Banks Goodfellow and John Tolson Goodfellow were both unmarried minors when they died, and one would have expected them to be buried with their father.[33] In Margaret's case, burying her alone in Plumbland churchyard, a place with no other connection to the Banks or Goodfellow families, and not with her father, seems most unusual, and perhaps almost cruel to the Victorian mind: consider, for example, the idea of reunion in death that is frequently expressed on headstones for those buried together in the same grave. This is as frequently encountered today as it was in the nineteenth century. All of this seems to be in the spirit of the terse death notice in the paper. There is something very sad about Thomas's death, burial and the break-up of his family.

In Thomas's will he bequeathed to his daughter Margaret all the real property he had inherited through her mother from Jacob Banks the elder's estate including the house Shorley Croft, which is specifically mentioned in his will. This is the house occupied by her mother, uncle and grandmother at the 1841 census. We do not know who owned the property in 1841, although it is quite conceivable that this was part of the real estate in Jacob Banks' estate that was held for the life interest of his wife. If this formed part of Margaret's share of the real estate on her mother's death, then, on Margaret's death in turn, it would be logical that it passed to her husband Thomas as her heir. The gift of this real estate to Margaret Banks Goodfellow showed her father to be passing her mother's property to her. How much income was produced by these properties is not known. John Gill, a letter carrier of Keswick, acted as agent for Margaret and collected the rents from these properties on her behalf (as she was under age, technically these rents were due to Thomas Goodfellow's trustees). He also suggested that Joseph Tolson took too great an interest in Margaret's income from these properties.

The Later Life of Margaret Banks Goodfellow

The 1861 census (the first after her father's death) showed Margaret Banks Goodfellow as a fourteen-year-old scholar boarding with a family called Watson in Eskin Place, Castlerigg, Keswick. George Watson was sixty-five and a road surveyor. Margaret was the only boarder at that address. She was also the only child. Mrs Watson was sixty-five, her unmarried daughter thirty-eight, her unmarried sister (a dressmaker) fifty-six and there was a servant, Mary Ball, aged eighteen – not much company of her own age for Margaret. Her half-siblings were shown in the same census as living with their maiden aunt, Frances Barron (sister of Sarah Goodfellow), in Main Street, Crosthwaite, Keswick. This prompts the question: why were the children split up after her father's death? Did Frances Barron, who was no blood relation to Margaret Banks Goodfellow, not want the responsibility of an eleven-year-old girl in addition to the two nephews and a niece (all under the age of nine at the time of their father's death) who were related to her by blood? Or did she just not have room for all four? Splitting up the children immediately after their father's death does look harsh. Frances Barron had been shown in the 1841 census as milliner, but by 1861 she was recorded as a 'gentlewoman'. The change in circumstances was probably a result of inheritance from her father,[34] but it could still be that her financial resources would have been too stretched by taking a fourth child.

The Death of Margaret Banks Goodfellow

Margaret Banks Goodfellow died in 1867 in the same house in Arkleby as her uncle John died, looked after by the same landlady, Mrs Routledge. Neither Margaret nor John was lodging in Arkleby at the time of the 1861 census. John moved there in early 1862 and, according to Joseph Tolson's evidence at the first trial, John Banks suggested to Margaret that she move to stay with William Thirlwall (his landlady's brother) at his farm in Parsonby, which adjoins Arkleby. The invitation was made in a letter, in John Banks' handwriting, of 20th August 1862, which was read at the trial. According to Tolson, Margaret moved to Plumbland after this letter. Margaret was certainly living at William Thirlwall's farm by at least late 1863. Her lodgings there were only a short walk from her uncle's lodgings. Margaret later moved from Plumbland to lodge with Mrs Routledge, probably after her uncle's death. How her rent was paid and who it was paid by is another of the family mysteries that are dealt with in Chapter Eight. The later disputes over her maintenance raise substantial issues about where money went in this family.

Margaret would have been fifteen or sixteen when she moved to Plumbland. But why John Banks suggested she moved there is unclear. It could have been prompted by Margaret finishing her schooling. If that was so, and with John Banks the elder being her only close adult relative, a move to be near him could have made sense, particularly if he was contributing in any way to her upkeep. Sadly, it is more likely that she moved to be near her uncle because no one else was interested in her care and upbringing. Whatever the reason for relocating, having been brought up and gone to school in the Keswick area, Margaret would have found the change from the small town to the comparative isolation of Arkleby (more a hamlet than a village) quite marked. Having been raised initially in her father's household, she would have experienced at least something of a normal family way of life in the first few years of her life. This would have been a contrast to later living in lodgings with an elderly family in Castlerigg and then in Arkleby, where her only family was her elderly, paranoid schizophrenic uncle. It is doubtful that she would have seen that uncle as a substitute father figure. When she moved in with Mrs Routledge at Gill Foot Cottage, the Routledges had two daughters aged approximately twenty and a child aged one, and between them they might have provided some female company or interest for her, but probably not friendship.

The future for Margaret after finishing her education would have been most different from today. The usually accepted role of Victorian women was to marry and raise a family. The position of women in society was almost unrecognisable from today's perspective. Any earnings of, gifts to, or inheritance by, a married woman became the property of her husband. On marriage, a woman's entire personal property became that of her husband. Her real property (land) remained with her, but the rights to the profits from the land were with her husband, and her rights to rent, mortgage or sell the property could not be exercised without his consent. A husband was not obliged to make any provision for his wife in his will. John Stuart Mill observed:[35]

> She can acquire no property, but for [the husband] the instant it becomes hers, even by inheritance, it becomes ipso facto his … This is her legal state. And from this state she has no means to withdraw herself. If she leaves her husband she can take nothing with her, neither her children nor anything that is rightfully her own. If he chooses he can compel her to return by law, or by physical force; he may content himself with seizing for his own use anything which she may earn or which may be given to her by her relations. It is only separation by a decree of a court of justice which entitles her to live apart without being forced back into the custody of an exasperated jailer.

Earlier, in 1866, John Stuart Mill had presented the first petition to Parliament, on behalf of the Women's Suffrage Committee, calling for the enfranchisement of all householders regardless of gender.[36] It failed. The political emancipation of women was years away, with equality with male suffrage coming only in 1928.[37] There was a long road of law reform ahead for women.[38]

Employment of women at this time was very much a class issue. Wives and daughters of men of independent means did not generally seek employment – and not much would have been open to them anyway.[39] Women of the lower classes would have sought work chiefly in industry, agriculture, the retail and service sectors or domestic service.

Margaret could, with her inheritance from her father and uncle, have supported herself and not have to follow the schoolteacher/governess route of many modestly educated single young women, but the expectation remained that the proper route ahead was marriage and motherhood.

It is certain that, after finishing her education, Margaret did not undertake paid employment. This might have been because income was available from her uncle, or from her father's estate. There might be another reason, the clue to which is to be found in an application made in June 1866 to the Court of Chancery for a guardian to be appointed to represent Margaret's interests.[40] In this Bill of Complaint, Margaret is referred to as being 'a person of weak, although not of unsound, mind'. This is the only contemporary clue as to Margaret's capabilities before her final illness the following year. There is no mention made in the Bill of Margaret having, or being suspected of having, other health issues at that time.

Margaret's being considered to have a weak intellect raises many questions that cannot be satisfactorily answered. Was this what would be described today as learning difficulty? Could she have been like her uncle in his youth: a child with a schizoid personality, but without the psychosis that he developed later in life? Did she suffer a degree of brain damage at birth? Given that John Banks' madness was well known within Keswick, any hint of Margaret having possible mental health issues, however slight, would no doubt have set tongues wagging about strains of madness within that family. On the other hand, it is also possible that the reference to a weak mind was an exaggeration designed to strengthen the application for funds to be released from John's estate to Mrs Routledge for her maintenance. She was seeking, and obtained, an order for £80pa, considerably more than the £50pa that had been paid by her uncle. That this application was made also raises troubling issues about her inheritance from her father (there is more on money issues in Chapter Eight).

As noted earlier, in her short life, Margaret would have known but a little of family life. Family life was central to most people in Victorian England, but the stark realities of family life for many at that time also involved untimely family bereavement or the individual's own early death. In 1850 male and female life expectancy at birth was forty and forty-two respectively. Although these figures started to rise during the second half of the century, by 1900 both figures were still under fifty.[41] It could conceivably be the case that bereavement, a split from her half-siblings and life with strangers had simply left Margaret a shy and withdrawn child. Timidity and a perhaps a reluctance to express her thoughts may have led to an assumption that she lacked intelligence.

Margaret never knew her mother or her maternal grandparents. Of her paternal grandparents there is nothing that shows any real connection. Thomas's father Archibald is thought to have died in 1857. Her father and step-mother were also both dead by the time she was barely eleven, and one half-brother died, shortly before her, when he was twelve. The first four years after her father's death were spent as a lodger, while she continued her education living apart from her half-siblings. Her closest relative, apart from the half-siblings, was her uncle, John Banks, but it is unlikely, given the severity of his illness, that she knew much of him, or spent much time in his company, when she was young and her father was still alive, or during her schooling. This isolation from her family sadly continued after her death. She was not buried in Crosthwaite churchyard where her father, uncle and maternal grandparents were buried; instead, she was buried in St Cuthbert's Churchyard, Plumbland,[42] on 9th May 1867. This church is under half a mile, on foot, from Gill Foot Cottage where she died. No other members of her family are buried there and there is now no identifiable marker for her grave, if there ever was one.[43] It is quite possible that no member of her immediate family attended the funeral, unless her seventeen-year-old half-brother, Edward Barron Goodfellow, travelled there from Keswick. It is to be hoped that he did, given that he was her heir.

We have no evidence of Margaret's emotions towards her parents, but it would not be uncommon for a child in her position to have had some feelings of guilt because her mother's death was a consequence of her own birth. The idea of the child blaming herself for her mother's death in childbirth is not a discovery of modern psychoanalysis: it is as old as the process of birth itself. The guilt will be made worse where others, siblings or the surviving parent or relatives, are sufficiently cruel or unfeeling as to assign any blame expressly or indirectly to the child. At this remove from the time of Margaret's birth it is not possible to be sure how the facts of her birth affected her as she grew up, but it would be a rare child that did not, to some degree, feel some guilt at living when her birth was the cause of her mother's death. Any guilt would make the sorrow for the loss of her mother much harder for the child to bear. Margaret could well have had a weighty cross to bear, particularly at Arkleby when, after her uncle's death, she would have seemed very much alone.

For Margaret, the loss of her mother was followed fairly closely by the death of her step-mother and then her father. The reaction to the loss of her step-mother would depend very much upon the quality of that relationship, which might have been close, but could have been more distant. Her father's death may have been significant for Margaret beyond simply loss. Margaret and her father were linked in death through tuberculosis. There is the possibility of either infecting the other, although, as her father's death was nine years before hers, Margaret is more likely to have contracted it from him rather than the other way round. As well as sorrow for the loss of her father, her approaching death from the same illness could easily appear to be retribution (divine or otherwise) for the death of her mother. It would be unusual for the circumstances of both her parents' deaths not to have left a profound mark on Margaret's life and personality. It would be a very resilient child that could have avoided a tendency to melancholy with this background.

Did John take on some responsibility for his niece following her father's death, or was this done by her father's trustees? Initially, there might be a clue in Thomas Goodfellow's will. He bequeathed his real property (in this context generally meaning land) to Margaret Banks Goodfellow. The extent and value of this property is not known, but he would have acquired it on his first wife's death. It was her inheritance of a share of her father Jacob's estate and it would have been distributed to Thomas the following year after the death of his mother-in-law, Margaret Banks the elder. It is likely from the terms of her father's will that the income from the property would have been sufficient to pay for Margaret Banks Goodfellow's lodging and education (see more below on the origin of this property). Her father concluded his will by requesting that John Banks 'look after' Margaret 'as well as his strength will allow'. In this context 'look after' could possibly be significant. John was not able to look after himself in the sense of his own everyday needs and he relied on paid strangers for basic care. The care that he could have provided for Margaret would, in practical terms, have been minimal, or none, other than ensuring that, one way or another, she was sheltered, fed and clothed. Thomas's will shows understanding of this in its caveat 'as well as his strength will allow'.

John would not have had much margin of income to pay for Margaret's education and lodging after paying for his own care, but it may have been possible, if this were needed. The most likely source of her support would seem to have been the income from her share of her father's estate. The income would have been in the hands of the executors and trustees, Joseph Dallow and John Scambler, and they would have disbursed it, as it was needed, for Margaret's support. There is the possibility that the estate might not have been as large as might appear from either her father's will or Jacob Banks the elder's will. The estate could have been diminished by any business difficulties and debts during Thomas's life, but on balance it looks as though the estate should have been large enough. Whilst all this looks logical, it begs the question why after her uncle John's death Mr and Mrs Routledge sought court approval for £80pa to be released from John's estate to maintain Margaret? The inheritance from her father appears to disappear from the story, although it should have been part of her intestate estate. This is odd, given that his will would have been made in the certain knowledge of his fairly imminent death from tuberculosis as it was made a little over two months before his death.

Was the consumption that would eventually kill Margaret at the age of twenty already apparent when her father died, and could his request for John to 'look after' her, imply more than paying for lodgings and education for the child? It is conceivable that Thomas had it in mind that care and nursing and ultimately somewhere to live would be required for her, if the disease was then known to be present. This is a difficult area, but on balance it seems very unlikely that Margaret's disease would have shown any identifiable symptoms until shortly before death. Apart from the absence of any comment that she was ill, it would have most unusual for the 1863 will to have not made alternative provisions if she was known to have a fatal and incurable disease. Also, according to evidence given at the first trial, both John and Margaret were able to travel the twenty-two miles to visit Carlisle on one occasion in the 1860s, and to make that journey there and back in day is not really consistent with the tuberculosis having progressed from being latent.[44]

Few of the questions about Margaret's short life can be answered, as the available knowledge of her is so little. There is something very sad about a young orphaned girl being split from her half-siblings and sent to a remote rural hamlet to live with her invalid uncle – and then to follow him to the grave less than two years later. Given the nature of her illness and the lack of close family, her years in Arkleby are difficult to see as being a happy time – one hopes her early childhood was better.

The White Plague

Margaret's cause of death, like her father's, is recorded as 'Phthisis'. Phthisis is the original Greek name for the disease and dates from the time of Hippocrates (c460 BC). Consumption was the more common name for pulmonary tuberculosis in the nineteenth century. The disease had been given the name 'consumption' from the idea that the body was consuming itself from within as the sufferer weakened and apparently wasted away. Today we know that the disease originates from infection by the bacterium *Mycobacterium tuberculosis*.[45] Both Margaret and her father contracted pulmonary tuberculosis – tuberculosis of the lungs – which is the most common form of tuberculosis.

In the mid-nineteenth century, tuberculosis was capable of being diagnosed only when there were observable symptoms. These were usually weight loss, fever, pallor, general debility, night sweats, breathing difficulty, chest pain and a chronic cough with the sputum often mixed with blood. These symptoms are widely portrayed in Victorian fiction, as well as described in contemporary accounts. The pale wasting away of an individual meant that the disease was too often portrayed in fiction as a romantic, almost elegant, death. To view it in this light overlooks both the pain and the more offensive symptoms. In some patients the lung damage became so severe that haemorrhage into the lungs would follow.[46] It is estimated that in 10–20% of cases where the infection is active, the infection passes out of the lungs into other parts of the body (extrapulmonary tuberculosis).

Mycobacterium tuberculosis was, and still is, transmitted by sneezing, speaking, singing, spitting, coughing, etc. All these actions will expel minute droplets from the mouth that are infectious. Tuberculosis infection can be produced by only a small quantity of droplets. This means that, as we know today but the mid-Victorians did not, there is a high risk of infection for those in close contact with a tuberculosis patient. With crowded or ill-ventilated houses, schools, factories, markets and places of entertainment, the mid-Victorians were living in conditions that were facilitating the spread of this then incurable disease.

Most who are infected with tuberculosis will not display symptoms, as the body's immune system will control the infection, often for long periods. In this period of latent tuberculosis, a person is usually not capable of infecting others. This period of latency, post the original infection, was not known in the mid-nineteenth century and therefore the disease was only recognised once the symptoms became visible.[47]

It is most probable that Margaret Banks Goodfellow and her father, Thomas, were infected with tuberculosis earlier in their lives and that the disease remained latent within them until shortly before their deaths. Thomas's symptoms were only diagnosed as being tuberculosis five months before his death from the illness in April 1858. For most patients, medical advice was probably not sought when the first symptoms were only slight, but instead only when the symptoms became well established. At this point in Thomas's illness, Margaret was still living with her father and it is quite conceivable that he could have been the source of her infection. We do not know when Margaret's symptoms became visible, only that tuberculosis caused her death in May 1867. It is noted that no reference is made to Margaret having tuberculosis or requiring money for medical treatment in the Chancery application of 25th June 1866 for a guardian to be appointed and funds to be released from John Banks's estate for her maintenance. It seems therefore that her symptoms were not yet visible and that, like her father, she would die within a short period of tuberculosis becoming apparent. The speed with which both Thomas and Margaret died after the symptoms first appeared was faster than the usual progress of the disease.

This fast progress was often spoken of as 'galloping consumption'. This can be contrasted with the usual progress of advance followed by apparent remission that took longer to kill. The natural advance/apparent remission progress was a god-send to the unscrupulous, who offered a wide range of treatments and regimes to no effect,[48] given the apparent remission was a natural feature of progress of the disease. Standard textbooks suggested that tuberculosis was fatal in 80% of all cases between five and fifteen years after symptoms were identified.[49] How little was really understood about tuberculosis in the mid-nineteenth century is encapsulated in the generally held view that it was an inherited and not an infectious disease.[50]

What can cause latent tuberculosis to become active? For Margaret, there are some grounds for possibly linking tuberculosis to puberty and hormonal changes. It is also possible that stress (loss of father, loss of uncle, removal to a remote hamlet) might be implicated.

As well as being a major killer, tuberculosis had a great influence on human culture especially in the nineteenth century. Enduring images of John Keats, or Edvard Munch's sister, of Mimi in *La Bohème* or of Violetta in *La Traviata* are with us still, as is the tragedy of the Brontë family.[51] Within Britain tuberculosis was a mass killer, particularly of the young and poor in the population. There seems to be a correlation between the industrial revolution and a surge in tuberculosis, until approximately 1840 when numbers began a slow decline. The cramped, ill-ventilated early factories and their cottage industry suppliers were ideal conditions for the spread of tuberculosis. Gradual reform and improvements produced an easing of the levels of tuberculosis deaths.[52]

CHAPTER FIVE

The Trials of the Will

Introduction

On first reading, much of the evidence produced in court against the will looks to be strongly in favour of John's illness being so severe as to render him unable to make a valid will. But this impression is misleading. The evidence tends to focus very much on John Banks's manner, appearance, habits and delusions throughout his life. All of these marked John Banks as different from those around him. Most of the claimant's witnesses said they considered him insane. For example:

- James Hope, tailor, draper and grocer, of Plumbland, regarded him as 'weak and imbecilic' and 'quite incompetent to make a will'. He added that 'his imbecility and insanity were evident and notorious'. These are strong views expressed in strong language that in fact told the court little or nothing about John's ability to make a will at the time that he did.
- John Hodgson, a commissioner of income tax living in Arkleby, said, 'he was in fact insane and out of his right mind … and always showed it'.

Today, opinions as to insanity given in court will be from those medically qualified to give them, not from the non-medically qualified. A non-medically qualified person can give evidence as to what he or she observed in terms of a person's behaviour and what conclusions he drew from it, but such a person cannot give evidence as to what it signifies in terms of a diagnosis. The witnesses for the claimant at this trial, as well as lacking any medical qualification, also tended to frame their evidence in the context of John

Banks' whole life, rather than focussing on what was really at issue – his mental ability at the time of his last will. A great deal of evidence relating to times both before and after the will adds little to the question of John's ability when he actually made the will, although it might help us now understand the illness itself.

It is difficult to escape the conclusion that John Banks was perceived by many witnesses as being too insane to make a will simply because he was mentally ill and behaved eccentrically. On the other hand, the evidence in favour of the will tends to admit John's eccentricities, but not the complete absence of understanding and ability. In fairness, some of the claimant's witnesses did admit to John having some capacity for short periods, but their evidence naturally tended to give much more emphasis to the evidence against capacity.

Further, the picture painted by the claimant's witnesses was generally aimed towards merely showing John's general insanity, as this was sufficient as the law stood then to prevent a valid will being made. As is commented on in more detail later, English law had reached a point where any mental impairment was thought sufficient to disqualify a person from making a will and this therefore accounted for the tone of much of the evidence. The claimant's legal team were surprised that at both trials the judges did not follow the supposed position that the law had reached. However, despite their partisan flavour, the witness statements and other evidence at trial enable us to form a better picture of John Banks' illness in his adult life, even if the evidence is not focussed on his abilities when he made his last will.

As *Banks v Goodfellow* was a matter of civil law, it appears odd now that the first trial was one before a jury, something that is mainly seen today in criminal trials. Jury trials still remained an option for some civil matters in 1869, although the number of cases heard before a jury was in decline. However, this was how the first trial of the validity of the will would be heard at Cumberland Spring Assizes. Before the Court of Probate Act 1857, the jurisdiction over estates was split between the ecclesiastical and common law courts – the former with regard to personal estate, and the latter with regard to real estate. The 1857 Act moved responsibility for non-contentious probate matters into the newly created Court of Probate. Contentious probate matters, including the validity of wills, were not yet placed within the province of this new court.

The dispute over John Banks the elder's will involved real property (essentially the only asset of his estate), and it therefore remained a matter for a common law court to resolve. Before 1898, the title to real property owned by a testator vested in his heir, or devisee, immediately on death (this contrasts with the position after the Land Transfer Act 1897 when title to land on death then passed initially to the executor and then, on distribution of the estate, to the beneficiary).

Initially, it does not seem that the death of John Banks caused any noticeable concern about the validity of his will. Having left all of his estate to Margaret Banks Goodfellow, his closest relative, and logical choice as beneficiary, it appears to have been considered, by those involved, that it was just a question of waiting for her twenty-first birthday when she could give a valid receipt for her inheritance. When she reached the age of twenty-one, she would be able to make a will disposing of her estate as she saw fit, but until then she could not make a will. There would have been some concerns about her estate once Margaret's fatal illness was identified, but the future plaintiff (today, claimant), John Banks the younger, was out of the country and probably unaware of her state of health until he was notified of her death.

As Margaret died intestate, her closest relatives and therefore her beneficiaries would have been her half-siblings Edward Goodfellow and Margaret Mitchinson Goodfellow (John Tolson Goodfellow had already died, under age). However, at this time, the intestacy law operated so that the male line would take preference over the female line for the inheritance of real property (land), meaning Edward was Margaret's largest heir – referred to in the judgment as the 'heir at law' – to the almost complete exclusion of his sister. It was therefore Edward's inheritance of Margaret's estate that seems to have sparked John Banks the younger, the testator's nephew, into his challenge to the will. The logic behind his challenge was that if John Banks the elder's will was to be declared invalid (because he lacked testamentary capacity) then John Banks the elder died intestate and his heir at law, after the death of Margaret, would be John Banks the younger, his nephew of the half-blood. Again, the male line would be preferred to the female for inheritance of land, thereby excluding all the nieces of the half-blood – John Banks the younger's sisters.

Probate was granted to the executors of the will of John Banks on 29th August 1865, without any challenge having been made to the will's validity. But, once it became apparent that Margaret had died intestate, and that John Banks' assets passed to the Goodfellow family, then the challenge to the will was made. This order of events detracts from the credibility of the challenge to the will. It shows that initially all potentially interested parties were content to accept the will's validity – indeed, both executors had stated this on oath when swearing their probate application. For this to be challenged later, when it became clear that the estate would pass to another, gives the inescapable impression that it was not the will that was being objected to but the ultimate beneficiary, Edward Goodfellow. This is an impression that should not have been taken into account by the Bench, but the jury could well have been influenced by it. It is not known if there was any animosity between John Banks the younger and Edward Goodfellow before the trial or if this was simply a case of John Banks the younger thinking that 'Banks money' should not go to a Goodfellow.[1]

The Initial Skirmishes

The first court application was made soon after John Banks the elder's death and it was not about the validity of the will. The application was to the Court of Chancery for the appointment of a legal guardian for Margaret Banks Goodfellow. Margaret's application was made on her behalf through her next friend Edward Highton (a local schoolmaster who later gave evidence for Edward Goodfellow at the trial of the will). A next friend is a person appointed to bring an action on behalf of a person who, through legal disability, in this case being under age, cannot bring the action in person. The Bill of Complaint lodged on her behalf also requested that the court order an accounting of the personal estate of John Banks the elder (i.e. that part of his property which was not land) in order to establish what it was, how it had been applied and why it was apparently insufficient to settle his debts without sale of any of the investment properties.

On 3rd August 1866 William Thirlwall and Elizabeth Routledge were appointed as Margaret's guardians by the court, and provision for £80pa was ordered to be paid from her uncle's estate for her maintenance. But, on 16th November 1866, on William Thirlwall's application, all litigation was stayed until after Margaret came of age. The reason for this stay is not immediately clear, but it could well have been because Margaret's illness was becoming apparent and that a dispute after her death was anticipated. On the other hand, it might have been because the award was substantial when compared to the £1 per week that Mrs Routledge was charging John Banks at the time of his death (and that had only recently doubled from 10/- because of the extra nursing he required).

On 4th June 1867, barely a month after the death of Margaret, a further Bill of Complaint was lodged. This fresh action was commenced by Joseph Tolson against his co-executor, William Thirlwall, and Edward Barron Goodfellow. Tolson's Bill of Complaint brought forward a dispute as to the due debts of John Banks and the money Joseph Tolson had spent from his own resources in supporting Margaret Banks Goodfellow. Further, in order to prevent creditors of John Banks forcing the sale of part of the estate's rental properties, Joseph Tolson claimed that he had advanced additional sums to the estate. He therefore sought an accounting, plus a settlement of costs incurred in litigation to date.

There is reference in a contemporary press report that the parties to the main action, John Banks the younger and Edward Barron Goodfellow, had already skirmished in the Court of Chancery before this matter was directed to be tried at the Cumberland Spring Assizes in 1869. John Banks the younger had apparently commenced his challenge to the will by filing, on 11th November 1867, his Bill of Complaint, which alleged that his uncle had showed signs of insanity as far back as 1841 and that:

> these symptoms increased towards the end of his life and for some years previous to his death he had but few lucid intervals and during the whole of the year 1863 he was incompetent to make a valid will.

He sought a declaration that the:

> Will of 28th December 1863 may be declared void and may be ordered to be delivered up to the plaintiff to be cancelled or that liberty may be given to bring an action of ejectment to recover possession of the said lands and tenements.

This is slightly curious drafting as, of course, it would not be sufficient to remove this will alone as that would have left the early December will to take effect. However, there are some other signs in the pleadings that indicate, initially at least, that there was some confusion in the mind of John Banks the younger's legal adviser as to the fact that there were two wills executed in December 1863.

It was as a result of these various applications to Chancery that the Master of the Rolls, Lord Romilly,[2] directed that the action should be taken forward as one of the validity of the will. The action was described in the Bill of Complaint as an action for ejectment (similarly in the head note to the appeal judgment law report). Ejectment was a common law action and, as its name suggests, it was an action to eject the occupier of land and to recover lawful possession of that land for the true owner. In addition, the action asked for an accounting for the wrongful withholding of the profits from the land during the time it was occupied by the person who was to be ejected.[3] Therefore, what was being sought by John Banks the younger was recovery of all the real property (and rents therefrom) that had been received by the executors of the will (for the benefit of the estate). The key issue, which would determine if John Banks the younger could succeed in the ejectment action, was the validity of the will, and without this no progress could be made regarding ownership of the property. Hence the direction was given by the Master of the Rolls that the validity of the will should be tried at Cumberland Assizes before judge and jury before any decision could be given on the question of ejectment.

Today, the costs of an action regarding the validity of a will are affected by the process of litigation, both pre-trial and trial, generally taking longer than it did in 1869. *Banks v Goodfellow* involved five separate days, or part days, in court: one full day and one part day at the Assizes and two part days for the appeal hearing in Queen's Bench[4] (ignoring the initial applications to Chancery), and a short time on the third day of the appeal for the Bench to deliver the judgment. A fairly recent reported challenge to a will, on grounds of capacity, involved five days at the first instance trial in Chancery Division of the High Court, with a further day in the Court of Appeal. The first hearing was five years after the death, and the appeal a further year later.[5] John Banks' will took less than two years to get into court after Margaret's death, and the appeal process was completed approximately eighteen months after the first trial. The modern process will involve expert evidence on the mental capacity question and a lengthier process of acquiring evidence and exchanging information between parties prior to the first hearing. The volume of paper will be significantly greater today.

The costs of a litigated testamentary capacity challenge to a will in the present day are not inconsiderable and, with a second hearing on appeal, a six-figure sum for the total costs is realistically to be expected (and this will be considerably into six figures on occasions). The shorter process of 1869/70 will have meant lower costs, but they would still have been significant, as five barristers (three of them silks[6]) were involved in the appeal alone. Additional legal costs were incurred over and above the eventual costs of the trial and appeal by the initial Chancery applications. If the costs of all parties were paid from the estate, it would have been greatly depleted by the end. Unfortunately, no costs orders survive, but it is likely that each side was left with the burden of their own costs – although there is the possibility that some of Edward Goodfellow's costs, particularly of the appeal, will have been awarded against John Banks the younger.

The Trials of the Will

The Cumberland Spring Assizes Trial in 1869

The Spring Assizes were announced in the local press as:

> NORTHERN CIRCUIT. Mr. Justice Lush. Mr. Justice Brett. Westmorland, Monday, February 15, at Appleby[7]; Cumberland, Tuesday, February 16, at Carlisle; Northumberland, Friday, February 19, at the Castle of Newcastle-upon-Tyne; Town of Newcastle-upon-Tyne, the same day, at the Guildhall of the said Town.

This rather prosaic press announcement contrasts with the reality of the opening of the Assizes sitting in Carlisle, which involved a considerable display of civic and judicial pomp.

The Commission of Assize and General Gaol Delivery was to be formally opened by Mr Justice Brett. He travelled to Carlisle from nearby Appleby by train,[8] arriving at five o'clock in the afternoon on Monday and he then used the station waiting room as his robing room. Duly enrobed as a judge of the Court of Common Pleas, he travelled from the station to the court in the High Sheriff's carriage accompanied by the High Sheriff and the Sheriff's Chaplain. The High Sheriff, John Ewart of Kingfield House, had only recently been appointed:[9]

> The High Sheriff's equipage was one of the most handsome that has been seen in Carlisle in recent years. The body of the carriage was painted a rich claret, picked out in fine lines of crimson, with the Sheriff's crest and armorial bearings emblazoned upon the door and quarter panels, the whole mounted complete in silver plating, fitted up with hammercloth,[10] made of blue cloth, with blue and drab[11] fringe, hangers and tassels and festoons to the doors and footmen-holders to match. The inside was lined with drab silk and cloth trimmings. The carriage was drawn by four very valuable grey horses, brought down from London, richly caparisoned with silver mounted trappings and driven by a powdered-headed coachman, who handled the ribbons after the approved London style.[12]

At the court, the Mayor of Carlisle, complete with his chain of office, met the carriage. The Mayor was accompanied by his Mace Sergeants and twenty members of Carlisle Corporation. After a brief opening ceremony, Brett J adjourned the court until eleven o'clock the following morning. He then retired to the judges' lodgings in Carlisle. Mr Justice Lush, who would also preside at the Assizes, was already there having walked from the station 'without ceremony'.[13] The following day began with both judges attending divine service at the Cathedral,[14] which was taken by the Sheriff's Chaplain. The Chaplain took as the text for his sermon 'Thy Kingdom come, thy will be done on earth as it is in heaven'.[15]

The *Kendal Mercury* of 20th February 1869 noted that there were only two civil matters to be heard at these Assizes – the matter of John Banks' will and a breach of promise action. The latter was a common law tort action for damages from loss of expectations, and damage to a woman's reputation, if a man[16] broke off an engagement without just cause. Such actions were widely used as comic devices by writers of the time, *The Pickwick Papers* and *Trial by Jury* being particularly famous examples.[17] At these Assizes, Miss Jane Robinson sought damages from Mr John Kirkbride, who had married another after jilting Miss Robinson. The action might have been prompted by Mr Kirkbride having inherited substantial property. Miss Kirkbride was awarded £250. A flavour of such trials is given in a press report:

> Evidence was produced, showing that the parties had been on the most intimate terms, and a large number of love letters and valentines, full of the usual expressions of ardent endearment, were put in and read, to the great enjoyment of the Court.[18]

Similar reports appeared widely in local newspapers throughout the country. This type of action was abolished by section 1 of the Law Reform (Miscellaneous Provisions) Act 1970.

By contrast, to the two civil trials, the criminal business of the Assizes was described as 'heavy' in the local press – there were nineteen prisoners for trial. The offences they were charged with included impersonating voters in the recent Carlisle election, five cases involving concealment of a birth,[19] seven cases of larceny, three of manslaughter and one of embezzling funds from the Carlisle Friendly Society.

The trial of the validity of John Banks' will was heard before Brett J, on Wednesday and Thursday, 17th and 18th February 1869, after the breach of promise matter was first disposed of. *The Westmorland Gazette*'s brief report refers to the will case as being 'of considerable length'. Two civil actions being dealt with in their entirety by the same judge within two days appears today to be speedy justice indeed. As noted later, *Banks v Goodfellow* did not close until 8.30pm on the second evening, and that was clearly an unusual length for a judicial day even then. The plaintiff, John Banks the younger, was represented by Mr Aspinall QC and Mr Kemplay. The defendant Edward Barron Goodfellow was represented by Mr Holker QC and Mr Crompton Hutton.

The trial opened with Mr Holker QC and Mr Aspinall QC making admissions before the court that:

1. John Banks the younger was the heir at law of John Banks the elder (i.e. the person who would be entitled to the estate on the intestacy of John Banks, if his will was invalid);
2. Edward Barron Goodfellow was the heir at law of Margaret Banks Goodfellow;
3. John Banks was indeed seized (in possession) of the fifteen properties in Keswick – the only assets in the estate.

The purpose of these admissions was to save time (and cost) by not putting each side to strict proof as to these facts when both sides were prepared to acknowledge them to be correct.

Evidence for the Defendant, Edward Goodfellow

Next, Mr Holker QC opened the case for the defendant Edward Barron Goodfellow. He said that although there were numerous parties involved in various ways in this litigation, he wished to focus the court's attention on the crucial question which would resolve the whole matter: the validity of the will. This seems a rather obvious point to make, but it was an important one for the jury to grasp – no matter what smoke and fury might be generated by the plaintiff's witnesses, the jury should remain focussed on this key issue.

Mr Holker QC drew attention to the terms of the disputed will, making the point that the gift of the whole estate to Margaret was an absolute gift; it was not conditional in any way. This meant that if she had attained the age of twenty-one, she would have been able to deal with the inheritance in any way she saw fit, including making a will leaving the property to whoever she chose. While this point might also seem somewhat obvious, Mr Holker QC was making two less immediately obvious points while explaining this. The first was that the testator John Banks himself was not concerned with any alternative gift to his half-nephew, or anyone else, if his niece did not survive – the inheritance was for her to do with as she wished as far as he was concerned. In an age when women were widely regarded as unsuitable to be property owners, John Banks could have left his wealth in trust for her: but he did not do this. Secondly, the absolute gift to Margaret also carried the implication that John Banks the younger was not high in his uncle's priorities, whereas his niece was. It was not spoken, but there was an additional implication that if Margaret had been able to leave her inheritance to whoever she liked, her half-siblings would have been the most likely to benefit as they were closest to her. Therefore, in the context of the terms of the will, the possibility of 'Banks money' ending up as 'Goodfellow money' was not so odd.

Mr Holker QC next put it simply to the jury that if the will was valid, Edward Goodfellow inherited all of Margaret's estate, including her uncle's bequest to her, as he was the heir on her intestacy. If the will was not valid then John Banks the younger would inherit his uncle's property as his heir on his intestacy. Both the question at issue and its implications were therefore clearly before the jury, and they could understand which individual stood to inherit from which finding.

Mr Holker QC also provided the jury with a description of the John Banks the elder. The *Carlisle Patriot* of 19th February 1869 summarised his remarks as:

> The testator was a man of great peculiarities. Unfortunately, for himself, he was a man whose health was not good. He was unhappily subject to some derangement of his stomach. He was subject to epileptic fits. He was a bookworm, a studious kind of man of a retiring kind of disposition. No doubt previous to his taking these fits and after he came out of them when he was getting round he was very violent, very extraordinary in his demeanour as persons subject to this unhappy calamity are. He used to behave in most violent manner and he used to strike himself and so on. No doubt too, when he was coming round he was subject to a delusion, as very often epileptic persons are. The delusion he had was that some persons with whom he was acquainted were pursuing him. His ideas were that a man of the name of Alexander another of the name of Goodfellow, and he (the learned counsel) believed a methodist minister of the name of Dudlow were pursuing him. That no doubt he was bound to confess was so. These were his peculiarities, but when healthy he was as sane a man as anybody else, and as capable of conducting his business as well and as orderly, and in as perfect manner as any man could well do.

While one must make allowances for the reporter's précis of counsel's remarks, what was understood by the reporter ought to be similar to what the jurors understood. The linking of the delusion to the epilepsy seems to be contrary to the evidence, but otherwise the general tenor is that which Mr Holker QC's witnesses would support.

Mr Holker QC further admitted that John Banks the elder had spent time in a lunatic asylum, but made the point (no doubt to diminish its significance) that this was 'as far back as 1840 or 1841'. It was, he said, organised by John's friends and that his stay was brief at eleven weeks. Furthermore, he had been discharged as being cured and had returned home. Again, a fairly simple resumé of what was going to be established by the evidence of his witnesses, but it made several important points to the jury. First, John Banks' illness could not have been too severe if confinement was for a mere eleven weeks and the professionals who ran the asylum recorded that John was cured. The jurors would all have known of people who were removed to an asylum and never came out, and this would contrast strongly with John's independent life.[20] Secondly, John's confinement in the asylum was not ordered by a court. The confinement was not that serious a matter and was simply the action of those who cared for him looking out for John's interests. John was not a danger to himself or others and did not have to be compulsorily removed from society for the protection of others. Thirdly, the fact he returned to the bosom of his family, among those involved in John's removal to the asylum in the first place, also draws attention to the point that once he returned to them, they made no further attempt to have John sent back to the asylum while they were alive. By implication they, too, not only accepted him as being cured, but did not consider afterwards that he should be returned to Dunston. None of this says anything about John's mental capacity to make a will – that would come later. But, by making the points to diminish the impression of madness, senior counsel was trying to take the sting out of the evidence that would be presented against the will involving generalised claims that John Banks was utterly insane.

Mr Holker QC moved on to draw the jury's attention to what John Banks did with the terms of his will, and that was what 'any man in the proper possession of his faculties would be expected to do'. That the terms of the will were consistent with what a sane man would have provided tends to support the point that John not only was capable of acting rationally, but did in fact act rationally in looking after the interests of his niece who would so tragically die before she could receive the benefit of her uncle's generosity. While the rationality of a will is not proof that it was made by a person with testamentary capacity, it does tend to support that conclusion. It also, importantly, supports the view that, even if he suffered from delusions, John was not influenced by them in making a will on these terms. In making this point, learned counsel was continuing to diminish the significance of John's mental health issues.

Mr Holker QC made the important point that, under the law, he believed that 'a man might have many delusions and still be capable of managing his property and affairs'. This point was fundamental to counsel's defence of the will, but it was by no means accepted by the courts of the day as a correct statement of the law.[21] However, his view, as the jury would have noted later, was supported by Brett J when he summed up for the jury.

The report in the *Carlisle Patriot* adds that 'the learned counsel argued at great length to show that the will was duly executed'. It is a little difficult to know quite what Mr Holker QC was 'arguing' about. The jury had not yet heard the evidence, chiefly from Mrs Routledge, that the will was not executed in accordance with the statutory requirements. It is therefore suspected that senior counsel was using his opening address to prepare the jurors' minds. What he could explain was what was required for the valid execution of a will – the testator's signature on the will in the presence of two witnesses, and the witnesses then each adding their signatures in the testator's presence. By establishing this simple procedure now, and telling the jury about what was on the wills to prove that this had been done correctly, he was preparing them to be critical of what would be alleged by Mrs Routledge. But, crucially, her allegations could not be supported, by what actually appeared on the will.

The first witness called for the defendant was George Ansell, the solicitor who took the instructions for the will. He had known the testator for over thirty years, having first met him in 1833, but he was not in Keswick when John was removed to the asylum. Mr Ansell gave evidence as to the circumstances of his going to Arkleby to take the instructions for the will. He was cross-examined at some length by Mr Aspinall QC and, during this questioning, Mr Ansell maintained that the testator was neither 'cracked' nor 'crazed'. He conceded that John Banks was eccentric, 'but he was held in great esteem and respect by his neighbours' notwithstanding his eccentricity. Mr Ansell's remark draws attention to the point that no attempt had been made by local citizens to have John Banks detained in an asylum on grounds of nuisance or public safety. Whilst this might not equate with 'esteem' it did indicate a level of respect (or at least tolerance).

Bringing Mr Ansell as the first witness was a significant move. First, he was a professional man with much experience of wills. Given his experience, his views on whether or not a man was mentally capable of making a will would be treated with respect by the court and jury. Secondly, an attorney in a small town was also a man of some consequence locally, particularly where his practice was of long standing. He was what would then have been thought of as a pillar of the community– an educated man of some consequence locally. His evidence, following on from senior counsel's address to the jury, would have helped to establish a logical and plausible narrative of events for the jury. It was also important in that the first explanation that the jury would hear about the execution of the wills was straightforward, cogent and supported by the will itself. First impressions count.

The defendant's second witness was Joseph Tolson. He was probably the most important witness in the whole trial, as he was the only person giving evidence for the will who was present at both meetings in Arkleby in December 1863. He was also responsible for making the arrangements for Mr Ansell to travel to see John for the instructions for the will. By the time of the trial, Tolson was fifty-eight years old, and he was a grocer and provision merchant in Keswick, as well as acting as John Bank's rent collector, while John was alive. Being a contemporary of John Banks, he had known him 'from a boy upwards' as he put it. His evidence followed a similar course to Mr Ansell's, in saying that John Banks was 'rather excited at times' but that he was capable of giving sensible answers if approached patiently. He accepted that John Banks was subject to a delusion about Featherstone Alexander. Tolson was still giving evidence at the end of the first day.

The trial resumed at ten o'clock the following morning, and Mr Holker QC continued his examination-in-chief of Tolson. He gave evidence of a letter that John Banks had written in August 1862, which was read out, suggesting that Margaret should move to lodge in Parsonby, near Arkleby. This letter would have been useful evidence not only of John's capabilities, but also that his concern for his niece exhibited the normal love and affection of any person in this position, i.e. that this would not appear to be the action of a deranged person. The evidence that would be given later against the will would paint a bleak picture of John's lack of ability to do things for himself or act in a rational manner and, while a rational letter does not of itself disprove that bleak view, it does undermine it somewhat. Although this letter was produced and read out in court, it is not among the surviving trial papers.

Tolson was cross-examined on his evidence by Mr Aspinall QC on the question of John Banks' delusions. Tolson admitted that John had delusions about Featherstone Alexander, both before and after Alexander's death. He denied any knowledge of a delusion about Thomas Goodfellow. He then went on to deny any knowledge of John having delusions about devils 'and never heard of him sitting with a poker in his hand to defend himself from some of them'. This issue was raised earlier in the cross-examination of Mr Ansell. Tolson also denied knowing anything about John seeing a regiment of soldiers (and, given he was not present when John was alleged to have seen this, Tolson's view does not seem unreasonable). Both this allegation and the earlier reference to the poker are allegations contained in the affidavits from witnesses against the will, which Tolson would have known about.

Tolson did say that he 'had heard of the testator behaving in a peculiar manner'. Tolson was cross-examined at length on the circumstances of the wills and John's mental state when he made them, but Mr Aspinall QC does not appear to have shaken Tolson's version of events. The report of this cross-examination ends with 'the signatures of the testator were very closely examined'. It is not surprising that the signatures were looked at carefully, but clearly no one succeeded in showing that they were not those of John Banks or the witnesses.

Dr Tweddle of Keswick was called next. He confirmed that mention of Featherstone Alexander would put John in a state of excitement, but apart from these times John was quite capable of talking rationally and conducting business. He had also, on a few occasions, seen John beating his head. He added one detail that is not found anywhere else, and that was that John's 'nervousness ... seemed to be worse when his stomach was out of order' (although it is far from clear what connection, if any, could have existed between his digestion and his schizophrenia). Dr Tweddle appears as a rather curious witness in that none of his evidence was relevant to the time the wills were made. However, his view of John's behaviour does support the views of Ansell and Tolson, the two chief witnesses for the will, and, coming from another pillar of the Keswick community, that would have been significant for the jury.

Mr Aspinall QC challenged the evidence of Dr Tweddle on Thomas Goodfellow, but again the doctor denied that John had any delusion about Goodfellow, but he did concede that John had a dislike of Goodfellow. The cross-examination continued, but probably did not help the case against the will. When asked about John's time in Dunston Asylum, the doctor said that he would have 'hesitated' to sign any certificate for John's committal. He then added that 'it is a very common thing for a person who has a delusion and who is not violent to be sent to an asylum'. Although the doctor was giving evidence about a time well before the wills, both points were useful to diminish the significance of John having been confined in Dunston. Mr Holker QC re-examined the doctor and he confirmed that he never saw John Banks have 'a true epileptic fit'. There does not seem to have been much point to this question, as all the other evidence on epilepsy was only of the time that John was at Arkleby – a period after the doctor knew him.

Mr Gibson, the assistant overseer for Keswick, next gave evidence that he had known John Banks for some years. Gibson appears to have taken the assistant overseer's post, with its responsibility for rate collection, around 1855. He said that he had frequent dealings with John from then until John went to lodge in Bassenthwaite, which is thought to have been in 1860.[22]

Gibson stated that he was able to conduct business with John regarding the rates on his properties. He said that John often had 'these beatings about his head', but if he waited John would calm down and would be able to conduct business.

A Keswick schoolmaster, Mr Edward Highton, was next to give evidence, and there were several helpful facets to his testimony. He stated that he had had knowledge of John Banks since 1852, but he was personally acquainted with him since 1856. Therefore, like Ansell and Tolson, he had known John for a number of years, and the likelihood was that John would have been calmer and more rational with those he knew and trusted and who were patient with him. Establishing this point in the minds of the jurors served to make a distinction between the evidence of a solicitor, a schoolmaster and council employee who were acquaintances of long standing and patient with John, and those who would give evidence later.

Like Mr Ansell, Mr Highton was a figure of some importance locally, being both schoolmaster and organist: an educator, as well as being educated himself, and also connected to the Church. Again, this was someone who would generally be looked up to in the community. His evidence, set out in Chapter Two, on John's ability to talk rationally in 1864 (the year before his death) on the subject of Martin Luther and the Reformation would have been in very stark contrast to the evidence on behalf of the plaintiff portraying John as delusional man incapable of looking after himself or conducting a rational conversation. Moreover, the subject of the book, Martin Luther, also served to make a useful point about the claim that John Banks saw the Devil and was being persecuted by him. Martin Luther too saw the Devil and was said to have thrown his inkstand at the Devil, to drive him away, when he believed that the Devil had come to visit him.[23] For the jury to have accepted that John was mad, just because he saw the Devil, carried the implication that the instigator of the Protestant Reformation must also have been mad, because he also believed he saw the Devil. This would not have been an acceptable conclusion to draw. While today Martin Luther and this story of the Devil might be less well known, we should bear in mind that in nineteenth-century Protestant England, such knowledge of the Reformation, and England's break with Catholicism, was a far more familiar, and serious, subject. The reference therefore helped to diminish, in the jurymen's[24] eyes, the implications of John seeing devils and demons, and to deter them from the simple acceptance that because John saw devils he must have been generally insane.

At this point Mr Holker QC advised the court that he had several more witnesses who could give similar evidence as to John's capacity, but he would restrict himself to two more and they were Mary Murray, a cousin of Edward Goodfellow, and Thomas Short of Carlisle. Mary Murray's evidence is simply reported as John being 'quite rational in ordinary business'. It is not reported for how long she knew him or under what circumstances. She was quite an odd witness to have called. Being a cousin of the defendant, the jury might have viewed her evidence with more scepticism (notwithstanding that it was given on oath) and what she did say seems to have been so unremarkable that in a lengthy report on the trial the reporter recorded no further details. However, Mr Thomas Short of Carlisle, the second of these two witnesses, was linked to her evidence.

Thomas Short was from Forster and Short, grocers of Carlisle.[25] John Banks and Margaret Goodfellow came into his shop in July 1863 and, he said, 'they came to see an assistant named Murray. Mr Banks talked rationally enough'. One must presume that in this context Murray was probably Mary Murray's husband or son (conceivably it was Mary Murray herself, but female shop assistants were less commonly encountered in the 1860s). Probably, the significance underlying this evidence is that Margaret and John were in each other's company for a day trip to Carlisle (most probably by train from Aspatria). This throws doubt on the evidence that would be given later against the will, that John was a madman who was incapable of behaving properly in company. It would also go against the evidence of Jane Clark, housekeeper to William Thirlwall, who had deposed in her affidavit that Margaret Goodfellow avoided John's company as she was afraid of him. In addition, it cannot have harmed the defendant's case for a Carlisle jury to hear evidence from two Carlisle witnesses, both conceivably known to some of them, particularly in the case of Mr Short. Having more trust in the evidence of those you know, as opposed to those you do not, is a not uncommon human trait.

Before moving on to the final witness for the defendant, it is worth noting that so far, collectively, the witnesses from Keswick were people of consequence who all had lengthy acquaintance with John. They had probably made a strong impression on the jury.

Mrs Routledge, John Banks's landlady at Arkleby, was then called to give evidence as to her signatures and those of her now deceased husband on the two wills. She confirmed that the signatures were authentic. She was called to give this evidence on behalf of the defendant as the authenticity of the signatures was essential to the validity of the will. Mr Holker QC had not wanted to call her as he regarded her as a hostile witness. Brett J, however, ruled that it was essential to call her in order to prove the authenticity of the will. Otherwise than on this point, Mrs Routledge was then going to be the key witness for the case against the will as she was the only person other than Tolson who was present during both meetings at Arkleby. If the evidence of Ansell and Tolson in favour of the will was to be undermined, it would have to be by her evidence. One would give much to know what kind of figure she cut in the witness box. By confirming the validity of her signature and as well as that of her husband, at the very least she confused the overall picture; the evidence of her earlier affidavit, sworn by her to be true, contained a statement that neither she nor her husband had witnessed the second will.

Mrs Routledge's cross-examination by Mr Aspinall QC essentially became the start of the case for the plaintiff against the will. After explaining that John was 'very unruly at times, knocking, shouting and saying the devil was in his head', she said that she did not know 'that he ever fancied he saw devils other than Alexander'. On the face of it, this is at odds with her earlier affidavits which refer to seeing him physically wrestling with the Devil and seeing imps. It is possible that when she used the word 'devil' in her affidavit that she was repeating what John might have called Alexander. But if it is the case that by 'devil' she was referring to 'that devil Alexander', then the implications of John's hallucinations would be reduced somewhat. However, this part of her evidence seems to be so much at odds with other evidence that, if it was reported correctly, it probably weakened her impression on the jury. The judgment from the appeal notes that 'he frequently believed that he was pursued and molested by devils or evil spirits, whom he believed to be visibly present', which does seem to be a reasonable summary in the light of all the evidence.

Mr Aspinall QC continued to take Mrs Routledge through matters covered in her affidavits; John's unruly behaviour when he perceived his persecutors were present and damage to his room. Her evidence then turned to the events surrounding the will (largely already set out in Chapter Three). Her version of the two visits in December 1863 for the wills is (as is also explained in Chapter Three) at odds with the Ansell/Tolson evidence. The effect of Mrs Routledge's narrative, if it had been accepted by the jury, would have been that:

1. John Banks was not mentally competent to make a will, and thus the execution of the wills was invalid.
2. John did not request the meeting for a new will and did not know why the visitors were there.
3. John trusted neither his attorney nor his rent collector.

4. John did not give instructions for his will, indicating that the solicitor had acted improperly, and that the will he drafted could not have derived from his client's instructions.
5. The manner of John's execution of the will, as described by Mrs Routledge, would indicate that John did not know and approve of the contents of the will, thereby rendering it invalid.[26] That a testator must know and approve of the contents of a will in order for it to be valid is not a statutory requirement but it is a common law requirement.
6. John's signature was not made in the presence of two witnesses together at the same time, thus rendering the execution of the will invalid as being contrary to the requirements of section 9 of the Wills Act 1837.[27]
7. The signature of James Routledge was not made in John Banks' presence, thus rendering the attestation invalid as being contrary to the requirements of section 9 of the Wills Act 1837.
8. Ansell and Tolson had conspired together to obtain John's signature on a false will, notwithstanding that they would receive no benefit from that will (alleging a conspiracy without an identifiable motive does not enhance a witness's credibility). There might possibly have been a motive for doing so, but not one that was discernible from the evidence heard by the jury (this is dealt with in a section on John's finances in Chapter Nine).
9. Ansell and Tolson had deliberately given perjured evidence.

In giving her version of events, Elizabeth Routledge was alleging either serious malpractice or utter incompetence on the part of Mr Ansell (on the basis of the numbered points above). To have approached a will in this way:

1. he would have been taking an extraordinarily cavalier approach to the law in this area, and his duty to his client; or
2. he was grossly ignorant of the law and what it required to make a valid will; or
3. he knew well what he was doing yet was prepared to procure, knowingly, a fraudulent will to ensure Margaret Banks Goodfellow's inheritance.

Without some level of corroboration from other witnesses, facts or circumstances known to exist that were consistent with such serious claims, Mrs Routledge's evidence was unlikely to have been accepted against the evidence of an attorney. It should not be overlooked that most of her evidence was focussed on the execution of what was the first of two wills executed in December 1863 and actually had little bearing on the validity of later will (the engrossed will). It is a valid question to ask why the plaintiff moved against the will when it was implicit in Mrs Routledge's claims that there had, at a minimum, been gross malpractice. The answer to this is probably that her evidence as to what happened was regarded as very much secondary to simply showing that John was, and always had been, insane. It is only because this approach was rejected by both courts that attention became very much focussed on the will executions. Nonetheless, her evidence should have been considered carefully as she would need to have been quite impressive when giving evidence in order for her narrative to prevail.

Mrs Routledge was re-examined by Mr Holker QC and she is reported to have repeated her claim that she considered John Banks to be mad. More significant, however, was her admission that 'I don't remember ever signing a will before'. That will probably have had an effect on the jury with its implication that the events surrounding the two December 1863 wills were an entirely novel experience for her, whereas they were not for Mr Ansell. To the mind of a juror, which version was therefore likely to be correct? At this point Brett J asked Mrs Routledge about the 1838 will and she replied 'I am quite sure the will of 1838 was not brought in. I never saw the will of 1838': an exchange that perhaps prompted jurors to ask themselves silently if Mrs Routledge even knew what a will looked like at the time of the meetings.

At this point Mr Holker QC recalled both Mr Ansell and Mr Highton. Mr Ansell said that since giving evidence he had rechecked his papers and found his draft of the memorandum of agreement of the terms of the lease (which provided contemporaneous evidence of the meeting with John Banks, the discussion of the lease and John Banks' signature). Mr Highton was able to identify John Banks' signature as being authentic by comparing it to the signatures of John in Highton's rent book – both points that supported the Ansell/Tolson evidence. This concluded the evidence for Edward Goodfellow, the defendant.

Evidence for the Plaintiff, John Banks the Younger

Mr Aspinall QC now addressed the jury and outlined the claimant's case. He laid particular emphasis on the 'condition' of John Banks in December 1863 and asked the jury if they could believe the evidence produced in favour of John Banks being capable of making a will. This was a rather direct challenge to the competence, or worse, the integrity, of the professional men who had already given evidence. At some point, and possibly during his address to the jury, Mr Aspinall QC suggested, according to *The Times*, that John Banks the elder:

> had taken a strong dislike to the plaintiff, who had, he had heard, been making inquiries whether or not he was his heir, should his niece die; and to satisfy him, the testator was allowed to make his will in favour of his niece, as she was heiress to him, it was thought it could do no harm.

A further attack on the integrity of Mr Ansell, but one that still does not really provide any motive as Margaret would have inherited John Banks' estate without a will.

Mr Aspinall QC first called Joseph Usher, a joiner aged seventy-eight from Keswick. His evidence was all about John before he moved to lodge in Bassenthwaite (1860 at the latest). John was as simple as a child, with no notion of business, according to Usher, and the children in Keswick used to call him 'Crazy John'. Usher was cross-examined by Mr Holker QC, who elicited the information that when John Banks lodged with him, John maintained cash books for the income and expenditure relating to his rental properties. Joseph Usher was followed into the witness box by his wife, and her evidence again related mainly to John's behaviour while he lodged with them. (Extracts from Mrs Usher's evidence were presented in Chapter Two, as they were relevant to John's illness.)

Margaret Bird, the wife of local policeman Superintendent Bird, then gave evidence, again mainly about John's behaviour. (Extracts from Mrs Bird's evidence were also used in Chapter Two as they were pertinent to John's illness.) But, as she had visited John after his move to Arkleby, and particularly after the onset of his epilepsy and his stroke, her comments about his time there had more relevance. In her view, John was not then in a fit state to conduct business. The first point established by Mr Holker QC in cross-examination was that Mr Routledge was Mrs Bird's cousin. This is not necessarily a point of importance in itself, but if Mrs Routledge had not proved credible to the jury, the relationship between the two witnesses might tend to weaken her husband's cousin's wife's credibility in the eyes of the jury.

Mrs Bird also said that John was 'very careful. I don't know anything about his property'. 'Careful' in this context suggests careful with money, which, if correct, is not usually an indicator of a lack of mental capacity. She expressed the opinion that John could never talk rationally for more than a minute or two at a time but added that he was 'very reserved'. 'Reserved' in this context is a curious word to have used, as it would usually indicate quietness in social conversation, which is not a picture usually painted of John. Brett J interjected at this point that he could not 'believe that Banks could talk sensibly for any length of time'. Whatever the reason for this remark was, it would certainly not have harmed the case against the will. Superintendent Isaac Bird had corroborated most of his wife's evidence, but added the very significant view that 'he had seen Banks sensible for an hour at a time. Sometimes he was capable of doing his business and at others not'. This comment was helpful to the defendant's case as it tended to show that John did not always appear to be insane and had lucid periods when he was rational – exactly the point that the earlier witnesses for the plaintiff had tried to make.

William Robinson, a miner, was next called and he gave evidence as to John's behaviour prior to John's move to Arkleby, including the incident mentioned in Chapter Three when John saw a regiment of soldiers before him while on the Bassenthwaite/Keswick road. Mr Holker QC's first question in cross-examination was to establish that William Robinson was the cousin of John Banks the younger. Later questions put to William Robinson produced the view that John Banks was 'not fit to collect rents' – a comment that conveys very little that was relevant to the making of the will. Next came Charles Christopherson[28] who had known John Banks the elder all his life. His evidence that John 'was occasionally fit to transact business, but more frequently not' was neither strongly for nor strongly against the question of John's capacity. He also told the court that he twice picked up and read a letter that John Banks had written to Her Majesty the Queen, but quite why this was thought to be relevant was not made clear. Writing to the monarch, is not *per se* indicative of mental illness – what was in the letter would have been more significant.

Two more witnesses, Ann Hammond and Mary Thwaites,[29] then gave evidence as to John's illness before he was at Arkleby. They were followed by the Reverend Sheppley Watson Watson of Plumbland, who met John shortly after he moved to Arkleby. He knew of John's delusions, and his evidence, as reported, seems to have been remarkably devoid of Christian charity, 'Saw it was no use talking to him as a clergyman, and [I] spoke to him as if talking to a child. From the appearance of the man altogether, anyone would take him for a person out of his mind'.

The last witness for the plaintiff was Dr William Jones of Aspatria. Comment has been made in Chapter Two about the inadequacy of his observations of his patient and his evidence about his treatment. Potentially, his evidence could have been very important to the plaintiff's case, but it was vague and lacked any reference to the stroke John Banks was said to have suffered during the time he was the doctor's patient. The press report of his evidence does read as though he was rather dogmatic, which may not have gone down well with a jury.

A curiosity of the plaintiff's case is that William Thirlwall was not called to give evidence by either side. He had earlier provided an affidavit in support of the plaintiff's case. He was present on the evening of the first visit for the will (after he returned from Bridekirk coursing), and he was present during the second meeting and witnessed the lease. Whether there was a falling out with his sister, Mrs Routledge, or he was simply unwell and could not attend we do not know. His non-attendance must have weakened the plaintiff's case.

Addresses to the Jury

Mr Aspinall QC, for the claimant, went first and outlined why a man as insane as John Banks could not make a valid will. He did not accept that a person as ill as John Banks was could have sufficient lucidity, 'A man attacked by incurable insanity could not have lucid intervals'. He concluded by asking the jury if they were prepared to say:

> that when a man is mad, when a man is possessed with all these fancies, when he indulges in all these antics, when he conducts himself in the irrational manner described, he was capable of making a will which would detach property from his own family and giving it to other people?

Mr Holker QC replied to this address and maintained, as Brett J had indicated during the trial, that 'though a man might be insane on all subjects ... yet sometimes he could be capable of transacting business and managing his affairs' and then be regarded by the law as being of 'a sound and disposing memory'; that is to say capable of making a valid will. He asked the jury to deal with the point at issue 'not according to the very learned definition of doctors and others who spoke about it, but by the guidance and dictates of common sense'.

He continued:

> What did it matter then when a man made a disposition of his property, whether he believed Fetherstone Alexander to be the devil or not. If he had left his property to Fetherstone Alexander it might have meant something.

In Holker's view, what the jury had to decide was whether Ansell and Tolson were telling the truth or whether Mrs Routledge was. In focussing on the conflict of evidence over the December visits, he was correctly drawing the jury's attention to the time that was relevant

A Point of Law and Directions to the Jury

There was an exchange during the trial between Brett J and Mr Aspinall QC that occurred while the witnesses for the claimant were being examined. The exchange reveals an important divergence of views on the law and the question of insanity and lucid intervals when applied to wills. The exchange, which took place immediately after the evidence of Charles Christopherson, was reported in the *Carlisle Patriot* of 19th February 1869 as follows:

> The judge here reminded learned counsel that the only question was whether the testator was in a sound state of mind when the will was made …
>
> Mr Aspinall – There is a difficulty, my lord, which does not strike one at first sight. It is not a question whether this man had rational moments, but what was the general state of his mind.
>
> The judge – Well, the evidence, goes to show that from time to time he was insane, no doubt. That is admitted.
>
> Mr Aspinall – My case is that he was in a state of chronic imbecility.
>
> The judge – Your own witnesses say that occasionally he could transact business. He might be so when the will was made. Your case is to prove the contrary.
>
> Mr Aspinall – I venture to submit not, my Lord. Every man in lunatic asylum may at times be in a state of mind fit to transact business.

The judge – They might make a will during brief intervals.[30]

Mr Aspinall – Lucid intervals is a term which requires a great deal of definition. With all deference to your Lordship, we will go on.

What this exchange was about was where the law on testamentary capacity stood in 1869 before this case was heard. It highlights what had already become apparent in the way each side had presented its case. The plaintiff was following judicial precedent that suggested that an insane person could not make a will, while the defence was based on the actual capability of John Banks when he made the will.

Brett J's directions to the jury contained the following advice:

> … the plaintiff and the defendant were both claiming this property, which was the property of John Banks. The plaintiff was entitled to the property, and their verdict, unless the defendant could prove to their satisfaction that John Banks made a will and a valid will. If the will was not a valid will, the plaintiff was entitled to their verdict. It is admitted that from time to time the testator was so insane that he was incapable of making a will. The question is whether, on the 2nd of December, 1863, or on the 28th of December, 1863, or on both, the testator was capable of having such a knowledge and appreciation of facts, and was so far master of his intentions, free from delusions, as would enable him to have a will of his own in the disposition of his property, and act upon it. The mere fact of his being able to recollect things, or to converse rationally on some subjects, or to manage some business, is not sufficient to shew he was sane. On the other hand, slowness, feebleness, and eccentricities, are not sufficient to shew he was insane. The whole burden of shewing that the testator was fit at the time is on the defendant in this case. In order to determine whether the testator had a lucid interval when the wills or either of them were made, it may be important to consider what was the extent and nature of his admitted general insanity.[31]

Brett J next read his summary of the evidence in detail, commenting upon it as he proceeded and concluded without giving any opinion on the various statements, but asked the jury to decide the question that had been put to them on the evidence adduced.

In this passage the judge was, as the appeal court would later do, going back to older principles in cases decided before the wrong turn taken by the law in *Waring v Waring*. What the judge said in this passage is consistent with the line he took in his exchange with Mr Aspinall, set out above. Given that there was not universal acceptance that Lord Brougham's views in *Waring* were correct, the slightly mischievous thought springs to mind that Brett J might have been perfectly well aware of what he was doing in not applying *Waring*. Further, he could have done this in the fairly safe knowledge that, whatever the jury's findings, one side or the other would appeal. Given that Sir Alexander Cockburn was the Chief Justice of Queen's Bench and given that his interest in partial insanity had been well known ever since his triumph, as a barrister, on this point in his defence of Daniel M'Naghten, Brett J must have realised that a chance to correct the aberrant approach in *Waring* could have been presented in this case. Did he even go further and alert Cockburn as to what was heading to his court on appeal?

What we know of Brett J's directions to the jury does seem to make it clear that the choice for the jury was fairly simple. By focussing on the events surrounding the wills, the question for the jury was: did John have the requisite mental capacity when executing the wills? This simple question makes most of the evidence presented in court for the plaintiff irrelevant. Was the account of Ansell and Tolson true, or did the jury think that Mrs Routledge was telling the truth? In those terms, the verdict becomes fairly predictable.

The report in the *Carlisle Patriot* contains additional remarks of Brett J:

> The whole burden of proving this to [the jury's] satisfaction [is] laid upon the defendant. It was the defendant who had brought forward this will. The defendant admitted that this man was insane at some time, but their case was that he was not insane at the time the will was made and that he had lucid intervals. Therefore the whole burden of proving that John Banks was sane when this will was made laid on Mr Holker, who appeared for the defendant.

The Jury's Verdict

The jury retired for only twenty-five minutes before finding that the will 'was a good and valid will'. It was by this time half past eight at night and one wonders if there was an element of hunger that might have speeded up the jury's deliberations. Previously, the rule in criminal cases was that juries were not allowed food, drink or fire after the judge's summing up, but this was abolished in 1858. A civil case such as this in 1870 would have allowed food, drink and fire, but the lure of home comfort would have been substantial.[32]

After the jury returned, there followed a further exchange between Brett J and learned counsel for the plaintiff, reported in the *Carlisle Patriot*:

Mr Aspinall – May I ask your lordship to stay execution?

The judge – In order that you may move for a fresh trial?

Mr Aspinal – I think that will be the course.

The judge – Very well.

Brett J is not apparently in the least surprised at the request, nor should anyone have been, given his earlier exchange with Mr Aspinall QC.

The Appeal

The scene was thus set for a strong appeal court[33] in the Court of Queen's Bench, in London, to hear the arguments on the correctness of Brett J's directions to the jury and the jury's conclusions based on the evidence that they had heard.

Queen's Bench was then nearing the end of its existence as an independent court. It was a common law court of considerable antiquity (dating from at least the early thirteenth century), and it had originally been known as the Court of King's Bench (becoming Queen's Bench during the reign of queens). Originally, the judges of the court would have travelled round the country with the King, sitting to hear cases wherever the King was. By the early fifteenth century it was based in London along with the other common law courts, the Court of Common Pleas and the Exchequer of Pleas. Over time, these three courts competed for work, although by the time of this trial they had near identical jurisdictions, principles and remedies. That they were so similar pointed to the rationality of formally merging all three into the new Queen's Bench Division of the High Court in 1875[34] – which Division continues to exist today. Sir Alexander Cockburn had been the senior judge – Chief Justice – of Queen's Bench since June 1859 – he was also the last Chief Justice of Queen's Bench.

Part of the function of Queen's Bench was to act as an appeal court from decisions of the County Assizes. Queen's Bench did not re-hear a case, with the same parade of witnesses and time taken with examination and cross-examination. The appeal trial would be based on the paper records of evidence (witness statements), the statements of case by the contesting parties and the judge's direction to the jury. In addition, counsel for both sides could address the court in legal argument and answer questions from the Bench when required. Similar principles apply today, in that an appellate court does not re-hear a case in full, but review the findings and the manner in which the law has been applied.

In this case there were two grounds for appeal to be considered by Queen's Bench: first that Brett J had misdirected the jury, and secondly that the verdict in favour of the will was against the weight of the evidence. If either was accepted a re-trial could be ordered. Cockburn CJ specified in his judgment that the misdirection pleaded was that Brett J, although leaving it to the jury to decide if when making the will John Banks was free from delusions, did not tell the jury that the delusions which John suffered from:

> might not have been present in his mind at the time of the making of the will, yet if they were latent in his mind, so that, if the subject had been touched upon, the delusions would have recurred, he was of unsound mind and therefore incapable of making a will.

The judgment of the court was given by Chief Justice Cockburn. There were no additional comments from the other judges, who sat with him in this case, and therefore, clearly, there were no dissenting judgments. Cockburn CJ's judgment still has admirers almost a hundred and fifty years later. Henderson J,[35] in a significant testamentary capacity case in 2007, observed that the judgment 'is a remarkable one, which repays reading in full. It is, apart from anything else, a masterpiece of English prose'.[36] Senior Judge Lush of the Court of Protection has said that:

> it exerts a gravitational pull on other tests of capacity ... There cannot be many other authorities this ancient that still command so much respect today.

In 2017, when the Law Commission consulted on possible reform to this area of law, the consultation document contained the comment that whilst many who responded said the test of capacity that Cockburn set out was 'well understood', it also noted that others said the language was 'archaic'. It would be a pity if the test disappeared simply because it was it was perceived as too old or that some readers today might struggle with the language of Dickens' time.

Cockburn proceeded on the basis that, given the jury's finding, John Banks, 'though generally of weak intellect', was able to manage his affairs, and, apart from his delusions, was, at least at the time of executing one or both wills, of sufficient testamentary capacity. Further, he accepted that during this period John was still subject to delusions but that they did not manifest themselves at the time of executing the will. Nonetheless, the delusions remained 'latent in the testator's mind' and could have surfaced if John was provoked. Because of the evidence of delusions continuing until John Banks' death, Cockburn considered the jury's finding, that he was free from delusions, to mean solely that the delusions were not manifest, not that he was free from them. This meant that the court must consider the extent to which the existence of delusions could deprive a person of the capacity to make a will. Cockburn found that the delusions were attested to by two witnesses 'whose evidence was above suspicion' – Dr William Jones and Reverend Shepley Watson Watson. (This was probably because of the individuals' status rather than any intrinsic value of the evidence.) He also found that there was a body of evidence which:

> if believed was strong to establish a case of general insanity. The jury, however, found in favour of the will, and must therefore have believed this evidence to be greatly exaggerated, or must have come to the conclusion that the will was made during a lucid interval.

Cockburn also accepted that John Banks 'managed his own monetary affairs (which were however on a limited scale) and was careful with his money'.

The legal difficulty at the heart of this case is an earlier decision relating to the concept of 'the unity and indivisibility of the mind'. Cockburn CJ drew attention to this in his judgment:

> in our day the doctrine has sprung up of the unity and indivisibility of the mind, but the ground on which insanity should cause incapacity appears to have been overlooked in the reasoning on which it is founded.[37]

This was a reference to the Privy Council judgment in *Waring v Waring*[38] in 1848. This judgment followed the, then fashionable, doctrine of the unity and indivisibility of the mind, which maintained that any unsoundness of the mind, no matter how slight or unconnected with the will, could be sufficient to prevent a person having testamentary capacity. We would now find it to be quite a reasonable view, on the part of Brett J, that a will made in a lucid interval can be valid, but learned counsel opposing the will seemed to doubt very much that this view conformed to the then existing law. The headnote to the law report of *Waring v Waring* summarises the four main points made by Lord Brougham[39] when he gave his judgment:

> If the mind is unsound on one subject, provided that unsoundness is, at all times, existing upon that subject, *it is erroneous to suppose such a*

mind is really sound on other subjects; it is only sound in appearance, for if the subject of the delusion be presented to it, the unsoundness would be manifested by such a person believing in the suggestions of fancy, as if they were realities: any act, therefore, done by such a person, however apparently rational that act may appear to be, is void, as it is the act of a morbid or unsound mind.

Delusion is the belief of things as realities, which exist only in the imagination of the patient. The frame of mind which indicates his incapacity to struggle against such an erroneous belief constitutes an unsound frame of mind.

To constitute a lucid interval, the party must freely and voluntarily, and without any design at the time, of pretending sanity and freedom from delusion, *confess his delusion.*

Where delusions are proved to have existed, both before and after the factum, the presumption is, that they existed at the time of the factum, and in such case, proof of a lucid interval, at the time of the factum, is thrown upon the party propounding a Will. *It is immaterial that the delusions do not appear on the face of the Will.*[40] (author's added emphasis)

Today, these views seem quite startling in their apparent complete denial of the ability of a person to make a will if he or she is suffering from any mental disorder. Although Lord Brougham's views were given in the context of a contested will, they are expressed in such sweeping terms that he appears to be speaking of any legal act done by anyone with a mental illness. The judgment was ostensibly addressing the subject of partial insanity or 'monomania',[41] as it was more commonly known then. However, the unpopularity of the rather extreme position that he took probably stopped these views leaching out of the area of wills into other areas of the law.

Reading Lord Brougham's full judgment, one is struck by both his utter faith in his own analysis and also his lack of any compassion:

> ... no confidence can be placed in the acts, or any act, of the diseased mind, however apparently rational that act may appear to be, or in reality be. The act in question may be exactly such as a person without mental infirmity may do. But there is this difference between the two cases; the person uniformly and always of sound mind, could not, at the moment of the act done, be prey to morbid delusion, whatever subject was presented to his mind; whereas the person called partially insane – that is to say, sometimes appearing to be sound, sometimes of unsound mind – would inevitably show his subjection to the

disease the instant the topic was suggested. Therefore we can with perfect confidence, rely on the act done by the former, because we can be sure that no lurking insanity, no particular, or partial, or occasional delusion, does mingle itself with the person's act, and materially affect it. But we can never rely on the act, however rational in appearance, done by the latter, because we have no security that the lurking delusion, the real unsoundness, does not mingle itself with, or occasion, the act ... the malady is there, and as the mind is one and the same, it is really diseased, while apparently sound, and really its acts, whatever appearance they may put on, are only the acts of a morbid or sound.[42]

Lord Brougham went further to stack the odds against the ability of a mentally ill person to make a valid will by adding later:

> So where any circumstances of grave suspicion arise at the outset of a case, as that a will is shown in the outset to have been made and published in a lunatic asylum (which I have known to happen), the burthen of proving, and very satisfactorily proving, the testator's sanity would be so clearly on the propounding party, that no further proof would be required to impugn it ... this clearly [makes] it incumbent on the party propounding, to show sanity by much clearer proof than would have been required had no such disease been admitted ...[43]

It has been drawn to my attention that the principle Lord Brougham was seeking to set out can be seen as analogous to, or developed from, the common law principle of *falsus in uno, falsus in omnibus* (false in one thing, false in everything). This, originally, was the principle that a witness who gave false evidence on one matter was not credible in giving evidence on others. While this principle was applied in the Stuart treason trials of the late sixteenth century, it is believed to have older origins. It was already regarded as not being a principle of universal application by the early nineteenth century; indeed Lord Ellenborough, in 1809, had expressed the view that:

> though a person may be proved on his own shewing ... to have foresworn himself as to a particular fact; it does not follow that he can never afterwards feel the obligation of an oath.

If Lord Brougham had sought inspiration from this concept, he had not noticed that its day had passed.[44]

These two extracts from his Lordship's judgment tell us a great deal about why the attack on John Banks' will was mounted the way it was. It explains why the evidence against the will was framed the way it was. It was mainly generalised evidence that, throughout John's adult life, he had been insane, which would have been sufficient to show, as per Lord Brougham's definition, that his will could not have been valid. The evidence of insanity would have been sufficient, following the second extract quoted above, to impugn the will. It explains why to the modern eye so much of the evidence against John Banks's will appears to lack focus on the crucial circumstances of December 1863 and the making of the two wills at Arkleby.

The inflexible and absolute approach to mental illness in Lord Brougham's judgment tends to make it seem that those attacking the will must have had very high hopes of success, particularly in the way that they portrayed John Banks. If the precedent set by the judgment in *Waring v Waring* was followed there would have been little hope of the validity of either of the December 1863 wills being upheld.

Significantly, one thing that immediately strikes the modern reader of Lord Brougham's judgment is the almost complete lack of legal precedent cited, and considered, in his judgment. This lack is readily apparent when Brougham's judgment is placed alongside Cockburn's judgment in the *Banks v Goodfellow* appeal. This lack of precedent, coupled with using the all-or-nothing approach to sanity (which clearly had not been necessary on the facts of the *Waring* case), made it easier for his judgment to be ignored by some later judges, and *Banks v Goodfellow* offered an opportunity to bury it completely.

Cockburn grasped this central issue early on in his judgment:

> The question whether partial unsoundness, not affecting the general faculties, and not operating on the mind of a testator in regard to the particular testamentary disposition, will be sufficient to deprive a person of the power of disposing of his property, presents itself here for judicial decision, so far as we are aware, for the first time. It is true that, in the case of *Waring v Waring*, the Judicial Committee of the Privy Council, and, in the more recent case of *Smith v. Tebbitt* Lord Penzance, in the Court of Probate, have laid down a doctrine, according to which any degree of mental unsoundness, however slight, and however unconnected with the testamentary disposition in question, must be held fatal to the capacity of a testator. But in both these cases, as we shall presently shew, the wide doctrine embraced in the judgment was wholly unnecessary to the decision, and we therefore feel ourselves warranted, and indeed bound, to consider the

question as one not concluded by authority, and on which we are called upon to form our own judgment. The question is one of equal importance and difficulty, and we have given it our best consideration.

This amounted to a blunt put-down of the views of Lords Brougham and Penzance.[45] The wording of the statements 'the wide doctrine embraced ... was wholly unnecessary to the decision' and 'we ... feel ourselves warranted, and indeed bound, to consider the question as one not concluded by authority' was not accidental or casually used. Cockburn CJ was known to spend considerable time on drafting his judgments and he took pride in the quality of the finished article.

Cockburn CJ also made the point that, to date, neither text books nor other court decisions had examined delusions, or partial insanity in the context of wills. Given his rejection of *Waring* and *Smith*, Cockburn felt that there was merit in looking back at the principal decisions that had preceded them,[46] noting at one point that the view of the court in the *Parnther* case showed 'a more indulgent view of the effect of insanity, as affecting testamentary capacity, was taken then than has latterly prevailed'.

Cockburn returned to *Waring* and summarised its principle as being:

> To constitute testamentary capacity, soundness of mind is indispensably necessary. But the mind, though it has various faculties, is one and indivisible. If it is disordered in any one of these faculties, if it labours under any delusion arising from such disorder, though its other faculties and functions may remain undisturbed, it cannot be said to be sound. Such a mind is unsound, and testamentary incapacity is the necessary consequence.

But, having said this, he again dismissed its relevance as it was not 'in any degree necessary to the decision' in *Waring* to decide this point. Both the *Waring* and *Smith* cases were concerned with general insanity, not partial. In both cases, the delusions were multifarious:

> and of the wildest and most irrational character, abundantly indicating that the mind was diseased throughout ... in both it was palpable that the delusions must have influenced the testamentary disposition.

Having made this important distinction, Cockburn felt that his court, being unable to concur with the *Waring* view, was then 'at liberty to consider for ourselves the principle properly applicable to such a case as the present'.

He further indicated, before setting out his test for testamentary capacity, that:

> there often are ... delusions, which, though the offspring of mental disease and so far constituting insanity, yet leave the individual in all other respects rational, and capable of transacting the ordinary affairs and fulfilling the duties and obligations incidental to the various relations of life.

Given the disarray of English judicial authority in this area, Cockburn and his colleagues had reviewed the position in other jurisdictions, but:

> we have, however, derived but little advantage from the inquiry. The Roman law, the great storehouse of juridical science, is as vague and general on the subject as our own.

He then noted that on the continent there was among current jurists 'a marked discordance of opinion'. French, Italian and German jurists were considered – this was unsurprising as Cockburn spoke these languages with some ease (he was accustomed to spending time on the continent each year).

Cockburn CJ's judgment moved on to what test should properly be applied, given that his court had a blank slate on which to create one. Acknowledging the moral responsibilities required for the disposition of property by will, it was vital that any test should recognise this in its requirements. Based on this he formulated the following:

> It is essential to the exercise of such a power that a testator
>
> shall understand the nature of the act and its effects;
>
> shall understand the extent of the property of which he is disposing;
>
> shall be able to comprehend and appreciate the claims to which he ought to give effect;
>
> and, with a view to the latter object, that no disorder of the mind shall poison his affections, pervert his sense of right, or prevent the exercise of his natural faculties—that no insane delusion shall influence his will in disposing of his property and bring about a disposal of it which, if the mind had been sound, would not have been made.[47]

This is the often-quoted test in *Banks v Goodfellow*. Less often quoted are Cockburn CJ's words in the subsequent paragraph:

> Here, then, we have the measure of the degree of mental power which should be insisted on. If the human instincts and affections, or the moral sense, become perverted by mental disease; if insane suspicion, or aversion, take the place of natural affection; if reason and judgment are lost, and the mind, becomes a prey to insane delusions calculated to interfere with and disturb its functions, and to lead to a testamentary disposition, due only to their baneful influence—in such a case it is obvious that the condition of the testamentary power fails, and that a will made under such circumstances ought not to stand. But what if the mind, though possessing sufficient power, undisturbed by frenzy or delusion, to take into account all the considerations necessary to the proper making of a will, should be subject to some delusion, but such delusion neither exercises nor is calculated to exercise any influence on the particular disposition, and a rational and proper will is the result; ought we, in such case, to deny to the testator the capacity to dispose of his property by will?

Taken together, these two passages set out principles that show far more humanity than the harsh and arbitrary approach of Lords Brougham and Penzance in *Waring* and *Smith*, respectively. The judgment in this case reflects the views and language of lawyers; there are no nineteenth-century medical expressions or ideas in the above test. What Cockburn CJ proposed was a test of understanding, not a medical judgment, that was set out in language that was accessible to all. It is a mark of how successful he was that this test is capable of being applied in the light of nineteenth-century psychiatry[48] or twenty-first century psychiatry. As this is a common law test of capacity it is capable of being amended by judges when circumstances require it.[49] The only thing that has changed during this time is the breadth and depth of understanding of the mind, but the basic requirements of understanding were correctly understood as written in 1870.

Cockburn CJ, in justification of his approach, made a further comment:

> It must be borne in mind that the absolute and uncontrolled power of testamentary disposition conceded by the law is founded on the assumption that a rational will is a better disposition than any that can be made by the law itself. If therefore, though mental disease may exist, it presents itself in such a degree and form as not to interfere with the capacity to make a rational disposal of property, why, it may be asked, should it be held to take away the right? It cannot be the

object of the legislator to aggravate an affliction, in itself so great, by the deprivation of a right the value of which is universally felt and acknowledged. If it be conceded, as we think it must be, that the only legitimate or rational ground for denying testamentary capacity to persons of unsound mind is the inability to take into account and give due effect to the considerations which ought to be present to the mind of a testator in making his will, and to influence his decision as to the disposal of his property, it follows that a degree or form of unsoundness which neither disturbs the exercise of the faculties necessary for such an act, nor is capable of influencing the result, ought not to take away the power of making a will, or place a person so circumstanced in a less advantageous position than others with regard to this right … It may be here not unimportant to advert to the law relating to unsoundness of mind arising from another cause—namely, from want of intelligence occasioned by defective organization, or by supervening physical infirmity or the decay of advancing age, as distinguished from mental derangement, such defect of intelligence being equally a cause of incapacity. In these cases it is admitted on all hands that though the mental power may be reduced below the ordinary standard, yet if there be sufficient intelligence to understand and appreciate the testamentary act in its different bearings, the power to make a will remains …

It is startling to read such a strong and clear defence of the rights of those with restricted or impaired mental faculties in a judgment written almost a hundred and fifty years ago. Only twenty-two years separate it from Lord Brougham's cold-hearted assault on the rights of the individual in *Waring*, and yet Cockburn then produced a defence of those rights in terms which would not be out of place in a modern human rights document.

The appeal judgment in favour of the will was a clear and unanimous view that the law had taken a wrong turn with *Waring v Waring* and that a more rational test must be set out. Had members of the appeal court, particularly Cockburn CJ, been looking out for a case such as this? Were they ready and waiting for the chance to steer the law back onto a more reasonable course? If so, Mr Aspinall QC does not seem to have suspected what might lay in wait for him.

As well upholding Brett J's application of the law in his direction to the jury, the appeal court also refused a re-trial, taking the view that, if faced with the same evidence, another jury would find exactly as the Cumberland Assizes jury did, particularly 'as to the absence of all connection between the delusions and dispositions made by the testator'. As a consequence, it would be 'worse than useless to put the parties to the expenses of a new trial'.

A Victorian Tragedy: The Extraordinary Case of Banks v Goodfellow

It does not seem to me to be a coincidence that Cockburn CJ chose to preside in this appeal. He had previously, and famously, made a name for himself in the area of partial insanity with his successful defence of Daniel M'Naghten. This acquittal ultimately led to the formulation of the M'Naghten Rules (1843) on the criminal accountability of the insane, which influenced criminal justice in many other jurisdictions for many years afterwards. Daniel M'Naghten was a Glasgow wood-turner who was subject to a paranoid delusion that he was being persecuted by the Conservative Government led by Sir Robert Peel. In 1843 Daniel M'Naghten shot and killed Edward Drummond, the Prime Minister's private secretary. M'Naghten had mistaken Drummond for Peel. His explanation of the murder was:

> The Tories in my native city have compelled me to do this. They follow me and persecute me wherever I go, and have entirely destroyed my peace of mind. They followed me to France, into Scotland and all over England; in fact, they follow me wherever I go. I can get no rest from them night or day. I cannot sleep at night in consequence of the course they pursue towards me. I believe they have driven me into a consumption. I am sure I shall never be the man I formerly was. I used to have good health and strength, but I have not now. They have accused me of crimes of which I am not guilty; they do everything in their power to harass and persecute me; in fact they wish to murder me. It can be proved by evidence. That is all I have to say.

A defence for M'Naghten was put together very quickly within little over a month after the shooting. Witnesses called by the defence included the Lord Provost of Glasgow, the Glasgow Commissioner of Police and eight doctors. Writing in 1977 Sir Roger Ormrod[50] noted:

> How this was organised and by whom is an intriguing question ... some person or persons must have been very strongly motivated to undertake and carry out so much work in so short a time.

The defence was led by Cockburn (then Alexander Cockburn QC). The immense effort that Cockburn put into this trial was undoubtedly, at least in part, because of his intense personal interest in the matter. At that time a number of medical and legal figures were concerned at how the law dealt with matters of insanity and partial insanity – particularly where capital offences were concerned. Cockburn ran a formidable medically based defence which the prosecution could not counter. The key was whether or not partial insanity could be a valid defence. Although M'Naghten was said to be generally sane, Cockburn succeeded in showing that the paranoid delusions under which M'Naghten was acting made him not responsible for his actions. Both in this case and the earlier *Hadfield* case the presiding judges accepted the defence with some alacrity, effectively stopping the trial with a direction to the jury to acquit.[51] The prosecution was conducted by the Attorney-General and he could not counter the defence's formidable array of medical evidence, admitting in a brief closing speech, 'I cannot press for a verdict against the prisoner'. Cockburn's proposition was put to the court as:

> The question is ... whether under that delusion of mind he did an act which he would not have done under any other circumstances, save under the impulse of the delusion which he could not control and out of which delusion the alone the act itself arose.

His argument for acquittal was therefore based on M'Naghten's partial insanity making him not responsible for his actions when acting under the influence of his delusions. This ran counter to the existing approach to insanity in the criminal law. Both his arguments in defence of M'Naghten and his later judgment upholding John Banks' will display the same understanding of mental illness.[52] By the strangest of coincidences, John Banks and Daniel M'Naghten both suffered from paranoid delusions and were almost exact contemporaries. M'Naghten was born in the year following John Banks and he died two months before him.[53]

In a retrospective of Cockburn's career, in the *Harvard Law Review* of June 1900, the author drew attention to Cockburn's work on the doctrine of partial insanity, linking his defence of M'Naghten with the *Banks v Goodfellow* judgment, which the author describes as 'beyond doubt one of Cockburn's most important judicial efforts'. Perhaps Cockburn CJ is, in the end, the real hero of this story. In achieving fundamental and long-lasting change to the judicial view of insanity, in both criminal and civil law, he contributed significantly to moving the law on insanity in a more modern direction. For one man to have brought about these changes through the court in two important areas of law is an achievement that should not be underestimated. His arguments on both occasions showed a greater understanding of issues of mental illness than was generally the case in his time. His approach was also far more humane and respectful of the individual's rights. His plain statement of the issue makes this clear:

It is said, indeed, by those who insist that any degree of unsoundness should suffice to take away testamentary capacity, that where insane delusion has shewn itself, it is always possible, and indeed may be assumed to be probable, that a greater degree of mental unsoundness exists than has actually become manifest. But this view, which is by no means universally admitted, is unsupported by proof, and must be looked upon as matter of speculative opinion. *It seems unreasonable to deny testamentary capacity on the speculative possibility of unsoundness which has failed to display itself, and which, if existing in a latent and undiscovered form, would be little likely to have any influence on the disposition of the will.* (author's added emphasis)

CHAPTER SIX

John Banks the Younger: The Claimant

Jacob Banks the Younger

As noted in Chapter One, Jacob Banks the elder's first son was Jacob Banks the younger. Jacob the younger was the older half-brother of John Banks the elder and he is believed to have been born in 1790s. Jacob Banks the younger became a pencil manufacturer, like his father. It seems likely that he started by working in his father's business and later took it over when Jacob the elder retired.[1] In 1815, Jacob the younger married Ann Robinson and, in due course, they had several daughters (some of whom died in infancy) and one son. Ann Robinson died in December 1835 and following her death Jacob married Sarah Dewey. There was no issue of this second marriage. Jacob's son from his first marriage was John Banks the younger, who was born in 1826. This John Banks was the plaintiff (claimant) in the legal dispute over the will of his uncle, John Banks the elder.

Jacob the younger appears to have been declared bankrupt in 1835 or 1836,[2] and he is thought to have died, intestate, in October 1846. The cause of his business failure, resulting in his personal bankruptcy, is not known but, in all likelihood, it was connected with Keswick having lost its monopoly on lead pencil production earlier in the nineteenth century. Competition from other countries would have changed the economics of manufacture and production, giving a harsher business climate for the whole Keswick pencil industry. It is likely that Jacob's business was not the only failure.

Frustratingly, we know nothing of the personal relationships between Jacob the younger and his father, and later between Jacob the younger and his half-siblings, John Banks the elder and Margaret Banks. As Jacob the younger died in 1846, the relationship between his children and John and Margaret Banks could be an important one for this story if we knew any of the details. All that is known is the allegation at the first trial that John Banks the elder had taken exception to John Banks the younger's enquiry about where the elder's estate would go if his niece predeceased him. This could suggest animosity between the half-siblings' families and that John the elder was not well disposed towards his namesake. Many a testator has, over the years, also taken offence at relatives who have expressed curiosity about the contents of a will while the testator is still alive. A testator can feel that this is presumptuous or a sign of greed – and often they have not been mistaken, on the latter point in particular. But this may not be the right conclusion to draw. Opposed to this was a claim from John the younger that his uncle was much attached to him, although on what grounds and when was not made clear.

John Banks the elder, as noted in Chapter Three, seems to have been determined that his niece should inherit his estate. Even if Margaret's later fatal illness was not diagnosed when the will was made, the wording in the will ensuring that Margaret, or her heirs if she died, would receive the estate is quite reasonable given his closeness to her. It is also quite a logical choice, given that Margaret was alone and probably incapable of earning a living. John the elder's decision about his will may say nothing about his feelings towards John the younger, merely that he believed that Margaret had more need of his largesse. Perhaps, today, the more careful draftsman would have more readily recognised the risk of Margaret dying before the age of twenty-one without issue and discussed the implications of this with John and, if required, provided definite alternate provisions in the will in the event that Margaret died before she attained twenty-one. It would be intriguing to know what John Banks the elder would have decided if that question had been put to him. Without expressly having his attention drawn to who should inherit if Margaret died without issue and before she could make a will, few in John the elder's position would have considered it. This is not being unkind to John the elder, as few testators today have the experience (or training) to think through the possibilities – and have the knowledge of devolution to understand both the problems and solutions. It is quite within the bounds of possibility that John the elder would have decided to keep his money within the Banks family and made provision for John the younger to inherit if Margaret did not – and then the whole dispute would have been avoided. Making provision for the half-brother's children would often be the choice of person in John's position in the absence of any major animosity towards them.

John Banks the younger

There is no record, or at least not one that can be traced now, that John Banks the younger, like his uncle, ever married. In the 1861 census John Banks the younger was recorded as a painter then living with his maternal uncle William Robinson (a pencil maker). The census entry actually reads 'Retired Painter'. At thirty-four he seems to be too young to have retired in the sense usually meant today. Given that the next census describes him as a painter, it is tempting to think that the 'retired' in the 1861 census means that he had left a more regular, or common, occupation in order to paint (presumably on the basis that the census taker did not regard painting as a real job). If that is the case, his previous occupation is unknown, but perhaps he ceased employment with his father's business when it failed. In his affidavit in the trial of the will,[3] John declared that he went to the USA in the spring of 1849. John remained in the USA until he returned to visit Keswick eleven years later in the spring of 1860. Why he made this visit he did not say, but it would not be unusual for an emigrant to North America, if he could afford the passage (it was after all cheaper, and a shorter journey, for someone from North America to do this than it would have been for an emigrant to Australia). In the autumn of 1861 (after having been present in Keswick for that year's census) John returned to North America, but this time to Vancouver Island, Canada. The census in Keswick had been taken on Sunday 7th April 1861, only a few days before the fall of Fort Sumter on 13th April signalled the beginning of hostilities in the American Civil War. The crisis over Southern secession in the USA had begun the previous year, and John may well have thought it best to try Canada for a time and stay away from the war and pressures to enlist. The introduction of conscription for the Federal Army in July 1863 would have made his decision look quite prescient.

In Canada, John lived in British Columbia until September 1867, at which point he was told of Margaret Banks Goodfellow's death and he decided to return to England to contest his uncle's will. Quite why he would have thought that it was worth returning to begin the litigation over the will is not known. It does seem a little too speculative to undertake the expense of the long journey in the hope that there might be a viable case. It is not outside the bounds of possibility that he was encouraged to return by others in Keswick who either disliked the Goodfellow family (particularly Edward), or at least were better disposed to John's interests.

The first Bill of Complaint in the dispute was filed on 11th November 1867. In it John is described as 'a gentleman of Keswick'. The use of the term 'gentleman', rather than giving an occupation, suggests that he had made sufficient money in North America to support himself in England without the need to work to this period. In his affidavit of 20th April 1868 John makes it clear that he came to England before taking legal advice. It is more than a little odd to undertake the journey without having had some legal advice about the circumstances of the will and his uncle. The decision to travel before receiving advice does point quite strongly towards the views of others having influenced him, and potential witnesses' apparent dislike of Edward Goodfellow must have been a factor. John the younger did not come back from North America when his uncle died in 1865, and at that time his grounds for challenging the will would have been exactly the same as they were when he made the challenge after Margaret's death. The only circumstance that had changed was the heir to the estate and that seems to be the factor that made his mind up (and probably also the encouragement from those who were prepared to give evidence on his behalf).

It is probable, but by no means certain, that John the younger returned to the USA after the litigation over his uncle's will was concluded, and this would then account for his absence from the 1871 census in England. In the 1881 census, well after the litigation over his uncle's will was finished, John the younger lived alone in Crosthwaite and was described in that year's census as a 'landscape oil painter'. In 1891, when he was sixty-four and lodging in Church Street, Keswick, he was described in that census as 'living on his own means'. This description would imply that John was at least moderately successful in earning enough from painting to support himself.[4]

John the younger had six sisters. Mary, Charlotte and Martha all died in infancy before he was born. The three sisters who survived infancy, Emma, Anna Bella and Lavinia (born 1822, 1824 and 1829, respectively) all emigrated at different times to the USA. Emma and Lavinia married in this country in 1851 and 1852, respectively, before leaving for the USA, and Anna Bella is known to have been living in the USA by 1855. It seems that all four siblings will have left England in a relatively short period after the death of their father and step-mother.[5] It would be natural for John to have spent some time with his sisters in the USA before returning to Keswick in 1860.

Evidence was given at the first trial, referred to in Chapter Five, that John's uncle, John Banks the elder, had spoken in 1861 of going to see his nephew in America in order to avoid the evil spirits that tormented him in England. He said the evil spirits would not be able to follow him there as they could not swim.[6] John Banks the elder never did make voyage to the USA. This evidence on the one hand could be seen as an illustration of John the elder's madness. But it could be seen as an attempt to point to some closeness between uncle and nephew and that could weaken any suggestion that John the elder had any animosity against his nephew.

At the time of the 1891 census, John was lodging in Keswick at 9 Church Street, and a fellow lodger there was a Richard Pendlebury, aged forty-four, described in the census as a 'Fellow & Lecturer of a Cambridge College'. He was, in fact, a noted mathematician and a collector of books and music manuscripts. After his death his library was donated to St John's College Library, and his collection of music manuscripts became part of the founding collection of the Cambridge Music Faculty Library. In addition, Pendlebury was a famous Alpine climber who is credited with being part of the first ascent of the Eastern Wall of Monte Rosa in 1872. He was born in Liverpool in 1847 and died in Keswick on 13th March 1902. Presumably, he was lodging in Keswick for the hill walking at the time of the 1891 census. One imagines that this interest would have provided the basis for conversations with his fellow lodger – a local painter of those hills who had also seen (and probably painted) the mountains of North America.

John Banks the younger died in Keswick on 19th May 1899, aged seventy-two. He directed in his will that he should be buried in Crosthwaite Parish Church. His grave is to be found on the north side of the church, further away from the church than Thomas Goodfellow's grave. The plain headstone refers to him as the son of Jacob Banks – a pencil manufacturer. Almost fifty years after Jacob the younger had died, the connection with a pencil manufacturer, even a failed one, was still a matter of importance to the family. John's will directed that his estate be held on trust for the income produced to be accumulated (i.e. retained within the trust fund) for twenty-one years[7] after his death. After the end of this period, the trust fund was to be distributed equally between his nephews and nieces. The will refers specifically to the ownership of rented properties, as well as dividends from three shareholdings in different banks and shares in the Central Pacific Railway of California.[8] The latter is an unusual asset for a Keswick man to own in the nineteenth century and it is probably linked to his earnings during his time in the USA. He appears to have prospered to a reasonable degree as an artist (unless this wealth came in part from any inheritance from his mother's family).

Coming from a family that would have suffered through their father's bankruptcy, the prospect of inheriting the fifteen cottages in Keswick must have been quite enticing to John the younger, but ultimately it would prove costly to him after the legal costs of two lost trials. The litigation would not have been cheap, although it may well appear so compared to the cost of modern probate disputes. As John was the failed litigant, he would have borne all of his own costs and may well have had a portion of Edward Goodfellow's costs awarded against him as well. Presumably, these costs would have made substantial inroads into John's capital (unless he left the legal bills unpaid and returned to North America, only returning to Keswick after the debts became statute barred).

CHAPTER SEVEN

Edward Barron Goodfellow: The Defendant

Edward's Inheritance

As already described in Chapter Three, Margaret Banks Goodfellow was the sole beneficiary of John Banks the elder's will. After his death there was no immediate challenge to the will and her inheritance under its terms. Although by surviving her uncle she became entitled to his estate, she was still under the age of twenty-one and, given she had not yet attained her majority, she could not take possession of that inheritance. This would have to wait until she was twenty-one, when she could give the executors a valid receipt for her inheritance. Further, and again because she was still a minor,[1] Margaret was not capable of making a valid will of her own to dispose of this inheritance (or any other property she had inherited) should she die before she reached her majority. The result of this legal incapacity was that when she did die under the age of twenty-one, she died intestate and, as today, the succession to an intestate's estate was a matter of the law directing who inherits, as opposed to the deceased having been able to direct who inherits by making a will.

When she died, Margaret was unmarried and she had no children, no parents or grandparents and no full siblings. Her closest relatives were her brother and sister of the half-blood (or half-brother and half-sister, i.e. they shared only one common parent with her), Edward Barron Goodfellow and Mary Mitchinson Goodfellow. Her second half-brother, John Tolson Goodfellow, had died before Margaret, without issue (he was only twelve when he died). In all these circumstances, Margaret's estate would pass unequally on her intestacy to Edward Barron Goodfellow and Mary

Mitchinson Goodfellow. The inequality came about as the male line was then preferred to the female line for the inheritance of real property (i.e. land). Any other property that was not land (and most of John's estate was in rented properties) would be split equally between Edward and Mary. Both would have come into their inheritances on attaining the age of twenty-one. Edward would therefore have been Margaret's major heir when he attained the age of twenty-one in June 1871 shortly after the litigation over John Banks' will was concluded and the appeal court delivered its judgment.

As well as Margaret Banks Goodfellow's inheritance from her uncle John, her estate would have been increased by her earlier inheritance from her father, Thomas Goodfellow. Thomas had bequeathed to her his silver watch and all his real property (which was almost certainly that which he had inherited from Margaret's mother). On Margaret's death this inheritance would also pass to her half-siblings Edward and Mary as part of her intestate estate. Again, it would have passed unequally, with the land going to Edward and the remainder (that was not land) split equally with Mary. Edward and Mary were also left an equal share of the remainder of their father's estate under the terms of his will, which they would receive on attaining twenty-one. Originally, the gift in Thomas's will was equally to his three children that he had by his second wife Sarah. As their brother John died intestate as a minor in 1865, his share of their father's estate would have been divided equally and added to Edward and Mary's shares. Edward took out letters of administration to John's estate on 7th June 1872. This enabled John's share to be dealt with in this way.

Edward's total inheritance was on his twenty-first birthday was:

- from his half-sister Margaret Banks Goodfellow's intestacy:

  - all of John Banks the elder's estate;
  - the properties specifically bequeathed to Margaret by her father, being the properties received from Jacob Banks the elder's estate via Thomas's first wife Margaret Banks the younger; and

- from his father's will:

  - a half-share of the residue of his estate.

There is considerable uncertainty as to how valuable this total inheritance was, but while it would not have been a vast fortune, it should have been of significant financial benefit to Edward and given him a degree of financial independence when he came of age.

Little is known about the early life of Edward Barron Goodfellow, apart from his being orphaned and afterwards living with a maiden aunt in Main Street, Crosthwaite. The aunt, Frances Barron,[2] the younger sister of Edward's mother Sarah, was born in 1821. How long he lived with his aunt is not known but it is likely that it was for the rest of his childhood. As to his education and early employment there is no information.

Edward's Marriage to Hannah Armstrong

The first significant event in Edward's adult life that has been found is his marriage to Hannah Armstrong on 6th April 1875 in Crosthwaite Parish Church when he was almost twenty-five and she was twenty-one. The location shows a continuation of the Banks and Goodfellow families' connection with this church. Hannah's family lived in Borrowdale and were either tenants or managers of the Borrowdale Hotel. It is possible that they could have owned the hotel, but no evidence of ownership has been found. Edward is shown on his marriage certificate to be 'of Independent Means' (giving some confirmation of the size of his inheritance). Hannah has no given occupation and is merely described on the certificate as a spinster, but what is known about her cause of death suggests that she may well have been an invalid and physically unable to work.

Hannah died, childless, on 20th August 1879, after almost four and a half years of marriage. Hannah's death was not registered by Edward, but by her aunt Martha Armstrong, who lived on Penrith Road, Keswick. At the time of her death, Hannah and Edward were living at the Borrowdale Hotel, in Borrowdale outside Keswick.[3] Edward was described on the death certificate as being the 'Hotel Keeper'. We do not know if Edward in turn had become manager, tenant or owner of the hotel, as 'hotel keeper' could cover any of the three. Owner would appear to have been unlikely. His occupation seems to be a major departure when compared to the pencil manufacturers and grocers encountered so far in his family and from his earlier description of himself as being of independent means.

There is evidence that this hotel was originally leased by Hannah's father and mother. Her father Benjamin Armstrong died in 1873[4] aged forty-five. His wife Mary was admitted to Garlands Asylum near Carlisle in 1876 where she remained until she died in 1881. Their eldest son Joseph survived them, but he died two years before his sister Hannah, aged twenty-three. The death of Benjamin would have been a blow to what appeared to be a successful business. The implications of this for the family pose several problems that are dealt with in Chapter Eight.

It is reasonable to surmise that Hannah was involved with the running of the Borrowdale Hotel after her father's death and before she married Edward in 1875. She was the eldest child, and her mother's mental illness would have prevented her having much involvement. It is then likely that Edward Goodfellow took over the running of the hotel shortly after the marriage (if he was not involved to some degree beforehand). Nothing is known about the circumstances under which Edward and Hannah first met. During Edward's time at the Borrowdale Hotel it is not known if he had any financial stake in the hotel or if he was only managing it on behalf of his wife's family – the latter being more probable.

Hannah Goodfellow's Illness and Death

Hannah's marriage to Edward was very likely from the outset to be of short duration, as Hannah appears to have been an invalid who was destined for an early death. Her death certificate shows three causes of death: chronic albuminuria (for four years before death), convulsions and coma (each for ten days before death). As noted earlier, in connection with John Banks the elder and Margaret Banks Goodfellow, Victorian death certificates too often record observable symptoms rather than the actual illness that caused those symptoms. In part this reflects the level of understanding so far reached in Victorian medicine. For Hannah, as for John Banks the elder, coma was not a cause of death, and it is unlikely that the convulsions were either, but more likely that both were symptoms linked to whatever was the underlying cause of the albuminuria.

Albuminuria is a condition that arises from an abnormal level of the protein albumin in a person's urine. The protein is important for the proper functioning of blood, and with healthy kidneys it is not filtered out. This excess of protein usually arises where the person has a disease affecting the functioning of the kidneys. Hannah's death certificate declares albuminuria to have been present for approximately four years (i.e. it was diagnosed very shortly after the time of the marriage). As is the way with these things, Hannah would quite probably have had the illness and some symptoms for a time before the diagnosis was made. Albuminuria today is often the first observable sign of a kidney condition. Later, albuminuria causes more visible symptoms of swelling of the ankles, hands, face or abdomen. The kidney damage causing albuminuria can often be caused by diabetes, but it would have been very unusual for someone aged twenty-one to have developed type 2 diabetes – this age is generally too young for this to develop. Type 1 diabetes also seems unlikely as a cause of the kidney damage, as death from diabetic ketoacidosis would have occurred quite quickly after a person developed the diabetic symptoms of thirst, polyuria (excessive passing of urine, and often also with excessive frequency) and weight loss, given the absence of any effective treatment for type 1 diabetes in 1879.

Renal failure looks to be the most likely explanation for Hannah's coma, and the convulsions, both of which occurred shortly before her death (and were recorded on her death certificate). Renal failure itself and albuminuria can, independently of each other, lead to high blood pressure sufficient to cause convulsions (renal failure) and a stroke (chronic albuminuria). It is also possible that all Hannah's symptoms could have been consistent with a much rarer genetic condition: Fabry disease. This disease has renal, vascular and cerebral complications among its characteristics, and they would fit with the death certificate's recording of albuminuria, convulsions and coma. Additional features of this disease are pain and fatigue. However, diagnosis of this disease would not have been possible during Hannah's lifetime – it was first described in 1898.[5]

At this remove it is impossible to be certain of the cause of the illness that resulted in Hannah's early death. But, whatever the true cause of the albuminuria and death, Hannah would have been in poor health while she was married and there would have been restrictions on her physical activity. It is also very unlikely she would have been healthy enough to conceive – and there were no children from the marriage. Her involvement with the running of the hotel would have decreased as time passed, and Edward Goodfellow would have increasingly managed the business.

On the one hand, one could view Edward's marriage to an invalid, with a limited life expectancy, as the act of a man devoted to his future wife. On the other hand, one wonders more than a little at the possibility of other motives, connected, perhaps, to maintaining control of the hotel. (See Chapter Eight for more on this issue.)

Edward's Marriage to Mary Armstrong

After Hannah's death, Edward remained as the hotel keeper at the Borrowdale Hotel – in the 1881 census (taken in April) he is still recorded as such. Significantly, the census also records Mary Armstrong, a barmaid aged seventeen, as being a resident at the hotel. Mary was a younger sister of Edward's wife Hannah. Mary and her slightly older brother Benjamin were the only two of her parents' three surviving children still living at the hotel at this time.[6]

On 26th July 1882, Edward married Mary Armstrong in Carlisle. The marriage certificate shows the groom as aged thirty-two and the bride as being nineteen. On 8th August (thirteen days later) Mary gave birth to their daughter, Clara Frances Barron Goodfellow. Clara's birth certificate recites her mother as 'Mary Goodfellow formerly Armstrong' and Edward Barron Goodfellow as the father, who is shown as 'Hotel Keeper'. For the place of birth and residence of the mother both show 'Main Street Keswick', not the Borrowdale Hotel. These bare facts of the marriage and birth appear to tell an all-too-familiar tale, but in this case the tale becomes a lot more complex and dangerous for Edward.

Edward and Mary's marriage took place in Carlisle, away from Keswick and Edward's family's previous connections with Crosthwaite Parish Church (in itself a curiosity considering how prominent this church is in this family's story). Given the almost certainly obvious advanced state of Mary's pregnancy, a marriage away from Keswick may not have been too surprising. The marriage was by licence, which avoided the necessity for reading of the banns, in Christ Church in Carlisle, and the witnesses were William Hall McVitie and Mary McVitie, a married couple of no known connection to either the Goodfellow or Armstrong families. The marriage certificate shows Edward as a widower, and 'gentleman', of Botchergate. There is a Botchergate in both Keswick and Carlisle, and this entry does not specify which, but it is highly suggestive of Carlisle rather than Keswick (which is specified in Mary's address). For Mary, the certificate shows her as a spinster, of no occupation, of Keswick 'in the parish of Crosthwaite'. Edward's description on the marriage certificate, omitting his usual occupation of hotel keeper, and using the Carlisle address, seem to be intended to hide his connection to the Borrowdale Hotel, particularly as he is shown as a hotel keeper on Clara's birth certificate just over a month later. Mary's particulars also show no connection with the Borrowdale Hotel.

The registration of the marriage was in the Carlisle Registration District, where one presumes little was known about either of them. The birth registration of Clara was in Keswick and there would have been little point in Edward not describing himself as what everyone there knew him to be. That Edward is clearly identified on the birth certificate as the father does not necessarily mean that it was an admission that the couple were married – nor does Mary's use of the name Goodfellow. Tongues may have wagged at the immorality of their position, but cohabitation was not a crime.

But, beyond the social embarrassment of the birth registration, the act of marriage of Edward and Mary raises more much difficult issues, both ecclesiastical and legal. These difficulties all stem from the well-known, indeed notorious nineteenth-century issue that marriage to one's deceased wife's sister was in law a void marriage at this time (and up until the early twentieth century). Furthermore, it was a marriage that the Church of England would not knowingly perform in England, as canon law forbade it because the Church regarded the relationship as incestuous. Therefore, Edward and Mary were not legally married and their marriage was a nullity.

The Marriage Act 1835

The consequences of the Marriage Act 1835, and the battle to reform it, are part of the fabric of the social history of Queen Victoria's entire reign, and almost all that of Edward VII as well. The starting point of this difficult part of Edward Goodfellow's history is therefore the Act itself.

Before the 1835 Act, any marriage that was in breach of the Church of England's rules of affinity could be challenged in court and declared void. The rules of affinity defined the relationships where marriage was barred because of kinship created by another marriage. Such a marriage was from the outset voidable – that is to say, it was a valid marriage until it was declared to be void after being successfully challenged in court. There was no time limit for a voidable marriage to be challenged in this way. While the Church of England maintained that its rules of affinity reflected God's law, the *Edinburgh Review*[7] sharply observed that 'the supremacy of the law of God was made dependent on the accident as to whether there was anyone spiteful enough or interested enough to procure the intervention of the law of man to give force to the Law of God'.

In 1835, the Lord Chancellor, Lord Lyndhurst, introduced a Bill into the House of Lords to put a time limit on challenges to have voidable marriages declared void. His Bill was intended to declare all such marriages, made prior to the commencement of new law, as valid. It was further intended to put a future time limit of two years during which any voidable marriages entered into after the passing of the Act could be challenged. In the absence of a successful court challenge, such marriages would automatically become valid two years after the date of the marriage. The motivation for this reform was said to be his Lordship's concern for the position of the Duke of Beaufort's heir – the product of the 7th Duke's marriage to his deceased wife's half-sister in 1822.[8] Any successful challenge to that voidable marriage would have disinherited the apparent heir, the Duke's only son.[9]

Given the opportunity of reform offered by Lord Lyndhurst's Bill, the House of Lords took the opportunity, in deference to the views of the Anglican Bishops in the House of Lords, to find a more radical solution. The Bill was accepted by the Lords in order to recognise the validity of all voidable marriages entered into before the new Act would come into force. Although the validity of these marriages was later recognised in *Ray v Sherwood*,[10] the judge expressed the opinion that while the ecclesiastical court could not annul what the law now recognised, those courts could still punish the parties involved for the ecclesiastical offence of incest.[11]

But their Lordships then amended the Bill so that *all* future marriages in England and Wales in breach of the prohibited degrees of affinity entered into after the Act's commencement would be void *ab initio*. These marriages being declared void from the outset[12] meant that no court judgment to declare them void would be needed. Further, being void, such 'marriages' would have never legally existed. When Lord Lyndhurst's Bill moved to the House of Commons, the Members there recognised the sweeping, and unwelcome, nature of this amendment, but their opposition failed as there were not sufficient votes to reverse the Lords' amendment during the rest of the Bill's passage through Parliament. The entrenched views of the Church of England will have influenced more than a few MPs. The Church of England not only wholeheartedly supported the passing of Lyndhurst's Bill and the Lords' amendment to it, but once enacted, it thereafter fought an extraordinary campaign in Parliament, and in the press, to prevent any reform during the remainder of the nineteenth century. The wealthy could evade this new prohibition by marrying their deceased wife's sister abroad.[13] Scotland was not an option for avoiding the 1835 Act as such marriages had been prohibited there since the Marriage Act and the Incest Act, both of 1567.[14]

The Church of England regarded marriage to a deceased's wife's sister as incestuous from the point of view of its doctrine. By contrast to this canon law position, and somewhat remarkably, during the nineteenth century there was no criminal punishment for incest – it was not a criminal offence. Incest was an ecclesiastical offence only, punishable in archdeacons' courts by fines, penances or public confessions.[15] Despite the absence of a criminal sanction, one imagines that the social opprobrium of a church punishment or public confession was considerable.[16] The civil law did not go quite as far as this. The legal consequences of any marriage 'within the prohibited degrees of consanguinity or affinity' after the 1835 Act[17] were that it 'should be absolutely null and void to all intents and purposes whatsoever'.[18]

A marriage to one's deceased wife's sister was at that time within the Established Church's definition of affinity. Affinity in canon law is a relationship which will be an impediment to marriage, because of the relationship that either party has as a result of kinship created by another marriage (or as a result of intercourse out of marriage). Affinity was defined by one opponent of reform as being the principle that:

> The man may not marry any of his wife's kindred nearer in blood than he may his own; nor the woman of her husband's kindred nearer in blood than of her own.[19]

Thus in the case of Edward and Mary, he was marrying his wife's sister, and the church viewed her as if she was also *his* sister by virtue of his marriage to Hannah. What constitutes affinity will vary between faiths. In an attempt to establish how other countries and other faiths viewed the Biblical texts in question (see below), the Earl of Dalhousie wrote to an assortment of foreign divines and professors, and the replies nearly all went against the Anglican interpretation of affinity. The view from Professor JS Blackie[20] at Edinburgh University was that:

> it is not Greek but common-sense that is required for the interpretation of the passage you mention; but common-sense is a quality with which most commentators and theologians are not specially dowered.

Most modern readers will probably share his view, having read this far.

The Anglican Church's support for this prohibition, and its argument against reform of it, was based on scriptural interpretation. One of the passages relied upon by the Church, and its supporters, was from Ephesians 5:31, '… shall a man leave his father and mother, and shall be joined unto his wife and they two shall be one flesh'. This, it was argued, had the consequence that if a man and his wife were of one flesh, they were of one flesh with each spouse's siblings. Being thus of one flesh led the then Bishop of Lincoln to observe that this meant that a man who married his wife's sister might just as well be marrying his own sister. However, at this time the Treasury took a far more pragmatic view and treated a gift by will from a man to his sister-in-law as a gift to a non-blood relative and taxed it at a higher rate for legacy duty purposes.

Other passages used in support of the Church's position were from Leviticus:

- in 18:8: 'None of you shall approach any that is near of kin';
- in 18:16: 'Thou shalt not uncover the nakedness of thy brother's wife'; and
- in 18:18: 'Neither shalt thou take a wife to her sister, to vex her, to uncover her nakedness, besides the other in her lifetime'. (The true translation of this verse from the original Hebrew was a matter of yet more heated dispute.)

These are references that may seem familiar from Henry VIII's annulment battle with his first Queen, Catherine of Aragon (previously the wife of the King's dead brother, Prince Arthur). In Henry's case, Deuteronomy 25:5:

> If brethren dwell together, and one of them die, and have no child, the wife of the dead shall not marry without unto a stranger: her husband's brother shall go in unto her, and take her to him to wife, and perform the duty of an husband's brother unto her

had been cited originally as authority to permit his marriage to Catherine, but Henry subsequently no longer accepted this as correct. He now believed that given the terms of Leviticus his marriage to Catherine was offensive to God, and as a consequence of this offence, God had denied him a male heir. Shakespeare was probably nearer the mark in *Henry VIII*, where, in Act 2, Scene 2 the Lord Chamberlain comments on the King that 'it seems the marriage with his brother's wife has crept too near his conscience', only for the Duke of Suffolk to demur 'No, his conscience has crept too near another lady' (lines that Shakespeare might not have written had Elizabeth I still been alive).

Deuteronomy 25:5 was now quoted by those advocating marriage reforms, much as those opposing Henry's 'Great Matter' had quoted it. Those in the hierarchy of the Anglican Church (that Henry had created over 300 years before) were still supporting his views on Biblical interpretation by opposing Deuteronomy and supporting the Leviticus texts. One difficulty which came from this dispute over Biblical texts was the fear that if the Anglican Church revised its position and accepted marriage to a deceased wife's sister, it would undermine the legitimacy of the English succession from Henry VIII to Victoria. This was not an area on which debate was welcomed then, but given that Parliament had settled the succession twice since Tudor times, arguments to the contrary were unlikely to be taken seriously.[21] The stance of the Anglican Church today is substantially altered from the time of the parliamentary battles of the nineteenth century (as is the statute law).

It is worth digressing a little further to observe that the campaign to reform this law is a wonderful example of the lengths to which the Victorian Church of England would go to defend what we would see as indefensible today. In the 1890s, over fifty years after the problem was created, when the tide was flowing strongly for reform, *The Freethinker* published a comment that 'On the whole the bishops of the Church of England are as obstinate a set of avaricious hypocrites as the world has ever produced'. The bishops had by then lost much public sympathy for their cause. The defenders of the status quo frequently let themselves be led into the realms of the absurd. Attempts began in 1842 to reverse the disliked provision of the Act, but this and the almost yearly attempts thereafter failed for over seventy years until one attempt was finally successful in 1907.

One of the main reasons in favour of reform was produced by the risks of childbirth in the nineteenth century (touched on in Chapter Four). Death in childbirth would often leave the father with an orphaned child or children to bring up. A conventional view was that an unmarried sister of the wife would be suitable to undertake this task because of her kindred feelings towards the children. Examples were quoted in support of reforming the law, citing the problems that could be created if the unmarried sister resided under the widower husband's roof. Apart from the appearance of impropriety of unmarried adults living in the same house, there was the actual possibility of temptation.

Gilbert and Sullivan, as was their wont, inclined to gently mocking the long-running campaign against reform, when the Queen of the Fairies in *Iolanthe* says of Strephon's power over the House of Lords, 'He shall prick that annual blister, marriage with deceased's wife's sister'.[22] But gentle musical mocking underestimated both the determination of the Church to resist change and the vehemence of the language used by the opponents of reform.

In 1876 the *Saturday Review,* in opposing reform, opined that, if permitted, marriages to a deceased wife's sister would be an example of the 'diseased craving for abnormal enlargements of personal liberty which is the seamy side of Liberalism'. This harsh language was relatively mild compared to the *Quarterly Review* where, earlier, in 1849, the view was put forward that:

> even popular discussion of the subject ... is an almost incalculable mischief. Thoughts which never would have occurred to the pure have been forced on the purest.

On yet another defeat for the reform movement, *The Church Review* was moved to be '… thankful to say that incest is in no danger of being legalised at present'. While no doubt this reference to incest was technically correct from the point of view of Church doctrine, it was absurdly inappropriate from the point of view of social usage. Matthew Arnold went further when he expressed the view, with surely a wildly over-heated imagination, and matching lack of logic, that reform would lead to bigamy and polygamy. Where would it all end? This was a theme in the opposition to change:

> that this first barrier having been broken down other marriages most undesirable, both of consanguinity and affinity, would follow and there would be a general and almost inextricable confusion of relationships.[23]

WE Gladstone thought reform would lead to 'the more horrible forms of incest' – which leaves one wondering what he thought qualified as the comparatively nicer forms of incest (but he had also expressed the view that rail travel on a Sunday was 'dangerous in its immediate and ultimate results to public morality',[24] so curiously, as the great liberal, he must have seen many and diverse threats to morality in social change). Parliament was assured on one occasion that any reform in this area would lead to 'enormities among peculiar sects of Christians' (thereby suggesting that Christians outside the Established Church were quite beyond the pale in their yearnings and implying that only those who attended the Established Church could be relied upon to resist the lure of 'enormities').[25] It was often the case that opponents of reform suggested that once a man could marry his sister-in-law there would be a temptation for him to murder his wife in order to marry her sister.[26] One is left rather mystified by the views held by some Victorians of their world.

The long fight for reform ended when it was achieved by the Deceased Wife's Sister Marriage Act 1907,[27] and thereafter the law permitted valid marriage to one's deceased wife's sister.[28] But until 1907 such a marriage remained void in law. To restate the point, void in this context means that in the eyes of the law this marriage was invalid, had no legal effect and did not legally exist; thus, Edward and Mary were not husband and wife. They were living in sin, with all the nineteenth-century social consequences and disapproval that went with that if their true status became public knowledge. As far as their children were concerned, they would be designated bastards, with a similar social stigma. Further, the children would have no property inheritance rights on their father's death, or, through Edward, from other members of the family (in the absence of any will specifically directing inheritance to them).

However, Edward's difficulties did not end here. His position was made more complex, and potentially dangerous for him, by how the marriage came about. For Edward and Mary to have gone through the ceremony of marriage, his prior marriage to Hannah and Hannah's relationship to Mary would need to have been deliberately concealed from the minister who officiated at their marriage. This, in all probability, was the strong argument for marrying not in Keswick but in Carlisle, where there was less chance of the relationship being known. Concealing the information from an officiating clergyman would be deceitful, but it would not be a criminal offence, only an ecclesiastical one. However, Edward's marriage was authorised by licence,[29] a convenient method for those in Edward and Mary's predicament of lack of time (but more expensive than a calling of banns). In applying for the marriage licence, Edward concealed who he had been married to earlier and what Hannah and Mary's relationship was. If he had not done so, no marriage ceremony with Mary would have been possible. His application for the licence therefore entailed a deliberate false declaration when he declared that he knew of no impediment to the marriage.[30] At that time, the Marriage Act 1836 provided that a false oath, or declaration, in order to obtain a marriage licence was an act of perjury.[31] By the terms of section 2 of the Perjury Act 1728, perjury was punishable by up to seven years' imprisonment.[32]

Edward's perjured marriage licence application therefore exposed him, if his perjury was discovered, to arrest and, if found guilty, a criminal conviction. While the maximum sentence of imprisonment was unlikely, a shorter custodial sentence was quite possible on conviction. This would not be a risk that was incurred lightly, and it does make one wonder at the pressures that were on the couple to marry. But if any members of either family were applying pressure for them to marry, they would also have known that the marriage was not a solution. The campaigns for reform of the marriage laws were a matter of wide public knowledge, indeed even public notoriety – and the reform debate had been going on for nearly fifty years by the time of Edward and Mary's marriage. It would have been widely reported in the national and local press, as well as debated (and condemned) in religious tracts. The subject would also have provided the topic for many church sermons. There is no realistic chance that Edward can have been unaware of the problem. So, what was the point of committing perjury and still not being married? This is one of the issues looked at further in Chapter Nine.

Edward and Mary's Children

Clara Barron Goodfellow, although born in 1882, was not baptised until 16th December 1888, and this was in Workington after her mother moved there, without Edward. Baptism in the Keswick area would appear to have been difficult as the void marriage could not have been disclosed to the local clergy. It would not have been impossible for Edward to appear as the father (but not the husband) in a local church, but this might have been unacceptable to the church, and Clara would have been baptised with her mother's surname of Armstrong. On the other hand, not having a child christened would also have made tongues wag. Edward and Mary had a further child, John Goodfellow (born 29th July 1883), and he was also baptised with his sister on 16th December 1888 in Workington.

Mary Goodfellow is to be found in the 1891 census living in Workington, Cumberland, but now as Mary Armstrong. She is recorded as being married, but no husband was present at the census. Her occupation was given as 'Office caretaker & seamstress'. In this census her children are also called Armstrong, not Goodfellow. Later, in the 1901 and 1911 censuses, she was still shown in Workington, but in both returns her name was given as Armstrong and she was recorded as a widow and 'dressmaker'. In fact, as at the 1901 census she was not a widow, as Edward was still alive, although whether she knew this is uncertain. This description could have been chosen because it was easier than explaining the continuing absence of Edward. However, his permanent absence, and the change of surname, does tend to point to a decisive break with her past, and her recognition of the reality of the void marriage.

Edward was absent from English census records after 1881 as he had emigrated to New Zealand in late 1887, a little over five years after his second marriage. He was thirty-seven years old when he left. Mary, then aged twenty-three, was left behind with children of five and four, apparently to fend for herself. Why Edward emigrated is not known, but there are several factors that may come into account: his void marriage and perjury, his departure from the Borrowdale Hotel and his finances. These issues are looked at in more detail in Chapter Eight.

New Zealand

Edward sailed as a third-class passenger with the Shaw, Savill & Albion Line on the SS *Doric*. He is recorded simply as Edward Goodfellow, a passenger booked through from London to Canterbury. He omitted his distinctive second name, Barron, when making the booking. As passports were not then in general use (their use was normally for commercial and diplomatic purposes at this time), there would have been no documentation tying this passenger to Edward Barron Goodfellow – although we can now do so. Third class, the new name for steerage,[33] was quite basic accommodation which was below deck. Consequently, there was usually reduced ventilation despite the often crowded conditions. Usually, this accommodation was bunk beds, with single men in one compartment and single women in another; the accommodation for married couples was between these two compartments. Dining was at communal tables. Steerage passengers would not have access to first- and second-class areas and facilities. There was often only a limited amount of water for personal hygiene, although the recent introduction of condensers allowed at least a steady supply of drinking water. Some more modern ships were replacing this type of accommodation with basic cabins.

The *Doric*[34] was a Harland & Wolff-built, steel-hulled ship, of just under 5,000 tons, launched in 1883. By later standards, the *Doric* was not a large ship for long-distance, mixed freight/passenger work. She had been designed and built specifically for the Great Britain–New Zealand route. She was built for the White Star Line[35] and made her maiden voyage on charter to the New Zealand Shipping Line, for this route, on 25th July 1883. By 1885 she was being used to operate a joint White Star Line and Shaw, Savill & Albion Line service on this route.[36] She is said to have been a passengers' favourite, particularly for first-class passengers.[37] Shipping advertisements drew attention to her 'modern appliances for the safety and comfort of passengers – electric lighting, baths in every compartment and perfect ventilation throughout'. Although this was now an age of iron- or steel-hulled ships, there was still much wood used for decking, etc. Electric light was potentially a way of reducing the real risk of fire at sea that came from oil lights.

The *Doric* was a three-deck ship powered by two steam engines advertised as developing 3,000 horsepower.[38] She was also reportedly capable of a top speed of thirteen knots. In addition to the steam engines, there were four masts which could provide sail-power in the event of engine failure or insufficient coal.

A maritime connection to Great Britain was of huge importance to a young colony like New Zealand. A feature of the colonial press was the attention given to the arrival and departure of shipping. Commercially, the timing and the forecast amount of shipping was important information for the export of agricultural produce (e.g. wool, butter[39] and mutton). It was vital to ensure the exports were ready to match the shipping departures and that the required cargo space was going to be available and booked. The arrival of imports was equally important for retailers, as manufactured goods were brought to New Zealand from Britain and retailers would want to advertise new stock as soon as possible.[40] Larger manufactured goods, particularly engineering products, would also arrive by sea. Apart from this, the arrivals at, and departures from, New Zealand ports of passengers was important social news, and lists of passengers and their destinations in New Zealand were often published in the newspapers. Letters to and from 'home' were a vital link, and local post offices would place press notices of last local posting dates for mail for departures on the mail boats. The information on shipping in passage was obtained from extensive use of telegraph messages on undersea cable.[41]

The ocean-going ships were an important lifeline and, despite the regular scheduled arrivals, the ships themselves could still be objects of great curiosity when they arrived. In December 1887, when the *Doric* was still in Port Chalmers after disembarking passengers:

> The steam launch Kate, which has recently commenced plying between Port Chalmers and Portobello, yesterday morning conveyed nearly 40 children of the Hooper Inlet School, with their teacher and several of the parents, to the Doric and other large steamers, which were inspected. Quite a number of the children had never been across the bay before, while a number of the parents were almost strangers to Port Chalmers. Mr E. Moss, who commands the Kate, has invited the school children of the Peninsula to take a free trip over to the Port on Friday, and the Broad Bay children go on Saturday.[42]

The *Doric*, in her later years, also made an impression on Rudyard Kipling, who wrote:

> ... it may help you to know that the ship 'McAndrew's Hymn' belongs to is the old Doric, once an Atlantic White Star I think and now a Shaw Savill, Albion boat running to New Zealand... in no sense a new boat with any special gear. When I was on her, her [low pressure] cylinder had a play of about an inch and a half on the columns and every piece of machinery had the muffled and protected look of a long-voyage boat. Not a bit like the shiny stuff on a racing Atlantic hotel; but lapped and swathed and junked up all white with salt-crust.[43]

British trade and foreign policy at this time were both hugely connected with the needs of Empire. The Empire, though important in world terms, had not yet reached its full extent. Many major territories were already part of it, although not necessarily in their final form. For example, Canada would not become a dominion until 1867 and even then it would not include Newfoundland. South Africa did not exist as a colony (although Cape Colony did), and several wars would occur there before South Africa became unified as part of the Empire. The Empire in Africa was far from its final extent. The Scramble for Africa, as the next phase of European colonisation is known, was not yet fully under way, and in 1870 there was only 10% of Africa under foreign control.[44] By the time of the First World War, that figure had risen to 90% and even then 'ownership' of areas would change as a result of the war. The Australian colonies would not come together to form the Commonwealth of Australia as a dominion within the Empire until 1901. New Zealand, which had first been a part of the colony of New South Wales, became a separate colony in 1841 and then self-governing under the Crown in 1854. New Zealand would not become a dominion until 1907. The protection of the Empire and the security of its trade and communications and the movement of passengers was a dominant factor in British government policy then and for many years to come.

The existence of its Empire was viewed in Britain as evidence of Britain's foremost position in world affairs. The Empire also played a huge role in the domestic economy by acting as an export market for British manufactured goods and as a source of raw materials for British industry. Additionally, the Empire provided an outward prospect of emigration, giving fresh opportunities for British citizens to start new lives in developing colonies. What occurred in the Empire (and lands that were added to it later) was not seen merely as news in Britain, it was something that directly affected the domestic economy and impacted on job prospects at home and abroad.

Some passengers have recorded that the departure of an emigrant ship from Britain could be quite a sombre event as the passengers contemplated their permanent departure from family, friends and homeland – usually with little prospect of ever seeing any of them again. While those emigrating no doubt had hopes for their new life in a new country, even the most optimistic probably viewed the journey, and the new start in life, with at least some apprehension. The sombre air would have been added to by a similar sense of separation on the part of those at the docks making their farewells to the emigrants. It was generally a time of tears, even for those who were leaving in the hope of escaping poverty. Some emigrants would stay on deck for a long time after the ship sailed, for a last look at 'home' and family before they were lost to sight. It seems unlikely that anyone was on the dockside to cry over Edward's departure.

The Voyage

The *Doric* sailed[45] at 1pm on Thursday 3rd November 1887 from the Royal Albert Dock, London, heading initially for Plymouth.[46] This was the eighth voyage that she had made to New Zealand. On leaving Plymouth, the *Doric* had on board forty-nine saloon, fifty-one second cabin and ninety-eight steerage passengers. After allowing for disembarkations and embarkations at Tenerife, Cape Town and Hobartt there were twenty-three saloon, twenty-nine second cabin, and seventy-one steerage passengers landed in the New Zealand ports.

Some of the details of this voyage are known, as the ship's purser, Mr WL Walters, was in the habit of preparing a press release to assist the local reporters on the arrival of the *Doric* in New Zealand.[47] The *Doric* was under the command of Captain JW Jennings:

> who brings with him as chief officer Mr Snowden. Mr Smith second, Mr Jones third, Mr Bell fourth; surgeon, Dr. E. A. Fall; purser, Mr W. L. Walters; and Mr Jones, the steward.

The engineering officer was Mr Barber, who seems to have had a good trip with no mechanical breakdowns to delay the ship – commendable for the early days of long-distance steam voyages.

The *Doric* went down the English Channel to Plymouth, where she arrived at 8am on 5th November. On arrival, the ship took on further passengers and probably topped up her coal bunkers, as well as taking on final fresh provender. Being a mail ship, there will also have been a last collection of mail for New Zealand and the intermediate ports. After leaving Plymouth at 1.46pm on 5th November, the *Doric* headed south to round Ushant,[48] then to cross the Bay of Biscay and steam down the Atlantic, off the Iberian coast, for Tenerife. Here and at the later stops at Cape Town, and Hobart, Tasmania, there would be more coaling, fresh supplies, and delivery and collection of mail. En route to Tenerife the *Doric* encountered a heavy gale in the Bay of Biscay, but still arrived, without undue delay, in Tenerife at 2.30pm on 10th November (meticulously recorded by the purser as a passage of five days, one hour and twenty-one minutes) and, after coaling, etc, left at 6.54pm the same day. The *Doric* then headed down the coast of Africa, passed Cape Verde, and, with easterly winds blowing, headed southwest across the Gulf of Guinea towards the Equator, which was crossed on 16th November. Thereafter there were fresh to strong southerly winds as they steamed towards the Cape of Good Hope.

The *Doric* reached Cape Town at 9.37pm on 26th November, then, as usual, coaled, landed and embarked passengers, mail and fresh supplies; and pushed on for Hobart at 12.42pm on 27th November. The *Doric* was now following the traditional sailing ship route to New Zealand. To head east across the southern Indian Ocean, ships went south to around the 40th parallel known for its generally westerly winds, frequently of considerable strength – giving the latitude between 40 and 50 degrees its name the Roaring Forties. For the same reason of using prevailing winds behind the vessel, on the return to Britain ships generally did not reverse the outbound route but sailed eastwards towards Cape Horn and then up the coast of South America before heading to Europe.

Rounding the Cape of Good Hope and going on into the southern Indian Ocean, the *Doric* initially met fine weather, now with a southerly breeze, which continued fresh to strong until 5th December, when she encountered another northwest gale producing high seas, continuing until noon on the 6th, when the storm and the seas moderated. This gale, like the one encountered in the Bay of Biscay, would no doubt have been uncomfortable and probably produced some seasickness but was unlikely to have been a threat to the ship. After this gale, there soon followed a fresh northwest breeze, accompanied by cloudy weather lasting until the 10th, when another gale set in for a short time. There were then fresh northwest winds until the 12th, when they dropped and shifted to the northeast. This light wind, with hazy warmer weather, continued until the *Doric* sailed up the River Derwent estuary to arrive in Hobart, Tasmania, at 6.40pm on 15th December. After disembarking the passengers who were going onwards to other Australian ports, the *Doric* left Tasmania at 9.10am on the 16th. The ship then steamed into the Tasman Sea, generally in a southeast direction to round the southern end of New Zealand's South Island and then headed north to its first stop in New Zealand. There was a moderate northwest breeze, which veered to north-northwest to west on the 18th December, with the hazy weather continuing. The ship passed the Nuggets[49] at 7pm that day and arrived off Otago Heads (the entrance to Otago Harbour) at 9.40pm on 19th December and entered Port Chalmers, Dunedin, early on the morning of Tuesday 20th December. The slight delay was probably caused by a reluctance to negotiate the entrance to the bay, and then the docks in Port Chalmers, at night. The passage from Plymouth to Otago Heads, including stoppage for the ports of call, had taken the *Doric* forty-two days, eleven hours and twenty-two minutes.[50]

Having left England with the approach of winter, Edward arrived on the South Island of New Zealand just short of the summer solstice. During the voyage there had been largely calm weather, no births or deaths on board and no sickness – or at least not enough to cause any quarantine issues when they arrived at Port Chalmers. The *Doric* left Port Chalmers on 21st December and arrived at 9am on the 22nd at Lyttleton, the port for Christchurch,[51] in the Canterbury Region. The *Star* for that day records the ship's arrival and lists the passengers disembarking, 'Mr. Edwin Goodfellow' (sic) appears in the list of the arrival of sixteen steerage passengers. *The Press* and *The Star* had, on 9th December 1887, both carried a report of the passengers booked in England for passage on the *Doric* to New Zealand up to 21st October 1887. Edward Goodfellow's name is not among them, suggesting, perhaps, that his decision was more last minute than planned well in advance. A last-minute booking in this way therefore avoided public notice of who he was and where he was going.

Edward's journey appears to have presented a similar prospect to other voyages to New Zealand at this time. Emigrant and mail ships to New Zealand were relatively expensive to sail in,[52] in part because of the length of the voyage, but also because of both the low numbers of passengers and the amount of freight that could be carried on the smaller ships built for this route. At this time large boats with greater cargo and passenger capacity also had much greater coal consumption than the *Doric*, and would therefore have had trouble making the New Zealand trip, given the distances between coaling stations. The larger steamers were used instead on the shorter North America route. A smaller vessel, such as the *Doric*, used less coal and had less danger from running out of coal if adverse conditions lengthened the journey and even then, if it did run out of coal, the *Doric* could resort to sail.

Although Edward's voyage was uneventful, a voyage to New Zealand could also have been a miserable and dangerous voyage.[53] However, more effective regulation of the New Zealand route by the time of Edward's voyage had resulted in better conditions on board than were often found on the mid-nineteenth-century transatlantic route. Fair weather could provide blue skies and calm seas, with some excitement coming from the birds or sea mammals encountered. The modern culture of sun worship and flimsier warm weather attire would have been alien ideas to most Victorians, so hot days and stifling clothing could be a trial for the passengers.

Bad weather during the passage could bring seasickness, misery, discomfort, injury from falls and even loss of a person overboard. There were no losses overboard on Edward's voyage, but there was no really bad weather. When sailing ships (which were still operating on routes to New Zealand) encountered severe gales, the conditions could provide additional mental stress from worry at the possibility of the ship foundering in a storm.

The travel writer Eric Newby made the journey to Australia (and back) fifty years later on a four-masted, square-rigged and steel-hulled barque of 3,200 tons, the *Moshulu*.[54] He wrote of the storms in the Roaring Forties rolling the ship through thirty degrees to port and starboard alternatively:

> My cross-ships bunk became a purgatory; at one moment I would be standing on my feet, the next my legs would be in the air with the blood rushing to my head … At supper the table rose to meet us in a most disconcerting way … Just before midnight came an even more extravagant series of rolls.[55]

Later, on the way home, he very narrowly avoided being swept overboard in another storm. Storms in the Southern Ocean could be a threat to any vessel and all those on her.

As with any confinement of a disparate group of people, squabbles and petty jealousies among the passengers could arise and would serve to make all on board even more uncomfortable – and no doubt make the journey feel longer. Not many of the smaller ships on the New Zealand run would have had a ship's doctor or medical facilities. Illness and injuries on long journeys were therefore a concern, as only rudimentary care (sometimes from the other passengers) would be available until the next port of call. Infectious diseases could spread more easily in the confined spaces of a ship, and in serious cases quarantine issues would restrict access to shore when coaling was required.[56] The presence of a doctor on the *Doric* was pointed out in the advertising for her sailings; this being seen as an advantage over ships that lacked a doctor.

Reports from other New Zealand-bound ships around this time comment on the boredom of spending six weeks, or longer, at sea. Food could be an issue on long voyages, becoming boring through repetition, as well as lacking in fresher ingredients the further the boat travelled from its last port of call. The quality of food was usually less of a problem for first-class passengers, but the cheaper the passage, generally the plainer the fare. To relieve the boredom, music helped, particularly in the evenings, to entertain and produce some bonhomie among the passengers. Parlour games, recitals, readings, storytelling and even amateur dramatics and dancing were also popular diversions at this time. Games could help – cards, chess or draughts, deck quoits, etc. The report of the *Doric*'s voyage also draws attention to regular 'Divine services' on board. Boat drills on the *Doric* were reported as being strictly carried out. Chance encounters with other ships, particularly those bound for 'home', could also produce excitement. There could be a chance to send a boat over with mail for family and friends in Britain and pick up any news or weather reports for their destination. Disappointment would result if sea conditions would not permit the rowed boats to cross between ships to deliver the mail. The meetings with ships would usually be in the more crowded waters of the Northern Hemisphere. Whatever Edward's reason for leaving England, his voyage to New Zealand would not have been a pleasure cruise, particularly in third class – but it would still have been an adventure to travel that distance, particularly for one who does not appear to have left the Lake District previously.

In Port Chalmers the *Doric* began to discharge the first of her New Zealand cargo and began loading the freight for the return voyage. She had brought some 2,360 tons of cargo from Britain. For Dunedin (and transhipment), 1,060 tons were unloaded; 490 tons would be off-loaded in Canterbury, 480 tons in Wellington and 330 tons in Auckland. In addition to this, eighteen bags of mail from Britain, one bag from Cape Town and four packets from Hobart were landed for the New Zealand postal service. Part of the Port Chalmers cargo was a consignment of brass instruments from Boosey & Co in London for the Port Chalmers garrison band:

> In all there are 25 instruments of first class quality, meeting the requirements of a full band, and the finish of one and all of them reflects great credit on the makers. Mr M'Connell, the conductor of the band, after issuing the instruments to the men, called upon them to perform some selections, which they did exceedingly well. Afterwards his Worship the Mayor (Mr. E.G. Allen) expressed the pleasure he felt at being called upon to assist at the testing of the new instruments. He complimented the people of Port Chalmers on possessing so excellent a band, and on their acquisition of such a complete set of instruments. His Worship added that in the bandmaster and conductor, Mr M'Connell, the men had a most able and efficient leader—one who, he was sure, would do his utmost to promote their interests in every way. Mr M'Connell, the bandmaster, thanked his worship and the other gentlemen who had honoured them with their presence that evening. He assured them that the band, individually and collectively, felt the compliment thus conferred upon them. After playing the National Anthem the band dispersed.[57]

Such different times.

At Port Chalmers the *Doric* took on board 1,200 bales of wool for export to Great Britain, and left there at 6pm on 21st December for Lyttleton, where she would take on a further 1,200 bales of wool and between 4,000 and 5,000 carcasses of mutton (besides cheese and butter for stowage in the cool chamber). The *Doric* then left for Wellington, where she would take in the bulk of her meat cargo, and finally sail for London (via Rio de Janeiro) on 7th January.

Edward in New Zealand

Although he landed originally on the South Island, Edward appears to have spent most of his time in Wellington, North Island. Wellington had been made the capital of New Zealand[58] in 1865 (when it had a population of 4,900) and had been created its first City Corporation in 1870 (although it was not officially designated a city until 1881). Edward arrived in a city that, in 1881, now had a population of 20,000 non-Maoris (that the population was counted omitting Maoris silently says much about Maori status after New Zealand was made a colony). The population was growing by around a thousand new immigrants each year. Unfortunately for those looking to create a new and prosperous life in this colony, there was a country-wide fifteen-year depression that lasted until around 1895. Civic morale in Wellington was boosted, to a degree, just before Edward arrived, by the celebrations for Queen Victoria's Golden Jubilee. Civic celebrations were also the order of the day in 1890 when the city celebrated its first fifty years of settlement. It is also worth recording that the Maori or New Zealand wars which began in 1845 were concluded only fifteen years before Edward arrived in the country. It was a different type of country to the Lake District that he had known – one that must still have had a frontier air, in the sense that it was new settlement for white Western Europeans with none of the infrastructure they were used to, being augmented by new immigrants with their futures to make.

Edward appears in official records as a groom in Wellington and in the 1890, 1896 and 1900 New Zealand electoral rolls. This seems to be a substantial drop in standing for the man formerly of independent means who had been a hotel keeper. It is not known if Edward took these jobs because there was nothing else to be had and he knew something of horses, or because he was actually knowledgeable about them. When Edward was living at the Borrowdale Hotel, he employed a William Ballential, who is listed in the 1881 census as a 'servant' whose occupation was 'Huntsman'[59] – not the usual hotel servant for a small country hotel. In the nineteenth century there were many packs of hunting hounds in the Lake District, and it is possible that Edward kept his own pack and Ballential was his huntsman. If Edward was a keen hunter it would explain his knowledge of horses, but also raise questions about his finances, given the notorious costs of the keen hunter.

Edward's Death

The new life for Edward in New Zealand was not particularly long and certainly not prosperous. He seems to have made little progress in improving his lot and remained a groom. He was killed, aged fifty-three, on Sunday 15th February 1903, just over fifteen years after his arrival from England. The *Wanganui Herald* for 16th February 1903 reported that he was killed by his horse while driving from Paraparaumu[60] to Paikakariki.[61] This was a journey of about six and a half miles down the coast a little north of Wellington.

Edward had started a new job for William Walter Harrison, a farmer in Paraparaumu, only a few days before his death. He had been taken on by Harrison as 'a weekly servant at £1 a week & found'.[62] Mr Harrison had promised to drive the Reverend Charles Theodore Pargiter to Paikakariki that afternoon, but because he had 'some oats to get in', Edward offered to drive the Reverend Pargiter instead. They set off at about 4pm in a spring cart pulled by an old horse, recently bought by Mr Harrison. The accident occurred about half an hour later.

The coroner's inquest was held before Coroner William Henry Simcox on 17th February in Paraparaumu. The Reverend Pargiter gave evidence to the coroner's inquest that:

> It was a warm day and there were a good many flies about. The horse kept twisting its tail about and the off rein got caught under its tail. Deceased leant forward to disentangle the rein. He lifted the tail with his left hand and the horse kicked out with one or both feet over the front of the trap & struck deceased on the chest leaving a mark just over the heart. As soon as deceased was struck he jumped out of the trap on to his feet on the left hand side, gave one or two staggers & fell on the side of the road. I laid him by the side of the road on the grass and unbuttoned his collar & shirt & looked to see any injuries. I found a slight discoloration over the heart & a feeling as if the ribs were broken in. Deceased gave no sign of life. He lay back with his mouth open making a gurgling noise for a few seconds. He did not speak or move after he once tumbled down. After I found I could do nothing for Deceased I turned my attention to the horse. When it kicked out it had fallen on its head and its neck bent under it. It got up and started down the road. I went after it brought it back & tied it by the reins to the steps … lifted deceased in the cart & took him back to Mr Harrison's & instructed Mr Bailey postmaster to inform the police at Otaki …[63]

Constable Timothy O'Rourke, who later examined the body, gave evidence that:

> I examined the body and found a semi-circular depression on the left breast over the heart. There was slight discolouration of the skin but it was not broken but the flesh underneath was parted the breast bone appeared to be sunken or broken. There was no other matter of importance on the body but the injury appeared sufficient to have caused instantaneous death.[64]

The verdict of the coroner's jury was:

> That the said Edward Goodfellow on the fifteenth day of February in the year aforesaid then driving a certain horse on a certain highway at Paraparaumu in the Colony aforesaid it so happened that the said horse kicked the said Edward Goodfellow with great violence, by means whereof the said Edward Goodfellow then received one mortal fracture on the upper part of the body, of which the said Edward Goodfellow then instantly died: and so the jurors aforesaid upon their oath aforesaid do say that the said Edward Goodfellow in the manner and by the means aforesaid accidentally, casually and by misfortune came to his death, and not otherwise.

Little seems to have been known of Edward's personal details by others in New Zealand. His death certificate shows him as being 'about 50',[65] with the section on his parents simply marked 'unknown'. For 'where born', the certificate is marked 'supposed Lake District England' and for the time he had been in New Zealand it shows 'since 1887'. He was buried in Otaki Public Cemetery, near where he worked, on 20th February 1903. There is no information on his death certificate about marriage or issue, the boxes are simply crossed through – no one even knew he had a second Christian name. That the heir to John Banks the elder's estate was working as a groom clearly confirms that he was no longer a man of any capital. At the time of his death he had just started a new job at £1 a week, and he died with only 8/6d in his pocket.

The absence of personal and family information on Edward's death certificate tends to point to a man who had not been forthcoming to others about his past or his reasons for starting his life anew when he emigrated at the age of thirty-seven. When driving the Reverend Pargiter, Edward had talked a little of himself and told Pargiter that he had been in New Zealand about fifteen years and that he was originally from the Lake District and had one sister 'at home married to a Wesleyan minister'.[66] At the time of his fatal accident it is a little ironic he was talking to a minister of the Church of England – the church that denied the validity of his marriage and would have held that he was guilty, in the church's eyes at least, of incest.

It is more than a little odd that in discussing family, Edward would choose to mention his sister and brother-in-law, but make no mention of his wives or children. But perhaps the reticence to divulge details of his past was through a desire to conceal, even fifteen years later, his real reasons for leaving England. It would have been difficult to explain his past without doing so. There could also be a reluctance to reveal how much he had lost in terms of status, wealth and family.

That someone would emigrate and look to start a new life in a colony in the nineteenth century was not at all unusual, nor would Edward be the first immigrant in a new country with something to hide. Did he not talk about his previous life through natural reticence, or through shame or embarrassment at his reason for fleeing, or even fear of discovery? Was this also a reason for shedding his distinctive middle name?

The possible reasons for abandoning his family and emigrating are explored a little more in Chapter Eight. The void marriage, perjury and finances are all issues that may have been involved.

The accident with the horse brought to an end Edward's complicated, and ultimately unsuccessful, life. The victor in the litigation ended his life with no property and no money, separated from the mother of his children, she and the children having already abandoned his name. A perjurer, cut off from his homeland, and his sister, he was no longer a hotel keeper, but an agricultural worker earning £1 a week. It is useless to speculate, but one cannot help wondering if the inheritance was really a benefit to him and whether he would have had a better life without it.

CHAPTER EIGHT

The Questions that still Remain

The Borrowdale Hotel

Almost five years after securing his inheritances, Edward Goodfellow married Hannah Armstrong in 1875. She was the eldest child of Benjamin and Mary Armstrong. Benjamin and Mary were both experienced in the hotel business, having both been on the staff at the Royal Hotel in Carlisle before they married.[1] By 1861 they were established at the Lodore Hotel[2] in Borrowdale, about half a mile away from the Borrowdale Hotel. For a time they appear to have run both hotels, probably from around August 1866, as the *Cumberland Pacquet* then carried an advertisement describing Benjamin as the proprietor of both hotels which were 'Patronised by their Royal Highnesses The Prince of Wales and Prince Arthur'. *The Kendal Mercury* for 17th November the same year carried an account of a ball and supper given at the Borrowdale Hotel:

> a recherché banquet well served and abounding in all the delicacies of the season, reflected the highest credit on the liberality and culinary taste of Mr and Mrs Armstrong, whose house-warming is unique in the annals of Borrowdale.

Even allowing for a local paper not wanting to upset local advertisers, this is a glowing report that suggests that Benjamin knew how to run a hotel.

Benjamin was the manager of the Borrowdale Hotel and he died in 1873, aged forty-four.[3] At this stage he appears to have given up the tenancy of the Lodore Hotel. This could have been because of his wife's mental health. On his death, Benjamin left his widow, Mary, and six children, who ranged in age from twenty to eight. Hannah was the eldest child and next in age was her brother Joseph, aged nineteen. Joseph died in 1877 aged twenty-two – the cause of his death was, not for the first time in this story, phthisis (which appears to have been diagnosed around August 1876).[4]

Benjamin did not name Joseph as an executor in the will which he executed on 16th May 1872 but appointed his eldest daughter Hannah instead. This was an unusual choice given the general male-centric view of business and allied matters in the nineteenth century, and it seems to imply more trust in her than in Joseph. One presumes also that Hannah had knowledge of, and an involvement in, the business while her father was alive. Using more distant family members as executors might have been considered, but the running of the hotel would probably have demanded too much of their time to make this practical.

As at 1873, Hannah and a local farmer Miles Wilson, a friend of Benjamin's, were the two executors of the estate, which included the hotel business. What comprised the business is not wholly clear. It is unlikely to have included the land and buildings as these were far more likely to have been taken by Benjamin on a tenancy agreement.[5] The stock, fixtures and fittings (depending upon the terms of the lease), carriages, linen, etc would be the tenants', as would the goodwill, stock and cash reserves. As Benjamin had taken on the newly built Borrowdale Hotel it is reasonable to assume that his time at the Lodore Hotel had been successful, but that he was then choosing to move to a newer and larger establishment. Photographs of the Armstrong family at the Borrowdale Hotel circa 1870[6] show a well-dressed and prosperous-looking Victorian family, giving the impression that Benjamin was successful.

The executors of the estate were also, together with Benjamin's widow Mary, appointed guardians of the infant children. Apart from Hannah and Joseph, the other children were aged fifteen, eleven, ten and eight. It is unlikely that Mary, the widow, was much involved with either the business or the children. Her mental health was declining and soon she was admitted to Garlands Asylum[7] in 1876. She remained there until her death in 1881. Benjamin Armstrong left his estate in trust to pay the income to his wife for life.[8] None of the children would have been entitled to receive anything from the estate until after their mother's death, when it was to be divided equally between them, subject to their attaining the age of twenty-one. The hotel business should have been capable of paying the fees for Garlands so that Mary would not have been cared for as a pauper patient.

When Edward married Hannah, he described himself as being of independent means, but when she died four years later he was described as the hotel keeper of the Borrowdale Hotel. Quite clearly, he had taken over running the business and had probably become involved in it either before

Questions that still Remain

the marriage or very soon afterwards, given Hannah's state of health. That the business was an asset of the estate there is no doubt, and it was probably the main part of the estate. It is most likely that Hannah and Edward would have asked Miles Wilson to retire from the trusteeship of the estate, and equally likely that he would have agreed to do so – a trusteeship is onerous, particularly one with a business as an asset. But if this surmise is correct, Hannah's early death would have then left Edward in control of Benjamin's estate as the sole surviving trustee, and in day-to-day control of the hotel in default of anyone else in the Armstrong family being old enough to manage it. After Benjamin's death in 1873, Joseph died in April 1877 aged twenty-two and Hannah died in 1879; Sarah, Benjamin junior, Mary and Eleanor all survived well into the twentieth century. The youngest of the last four attained the age of twenty one in 1886.

Edward's reasons for marrying an invalid were touched on Chapter Seven: was it love or money? It is not hard to see that Edward's progress, through this marriage, to the control of the Borrowdale Hotel business would be the subject of local gossip (and local gossip rarely dwells for long on the good side of a person's character). Hannah's early death, and Edward's inheritance of her share of the estate, would not have silenced any rumours about his motives for marrying an invalid.

Nonetheless, whatever the truth might have been about his motives, Edward remained at the hotel after her death, no doubt assisted by being in possession of Hannah's share of her father's estate. He also seems to have been the only adult within this branch of the Armstrong family in a position to try to run the hotel business, and it is worth remembering that Benjamin's widow was by this time in Garlands Asylum and would die two years after Hannah. Edward's later marriage to Mary Armstrong would have also brought him effective, but not actual, control of her interest in the estate.

It is worthwhile, at this point, summarising the events in chronological order.

May 1873	Benjamin Armstrong dies
April 1875	Hannah Armstrong marries Edward Goodfellow
1876	Benjamin's widow Mary admitted to Garlands Asylum
April 1877	Joseph Armstrong dies
August 1879	Hannah Goodfellow dies

1881	Benjamin's widow Mary dies in Garlands Asylum
July 1882	Mary Armstrong marries Edward Goodfellow
August 1882	Clara Goodfellow born
July 1883	John Goodfellow born
1884	Edward Goodfellow leaves the Borrowdale Hotel
November 1887	Edward Goodfellow sails for New Zealand

Until Mary, Benjamin's widow, died in 1881, her husband's estate would have been held to pay the interest to her. After this point the estate became distributable to his children. The practical problem here is that there were three children still under the age of twenty-one at that time and they could not receive their shares of the estate until attaining twenty-one. Edward would appear to have taken the view that the hotel business should keep going until the children's shares were able to be handed to them. It is quite likely that the business could not have functioned after the cost of withdrawing capital to pay the adult children's shares when they were twenty-one. If Edward argued that the business should be kept intact and realised when the youngest child attained twenty-one, that would have meant a disposal in 1886. But Edward left the hotel sometime in 1884, as in that year a Mr Gregory and a Mr Askew became tenants of the Borrowdale Hotel. These two present a curious tale. Mr Gregory was clerk to the Birkenhead Guardians and superintendent registrar for Birkenhead and district. He lived way beyond his means and in 1886 appeared at his own bankruptcy hearing (which eventually led to criminal charges for concealment of assets and falsely obtaining credit). Perhaps in the hope of clearing some of his difficulties he was persuaded by a Mr Askew to join him in the tenancy of the Borrowdale Hotel in 1884. Neither had the £2,200 necessary to enter into the tenancy and purchase the furniture, carriages, linen, etc in the hotel. A sum of £1,000 was borrowed from the Cumberland Banking Company, and Coward's trustees, then described as the owners of the Borrowdale Hotel, agreed that the balance could be paid in instalments. The security for the bank was various deeds to properties that Gregory claimed to own, but in fact did not. The hotel venture predictably failed. Gregory said on his arrest, 'I have correctly accounted for money and everything belonging to me. I will make somebody pay for this if I am locked up'. He went to jail for three months. Of Mr Askew, if that was indeed his real name, there seems to be no further trace.

That £2,200 was required to enter into the tenancy to purchase furniture, carriages, linen, etc suggests either that these were not the assets of the tenant when Edward was the tenant or that they might have been seized by the landlord if Edward was in serious default of his tenancy terms.

So why did Edward give up the tenancy at that time? It was a further three years before he departed for New Zealand, but by then he had little or no money. He sailed on a third-class passage and then worked for the rest of his life as a groom. It is unlikely that he left Mary, his wife, with much, if anything, as she moved away to a small terraced property in Workington and thereafter worked as a caretaker and seamstress. That there was no money left leaves several possibilities.

First, and probably most likely, Edward was not a good businessman and the hotel slowly declined, perhaps also swallowing his own capital. If this was the case, then the shares of the Armstrong children in the business will have amounted to nothing. This in turn would have caused strained relationships with the rest of the family. Secondly, the same result might have been achieved simply through Edward living beyond his means – he would be by no means the first hotelier to do that – and that again would lead to the loss of his properties to satisfy his creditors. The third possibility is more sinister and goes back to his marriage to Mary. There was always going to be the risk of the true facts of this marriage being discovered and that he would be exposed as a perjurer, which could then have led to a prosecution. Being blackmailed over the marriage to buy off the threat of exposure does look rather dramatic, but it could account for Edward absconding when the money ran out (and also his continued reticence about his family when he was in New Zealand). It is unlikely that an accidental discovery by others of the marriage would have led to Edward's departure from the hotel as he remained in England for the next three years. If the circumstances of the marriage were discovered, it is far more likely that this was immediately before he sailed to New Zealand.

For whatever reason, from coming into his inheritance in 1871 to his departure in late 1887, all Edward's inheritances were gone, as was any interest he got from his wives in the Borrowdale Hotel business. One cannot imagine that the Armstrong family looked back on their involvement with him fondly. His departure might have given some satisfaction to those who were so keen to give evidence opposing his inheritance of John Banks the elder's estate.

Why did Edward and Mary Marry?

By the time of the 1881 census Hannah's younger sister Mary was the only Armstrong child left at the hotel. The whereabouts of her youngest sister Eleanor (aged sixteen) or her brother Benjamin (aged nineteen) are not known. Mary's pregnancy in 1882 aged nineteen would have led more awkward gossip, even if Edward did not acknowledge his responsibility at the time. The marriage of Edward and Mary in August 1882 was apparently conducted away from Keswick to hide the fact of the marriage and Edward's act of perjury in connection with the marriage licence (see Chapter Seven). Afterwards, Edward returned to the Borrowdale Hotel and Mary lived in Keswick (possibly in one of Edward's inherited properties, if he still had them). On both their children's birth certificates in 1882 and 1883 Edward is described as 'hotelkeeper' and Mary as resident at Main Street, Keswick. But how was Mary's new residence and child explained in Keswick? It could be that Edward and Mary were open about the relationship, and Edward's paternity of the issue, but not the fact of their marriage. While an irregular relationship would have caused gossip and disapproval, it would hardly have been the first such ménage in Keswick.

For the two children born of this relationship, both births were registered by Mary and both certificates show the mother as Mary Goodfellow 'formerly Armstrong', the father as Edward Barron Goodchild and each child having the surname of Goodchild. None of this information necessarily equates to a public disclosure of a marriage, as Mary was entitled to adopt and use whatever surname she chose, and this is still the position today, provided it is not done with the intention of perpetrating a fraud.

The father's name being on the birth certificate means simply that he acknowledged each child's paternity and justified the use of the Goodfellow surname for the children – it was not a declaration that the parents were married. So, it could be that Keswick people knew of the relationship, but only as being one outside of marriage because of Edward's previous marriage. The registrar who registered both births was Matthew Knubley. He had also registered the deaths of Edward's mother, father, younger brother, first wife and brother-in-law. It is not likely that he would have been unfamiliar with Edward's family history. The births of the two children were not announced in the local press.

The effect of the marriage in Carlisle was none – being void, it was of no effect whatsoever. But Edward was potentially exposed to up to seven years in jail for his perjury on the licence application if it was discovered. So, what was the purpose of the wedding ceremony? It created no legal relationship, it gave Edward no rights over his wife's property and it could not be celebrated with family or friends. Edward could give his children his name by appearing on each birth certificate as the father, but that could have been done without marriage. Mary could adopt his name, as she did, but this would have been taken by Keswick for what it actually was: a cohabitation. Was the ceremony simply to give Mary her day in church, even though she could not tell others?

The ceremony could not be disclosed to those in Keswick; it was only seven years since Hannah's death and Edward is unlikely to have been so popular locally that no one would have wanted to draw the authorities' attention to the irregularity. Were Edward and Mary so ignorant of what obsessed the rest of England in that century as not to know of the endless debates on the deceased wife's sister issue? This is unlikely but, if it was the case, the logical thing for Edward and Mary to have done when they decided to marry would have been to approach the church in Crosthwaite, and upon doing so they would have been refused and told why. If it was the case that as far as Keswick was concerned they were cohabiting, then again what was the point of the void marriage (and, more importantly, Edward's allied act of perjury)?

It is difficult to understand why Edward took the risk that was inherent in the perjured application for the marriage licence, as he appeared to gain nothing by it. If he and Mary were prepared to cohabit, why go through with the marriage? This remains one of the events in this story that appears to defy a rational explanation, but given how irrational human nature can be, we probably must just accept that it was an irrational act that brought him no benefit.

Five years after his marriage, Edward left for New Zealand in 1887. He travelled alone leaving behind his twenty-three-year-old wife, and children aged five and four. Beyond his one-way third-class ticket, he appears to have taken little or no money with him. He earned his living in New Zealand as a groom and at the time of his death he was employed at £1 per week and only had a small amount of change when he died. Between 1871 and 1887 his inheritances from his sister and father had gone, together with whatever he obtained from his father-in-law's estate via both marriages. There seems to have been nothing much left for Mary, as she moved away to Whitehaven and earned her own living as an office caretaker and seamstress. The possibility of Edward remitting any money from New Zealand to help her seems unlikely on a wage of £1 a week.

Why did the Litigation Occur?

The reason why this dispute began when it did is worth considering. While Margaret Banks Goodfellow was alive, and was her uncle's heiress, no challenge to the will was forthcoming from John Banks the younger. On her death, and the inheritance then passing to Edward Goodfellow, the challenge was made. This acceptance, and then change of heart, at first blush weakens John Banks the younger's case against the will, in that he appears to have been prepared to ignore the issue and accept Margaret's inheritance under John Banks the elder's last will as valid. However, challenging the will while Margaret was alive would have given rise to questions of his standing to do so. Margaret would be John the elder's heir either under the will or on his intestacy as his heir at law if the will was not valid. John Banks the younger could only inherit if Margaret died under the age of twenty-one and his uncle died intestate. Realistically, the costs risk of litigation against the will was only worth taking if Margaret died before reaching her majority.

On Margaret's death, John Banks the younger was notified and he returned to England from North America fairly promptly. Who told him of her death and why? It does not appear that any of his close relatives were still in England at this time. It was therefore possibly a friend with whom he was still in touch who contacted him. Conceivably, it was also someone who disliked Edward Goodfellow sufficiently to encourage John's return. If this was the case, it must have been a dislike of Edward, rather than simply of all Goodfellows, as, of course, Margaret was herself a Goodfellow. But on the other hand, what would have caused such dislike of someone not yet twenty-one? However, there is also the possibility that John was waiting for this event. He had made enquiries about his uncle's will during his previous visit. Had he then taken legal advice and been told of the potential to attack his uncle's will if Margaret died under the age of twenty-one? If this was the case, her death would have been the starting pistol for the work to commence. In Chapter Four it was speculated that the difficulties of her birth could have led to Margaret being a sickly child if she was underdeveloped and weak, so that her death before the age of twenty-one would not necessarily have been that remote a prospect in the nineteenth century.

The letter from England telling John of Margaret's death would make interesting reading if it had survived.

Questions that still Remain

Mrs Routledge

Mrs Routledge is something of a problem in that her evidence seems so fierce and almost personal against the will and in her assault on the integrity of Tolson and Ansell. There were few points that the evidence of the three actually agreed on. But Mrs Routledge was prepared to give her evidence regarding the execution of the will even though the presence of her signature on the engrossed will flatly contradicted this evidence. This point is considered more in the following section.

Where did John Banks the Elder's Money Go?

John Banks the elder's annual rent from his properties comfortably exceeded his expenditure on board and lodging. There would, of course, be repairs to the properties and local rates to pay, but there is no suggestion in the evidence that John found it difficult to meet his outgoings. There is evidence which hints that John was frugal and also that he maintained a bank account in Keswick (which would scarcely have been needed if his existence was hand to mouth). The evidence of Mary Usher was that John paid 10/- per week on board and lodging and he spent little on clothing, but his rents amounted to £80 pa. In the last year of his life there would have been medical expenses which would have probably prevented there being any surplus income that year. But in the preliminary skirmishes in the litigation some odd allegations surfaced about the state of his finances. John Banks the younger claimed that Joseph Tolson told him in September 1867 that John Banks the elder died in debt. Given the surplus income throughout almost all his life by himself, this is rather startling.

Grenip Cartmel's evidence against the will contained a passage relating to a loan he claimed to have made to John Banks the elder in 1861. This was for £70 and was made at John Banks' request. It was still outstanding at John's death. Cartmel was a tenant of John's and earned his living as a tailor. It is curious that a tailor had £70 available to lend for an indefinite period and for an unstated reason to a man who he considered was 'insane and out of his right mind'. Cartmel also helpfully added that John 'was like a child and not a man' and that he could have persuaded John of anything. Cartmel's evidence contained no detail about the rate of interest on the loan or any payments of interest or capital that had been made. Other evidence, from William Robinson, was that John Banks the elder 'was easily imposed upon and people who knew him could get him to do almost anything'. Dr Jones of Aspatria gave similar evidence, 'I could have got him to sign anything. I had only to ask him'. Mary Usher also averred that 'he could easily be imposed upon and people who knew him could get him to do almost anything'.

Elizabeth Routledge also touched on John's finances in her evidence, alleging that Joseph Tolson had failed to pay £11 of John's rent into John's bank account and instead spent it buying bacon. This is the same amount as the cheque, referred to in Chapter Three at the meeting for the first will, which Tolson was to pay into John's bank account or encash – the evidence is unclear which was actually done. Mrs Routledge's evidence does not explain how she knew of the £11 and that it was not in John's bank account. She also claimed that Mr Ansell the attorney had borrowed £60 from John Banks and that she had seen a promissory note for this amount. Ansell's evidence was that he gave John his promissory note as security for £60 which John 'had placed in my hands a few years before his death and I regularly paid interest for it. He never lent me any other sum'. No reason is given as to why an attorney had found it necessary to borrow £60 from a client.

None of this proves that John's naivety was exploited by others, but it certainly raises an ugly suspicion that it was. Furthermore, Cartmel and Ansell were on opposite sides of this dispute, but neither side seemed inclined to explore what had transpired in order to discredit the other's evidence. Elizabeth Routledge's too detailed knowledge of John's finances also points uncomfortably towards too many people perhaps knowing too much about John's money.

Mrs Routledge also alleged that around Whitsuntide 1863 Joseph Tolson had removed from Arkleby John's writing desk, private papers and pocket book. The latter, she said, contained the promissory note for £60 from Ansell. In June 1863, she, her husband and John Banks visited Tolson's house to ask for the return of the promissory note as 'it would be safer at our house', but Tolson denied ever having seen it. They all then went to Ansell's office and he handed the promissory note to John Banks. Joseph Tolson returned the desk and pocket book. Ansell's version is that a visit took place in 1864 when John Banks asked what sum would be due on the note. He said that nothing was said about repayment and he expressly denied that the promissory note had ever later been in his possession after he returned it to John. The evidence of Tolson on this matter was also that this visit occurred in 1864, not 1863. Tolson's daughter Jane also gave evidence of a visit in July 1864 (dealt with in Chapter Three), although she says nothing of a writing desk and a visit by John to Mr Ansell. Ansell added that the writing desk (which he said was more of a box) had been handed to him for safe-keeping by John. Tolson was also asked to get the box repaired for John in Keswick.

Questions that still Remain

Left with the box was the promissory note and various other papers. The box, papers and promissory note were all handed back to John by Tolson before he returned to Arkleby. Tolson also concurred with Ansell that the promissory note, so far as he was aware, had never been in Ansell's possession after Ansell had signed it and given it to John. The position with John's finances becomes more opaque with each piece of evidence. Tolson added that there was no visit to Ansell's office, but that he and John went out to look at John's properties for any repairs that were needed.

Whatever was alleged, and the truth will not at this stage be found, the key points are:

1. We know that, until the last year of John's life, there should have been an annual surplus of income over expenditure, and therefore there should have been a surplus of cash at his death
2. It was claimed that there was in fact not enough money to clear his debts, and it was proposed that properties be sold to raise cash before Margaret Banks Goodfellow died.
3. We know of no circumstances in which John needed to borrow money from others.

Did any of those close to John take advantage of him, e.g. falsify accounts, overstate what was due from John, or just plain steal from him? We cannot now know the answer, but the lack of savings and ready cash is suspicious. The shortage of income to support Margaret after John's death also lends some weight to this suspicion. But at this remove in time we will never know the truth as to where John's surplus income went, and I am left with the uncomfortable feeling that the witnesses on both sides of this dispute knew far more about the money that was said in evidence at the trial. Indeed, one wonders if the two sides in this dispute might actually have been arguing over the money and who might gain an advantage by covering up their financial 'dealings' during John's lifetime.

Margaret's inheritance from her father seems to have been sufficient to support her after his death while she was at school and lodging in Kendal. There was nothing said about her income after she moved to Arkleby, when, after John's death, an application was made to the Court of Chancery. This was for provision for Margaret's maintenance during her minority. The Court directed in 1866 that £80pa be released to Mr and Mrs Routledge for this purpose. Two things stand out about this award. The first is its size when compared to her uncle's position. In 1863 he was paying £26pa (10/- per week) for board and lodging. This was doubled in December 1863 to £52 after Mrs Routledge's negotiation with John. Now, less than three years later, board and lodging for Margaret was increased to £80pa (almost £1 11/- per week), or three times John Banks' rent in 1863. Secondly, in awarding this sum, the Court took no account of the income produced by the property Margaret inherited from her father's estate, which one presumes was enough to keep her while lodging in Keswick four years before. The rents on the property were collected for her until her death by John Gill. It appears the properties from her father were still intact at Margaret's death and that these will have passed to her half-brother. But it seems unlikely that there was any cash or savings as well. Quite why Margaret's board and lodging at this point was more expensive than that of her invalid uncle had been is unclear. Nothing was said in the Chancery application that Margaret was known at that stage to be ill with pulmonary tuberculosis. Mrs Routledge would look to have made more from her teenage lodger that she ever did from John. Why was Margaret's own income not mentioned?

Valediction

This then is as much as I have been able to draw together from reports and records of the Banks and Goodfellow families' history and the trials. The central characters leading up to the court case were a mentally ill middle-aged man and a consumptive young woman. Neither appears to have had much joy in their life. With no close family around them, they relied instead on the paid comfort and care (such as it was) of strangers. At the end they were both alone, John Banks isolated by his illness, and Margaret Goodfellow, an orphan, isolated from what few relatives she had left.

Of the protagonists in the trials, one lost the case and the other ultimately ended penniless.

Incurable diseases and early death – at least early by our standards today – were very much the lot of many mid-Victorians. Historical events do not necessarily single out those who look or act like heroes of stories, but here John's and Margaret's joint legacy from their illnesses and deaths is a legal test that still bears their families' names. I am sure they would have both swopped their posthumous link to this legal test for more normal and fulfilled lives – and who could possibly blame them? However, we are today grateful to them for the sensible piece of law that arose from their troubled lives.

APPENDIX I

Information

Cast of Main Characters

Banks Family

Jacob Banks the elder	The father of two sons, Jacob Banks the younger and John Banks the elder
Jacob Banks the younger	The only son of Jacob Banks the elder's first marriage. He was a half-brother to John Banks the elder and was also the father of John Banks the younger
Margaret Banks the elder	The second wife of Jacob Banks the elder and the mother of both John Banks the elder and Margaret Banks the younger
John Banks the elder	The second son of Jacob Banks the elder. John is the central character in this narrative
	It was his will that was the subject of the litigation
Margaret Banks the younger (later, by marriage, *Margaret Goodfellow*)	The daughter of Jacob Banks the elder and Margaret Banks the elder, and younger sister to John Banks the elder. She was the first wife of Thomas Goodfellow, and the mother of Margaret Banks Goodfellow

John Banks the younger	The only son of Jacob Banks the younger, and therefore nephew of the half-blood of John Banks the elder
	He was the plaintiff (claimant) in the will dispute

Goodfellow Family

Thomas Goodfellow	The husband of Margaret Banks the younger
Margaret Banks Goodfellow	The only child of Thomas Goodfellow and Margaret Goodfellow
	She was the beneficiary of the disputed will
Sarah Goodfellow (née Barron)	The second wife of Thomas Goodfellow
Edward Barron Goodfellow	The eldest son of Thomas and Sarah Goodfellow, and heir to the estate of his half-sister Margaret Banks Goodfellow
	He was the defendant in the will dispute
John Tolson Goodfellow	The second son of Thomas and Sarah Goodfellow
Mary Mitchinson Goodfellow	The only daughter of Thomas and Sarah Goodfellow
Hannah Goodfellow (née Armstrong)	The first wife of Edward Barron Goodfellow
Mary Goodfellow (née Armstrong)	The second wife of Edward Barron Goodfellow

Appendix I

Others

James and Elizabeth Routledge — John Banks the elder lodged with this couple at the end of his life, as did Margaret Banks Goodfellow at the end of hers

William Thirlwall — The brother, neighbour and landlord of Elizabeth Routledge. He was also an executor of John Banks the elder's disputed will

Joseph Tolson — A Keswick grocer who collected rents for John Bank the elder and was an executor of John Banks the elder's disputed will

George Ansell — A long-established attorney in Keswick who prepared John Banks the elder's disputed will

The Principal Judges

Mr Justice Brett — Presided over the first trial of the will at Cumberland Assizes

Sir Alexander Cockburn, Chief Justice of the Court of Queen's Bench — Delivered the judgment of the panel of judges who heard the appeal in the Court of Queen's Bench

The Banks/Goodfellow Family Tree

| Jacob Banks the elder
d.1830 |

| Martha
Hurstfield |

Married (1)

| Jacob Banks
the younger
1796–1850 |

Married 1815
Anne Robinson

| John Banks
the younger
1826–1899 | Six daughters |

```
Margaret Newby
   1781–1848

Married (2)
   1810

        John Banks the elder
            1812–1865

                Margaret Banks the
                    younger
                   1815–1847

                        Married 1846
                        Thomas Goodfellow
                           1820–1858

                                Margaret Banks
                                  Goodfellow
                                   1847–1865

                                        Married 1848
                                        Sarah Barron
                                          1817–1857

                                                Edward Barron
                                                  Goodfellow
                                                   1850–1903

                                                        Two other children
```

A Victorian Tragedy: The Extraordinary Case of Banks v Goodfellow

Chronology

Birth of John Banks the elder	July 1812
Birth of Margaret Banks the younger	September 1815
Death of Jacob Banks the elder	December 1829
John Banks the elder in Dunston Asylum	Early 1841
Marriage of Thomas Goodfellow and Margaret Banks the younger	16th March 1846
Birth of Margaret Banks Goodfellow	8th January 1847
Death of Margaret Goodfellow	12th January 1847
Death of Margaret Banks the elder	18th January 1848
Marriage of Thomas Goodfellow and Sarah Barron	7th March 1848
Birth of Edward Barron Goodfellow	21st June 1850
Death of Sarah Goodfellow	6th April 1857
Death of Thomas Goodfellow	6th April 1858
Instructions for John Banks the elder's last will and execution of a draft will	2nd December 1863
Execution of John Banks the elder's engrossed will	28th December 1863
Death of John Banks the elder	28th July 1865
Death of Margaret Banks Goodfellow	6th May 1867

Appendix I

First trial of the will at Cumberland Spring Assizes	February 1869
Appeal judgment in Queen's Bench	6th July 1870
Marriage of Edward Barron Goodfellow and Hannah Armstrong	6th April 1875
Death of Hannah Goodfellow	20th August 1879
Marriage of Edward Barron Goodfellow and Mary Armstrong	26th July 1882
Birth of Clara Goodfellow	8th August 1882
Birth of John Goodfellow	29th July 1883
Death of Edward Barron Goodfellow	15th February 1903

Note on Geography

Keswick is today a market town and tourist centre on the River Greta in the modern county of Cumbria. Keswick lies within the English Lake District between Derwentwater to the south west and Bassenthwaite Lake to the north west. The Lake District was established as a National Park in 1951 and was designated as a UNESCO World Heritage Site in 2017. The climate of the Lake District is the wettest in England, but the rainfall has contributed to its lush valleys whose greenness contrasts with the starker mountains and fells which provide a major attraction for climbers and walkers.

Skiddaw, the fourth highest mountain in England, lies to the north of Keswick and makes an impressive skyline above the town. Blencathra, or Saddleback, lies to the north east. Keswick is sixteen miles west of Penrith and just over forty miles north west of Kendal.

In the nineteenth century, the county of Cumbria did not exist, and the area in which the events in this book took place mainly lies within the older county of Cumberland. Keswick had a population of slightly over 2,600 in the mid-nineteenth century[1] (today this is around 5,000 but is swollen considerably by visitors, particularly in summer).

A mid-nineteenth century guide to the Lake District was less than flattering about Keswick:

> There is no beauty in the primitive little town itself; but it has its attractions besides the convenience of its central situation among so many mountains and valleys. Of these attractions the first is undoubtedly Mr. Flintoff's model of the Lake District, which is within a few yards of all the principle inns, and may be seen during a shower, when, otherwise, the stranger may be losing temper in hearing the rain drip.[2]

Arkleby is a hamlet in the parish of *Plumbland*, as is *Parsonby*, and Plumbland was in Cumberland. Arkleby lies north west of Keswick and Bassenthwaite Lake, and just south of the small town of Aspatria. Arkleby is about sixteen miles north east of Keswick, and about twenty-one miles south west of Carlisle. Arkleby appears as 'Arcleby' in some of the trial documents.

Borrowdale is a valley south of Keswick along the western shore of Derwentwater. At its southern end is the Honister Pass leading to Buttermere. The Borrowdale Hotel is in this valley, four miles south of Keswick near where the River Derwent enters Derwentwater.

Carlisle is a city and the county town of Cumbria. It is just south of the border with Scotland and about forty miles, by road, north east of Keswick.

Crosthwaite is a parish on the north western edge of Keswick.

APPENDIX II

Biographical Sketches of the Judges and Principal Barristers

The two trials involved a notable selection of members of the Victorian Bar and Judiciary. Some short biographical details of them are set out in this appendix.

Judges

The Cumberland Assizes

MR JUSTICE BRETT PC QC, 1ST VISCOUNT ESHER (1815–1899)

William Baliol Brett had a very long and fairly distinguished legal career. He was born in 1815, the year of Waterloo, the second son of the Reverend Joseph George Brett of Chelsea. He was conventionally educated, first at Westminster School, then later at King's College London and Gonville & Caius College, Cambridge.[1] While at Cambridge he was part of the successful 1839 Boat Race crew. In 1837 and 1838, when there was no Boat Race, he was part of the Cambridge eight who beat the Leander Rowing Club.[2] He graduated with a BA in 1840 and an MA in 1845.

Brett was admitted to Lincoln's Inn in 1839 and called to the Bar on 28th January 1846.[3] He then initially practised his advocacy on the Northern Circuit. The judicial circuits of England originated in the twelfth century, when Henry II sent royal judges out to dispense justice in different regions of the country in the King's name. The practice later arose for a barrister to develop his[4] own practice around one particular circuit.[5] This practice allowed him to build his reputation with local solicitors, whose work was the province of that circuit. The judicial circuit system continues today.

Brett first began to make a name himself in mercantile and marine cases, later extending his expertise into bankruptcy. He was thought of as a sound lawyer, although it was said that he was hardly a profound one. But when in court he was an easy speaker, and, above all, was said to have used the approach of a clear-headed and experienced man of the world. He was especially at home when addressing juries, who understood his approach, and his effectiveness with them probably naturally led to him forming an unusually high estimate of the value of jury verdicts. He took silk in 1861 and was made a Bencher of Lincoln's Inn in the same year.

Brett also had a keen interest in politics, and his views are described as having been ardently conservative. He first stood, unsuccessfully, for Parliament in 1865 at Rochdale. The following year Brett was returned for Helston in Cornwall under most unusual circumstances. Both Brett and his Liberal opponent, Robert Campbell, polled the same number of votes. The mayor of Helston, as returning officer, had a casting vote in such an eventuality, and he used this in favour of Brett's opponent. The casting vote was successfully challenged by Brett on the grounds that it was cast out of time. It therefore fell to the House of Commons to decide who should take the seat. The House settled the dispute by allowing both candidates to sit in Parliament for Helston until the next election.

Once in the House, Brett's political career prospered and he was appointed Solicitor-General in Disraeli's administration in 1868 (and received the customary knighthood). His time as Solicitor-General was short, although in Parliament he also took a leading part in law reform including the abolition of public executions. In August 1868 he left Parliament on his appointment as a Justice in the Court of Common Pleas.[6] His work in this court was not without criticism, particularly as regards the severity of his sentencing in criminal matters. As well as sitting in Common Pleas, he also returned to the Northern Circuit as a judge sitting at Assizes. It was in this capacity that he heard *Banks v Goodfellow* a few months after being appointed to the Bench.

After the creation of the Court of Appeal,[7] Brett J became a Lord Justice of Appeal in 1876 and was also appointed a member of the Privy Council. In 1883, following the death of Jessel,[8] Brett succeeded him as Master of the Rolls.[9] It was said that he was not always courteous in his interventions in court and was harder on younger counsel in particular.

Brett was disappointed, even angry, at being passed over as Lord Chancellor in 1885, when Hardinge Giffard QC was appointed.[10] The reminiscences of Ernest Bowen-Rowlands[11] quote Sir Harry Poland[12] on this appointment, claiming Brett had become unpopular within the Conservative party, and that the party establishment were strongly for Giffard, he being 'the better man'. Poland also claims that creating Brett Baron Esher in 1885 was to mollify him after being passed over as Lord Chancellor.

By the time of his retirement in 1897, the general view of Brett's interventions in court was that he had mellowed with age. As a judge, Brett tended to approach issues with a robust common sense which could make him heedless of some legal or judicial technicalities if they impeded justice. To his credit, although not necessarily to the pleasure of his fellow judges, he was prepared to hold his ground against the other members of the Court of Appeal. His obituary in *The Times* cites several of the notable occasions where he was proved right in his views on appeal to the House of Lords. Less to his credit was his utter faith in juries, which strengthened later in his career when applications before him for new trials became almost hopeless.

As he aged, his irritability and near-contempt for House of Lords' decisions with which he disagreed became greater. It was said of him that overall he was a sound and accurate judge, but not a legal giant, and *The Times* obituary of him lamented his lack of literary, grace or 'epigrammatic point'.

Of being created Baron Esher in 1885, it is noteworthy that his obituary recorded this honour as being 'in well-merited recognition of already prolonged service' – note 'prolonged', and not notable, service. He retired in 1897 and was created the 1st Viscount Esher. This was a most unusually high honour to be given to any judge for legal services, other than a Lord Chancellor. He died on 24th May 1899 from heart failure, following a chill that gave rise to congestion of the lungs, complicated by 'dropsical features'. His obituary in *The Times* said that his death brought to an end 'one of the most remarkable legal and judicial careers of our time'. Esher himself, with a little, perhaps pardonable, exaggeration, described his length of time as a judge as without parallel since Lord Coke.[13]

Late in his life, his portrait was painted by John Everett Millais[14] and it was exhibited at the Grosvenor Gallery in 1887.

Brett had married Eugénie Mayer on 3rd April 1850. It has been rumoured that she was the illegitimate daughter of Napoleon Bonaparte[15] and Fanny Mayer rather than being, as is otherwise recorded, the daughter of Louis Mayer. She was born on 13th August 1814[16] and died on 4th June 1904. The highly ornate Edwardian tomb for Viscount Esher and his wife is in Christ Church churchyard, Esher. His effigy shows him in his judicial robes. There were three children of the marriage.

The arms granted to him as Viscount Esher bear the motto *Vincimus* (We have conquered), which does not seem terribly fitting for one whose career involved impartial assessment.

Queen's Bench

SIR JOHN WILLIAM MELLOR PC DL QC (1809–1887)

Mellor was born at Hollinwood House, Oldham, on 1st January 1809 into a family of wealthy Lancashire manufacturers. He was raised in Leicester, where his father became both Lord Mayor and a Justice of the Peace, and was educated at a Leicester grammar school and a local private school. Mellor was a non-conformist with Unitarian beliefs and this meant that he could not agree with the Thirty-nine Articles, which were the founding principles of the Church of England. Adherence to these articles was, before 1871,[17] a prerequisite for anyone taking up a fellowship at Oxford, Cambridge, London or Durham universities. Mellor had been accepted at Lincoln College, Oxford, but this inability to subscribe to the Thirty-nine Articles meant that he could not attend. Instead, he started to study law, first with a country attorney and then, in June 1828, at the Inner Temple. He was called to the Bar in June 1833 and joined the Midland Circuit. Thereafter he had a successful career as barrister. He authored *Suggestions as to Oaths*. He was appointed Recorder[18] of Warwick (1848–52) and later Recorder of Leicester (1855–61). He took silk in July 1851 and in the same year became a Bencher of the Inner Temple. He became a serjeant-at-law prior to his appointment to the Court of Queen's Bench in 1861 and was knighted in June 1862. In Queen's Bench he was a little overshadowed by the learning of Blackburn and the brilliance of Cockburn, but he brought great patience and acumen to his work. On his retirement in 1879,[19] he was then appointed to the Privy Council in June. His time on the Bench was held to have been characterised by patience and good sense.

In 1867, he presided at Winchester Assizes in the trial of Frederick Baker for the murder of 'Sweet' Fanny Adams. This eight-year-old girl was horribly butchered into many pieces. The defence was that Baker was not responsible by reason of insanity, maintaining that this was a consequence of Baker's father having been violent, a cousin having spent time in asylums, his sister having died of a 'brain fever' and Baker himself having attempted suicide after a failed love affair. An expert witness called by the Crown, Professor Alfred Swaine Taylor,[20] suggested in support of this contention that homicidal maniacs who had no previous history of mental illness often came from families that did. He was then asked if he thought the accused was mad.

Appendix II

This led Mellor to intervene with the sharp observation that he would not accept that the utter brutality of the crime was evidence of the accused's insanity.

Mellor was one of three judges, with Lush J and Cockburn CJ at the 188-day-long perjury trial in 1873 of Arthur Orton, 'the Tichborne claimant'. In his description of the case, James Beresford Atlay[21] described Mellor as 'second to none amongst the Common Law judges'. His entry in the *Dictionary of National Biography* notes that he 'often amused the jury with his dry humour'.

Even allowing for the usual generosity of Victorian obituaries, Mellor's obituary in *The Times* clearly shows a high regard for his abilities as a judge. He died at his house in Sussex Square, London on 26th April 1887 shortly after returning from Cannes where there had been a minor earthquake. *The Times*, in reporting his death, says that after a chill 'his old enemy asthma returned, congestion of the lungs[22] set in' and he succumbed to 'years and the British climate'. In his retirement Mellor had spent much of his time at his second home, Kingsdown, on the cliffs near Dover, and he was buried in a vault at Kingsdown, Kent.[23] His pall-bearers were local lifeboatmen, as Mellor had been a great supporter of them and their work. He left an estate of £97,000. He had married Miss Elizabeth Moseley in 1833 and claimed to have spent his first brief fee on the wedding ring. There were nine children of the marriage, eight of them sons.

During his legal career Mellor was also active in Whig (Liberal) politics. Following failed attempts at Warwick (1852) and at Coventry (1857) he was elected to Parliament to represent Great Yarmouth 1857–59 and subsequently Nottingham 1859–61. He resigned his seat on being appointed a judge in 1861.

JAMES HANNEN PC FRS, BARON HANNEN (1821–1894)

James Hannen was the son of a London wine merchant of the same name, and was born in Peckham on 19th March 1821. He was educated at St Paul's School and at Heidelberg University (an unusual choice for an aspiring English lawyer, but it was at the time famous for the quality of its school of law). The experience at Heidelberg, according to his obituary in *The Times*, 'distinctly coloured his way of thinking … It probably gave him a love of principle, a taste for philosophizing, if not philosophy and a larger horizon as to jurisprudence than is common on the Bench'. It also left him with a profound regard for Germany and German culture. The obituary noted that at his death there were not more than two or three others 'who came nearest to the highest ideal of an English judge'. It also contained the view that he had not risen as high as his talents warranted and suggested that this was because of the time he spent in the 'backwater' of the Probate and Divorce Court, 'What would have been Lord Hannen's fate if he had not been created judge of the Probate and Divorce Court or if he had not held that post for the best years of his judicial life?'. He was further praised for 'the absence of self-seeking and single minded love of truth which marked his public life'.

Called to the Bar at the Middle Temple in 1848, he joined the Home Circuit – then of greater importance than its successor, the South East Circuit. At this time he also supplemented his earnings by writing for the press, and supplied special reports for the *Morning Chronicle*. He was not eloquent in speech, but clear, accurate and painstaking, although still regarded as a 'frigid and passionless speaker'. Despite this, he quickly advanced in his career, passing many more brilliant competitors. His progress was assisted no doubt by his markedly sound common sense. Serjeant Ballantine wrote of him that 'I have been engaged with and against him in many cases while was at the bar, and I never knew a more conscientious or painstaking advocate'.[24] Contemporaries marked him early on for high judicial office. He became junior counsel to the Treasury in 1863. He appeared for the successful claimant in the long (and expensive) Shrewsbury peerage case in 1860, when the will of the 17th Earl was challenged and Lord Howard (son of the then Duke of Norfolk) was declared to be entitled to the earldom of Shrewsbury.

Hannen was appointed as a judge of the Court of Queen's Bench in 1868. He did not appear to shine in this role and, initially, was perhaps overshadowed by Cockburn and Blackburn, both more eloquent and forceful personalities. Hannen became a judge of the Court of Probate and Court for Divorce and Matrimonial Causes in 1872. By virtue of being the Probate Judge, he became President of the new Probate, Divorce and Admiralty Division brought into operation by the Judicature Acts 1873–75 when those three courts became part of the new High Court of Justice. Here, it is said, he showed himself a worthy successor to Cresswell[25] and Penzance,[26] if not in legal brilliance, then in patience, good sense and sober judgement – and the ability to control his known fierce temper. It is said that he accepted little levity in his court.

He produced a stream of consistent, well-drafted decisions in the area of probate and divorce law – see his classic definition and description of undue influence on a will in his direction to the jury in *Hall v Hall*,[27] which is still to be found in text books and is much cited today. Hannen's obituary makes reference to his involvement in the law of testamentary capacity (citing *Boughton v Knight*[28] and *Smee v Smee*[29]) but it makes no reference to his role in the appeal in *Banks v Goodfellow* (although perhaps this was included in 'other cases relating to the capacity to make a will'). Within the area of wills, his judgment in *Parker v Felgate*[30] on the deterioration in mental capacity between will instructions and execution of the will is still widely cited and applied today.

Many important causes came before him during his time in this court, but he also gave notable service more widely – particularly in ably presiding over the Parnell Special Commission (September 1888 to November 1889).[31] The hearings lasted 189 days, and Hannen conducted it with tact and great calm. His influence pervaded the whole proceedings, and it is understood that he personally drafted a large part of the final report. In January 1891 he was appointed a Lord of Appeal in Ordinary with the dignity of a life peerage as Baron Hannen of Burdock in the County of Sussex, but in that capacity he had few opportunities for displaying his judicial ability, and he retired at the close of the session of 1893. His declining health will have also been a factor in this decision.

Hannen's last major public service was in connection with the Bering Sea Arbitration of 1893 in Paris, when he acted as one of the British arbitrators. This was the resolution of a dispute which originated in the 1880s following the USA's purchase of Alaska from Russia. The USA claimed exclusive jurisdiction over the sealing industry throughout the Bering Sea and this claim was disputed by Great Britain (which still had charge of foreign affairs for the Dominion of Canada). The decision was in favour of Great Britain. Hannen's obituary observes that the outcome of the inquiry was in no small part due to Hannen's diplomacy, patience and skill.

In 1865 Hannen had stood, unsuccessfully, as the Liberal parliamentary candidate for Shoreham. His obituarist suggested that this defeat was fortunate, as his talents could well have been wasted in Westminster. He was elected a Fellow of the Royal Society in March 1891. He died in London, after a prolonged illness, on 29th March 1894 and was interred in the catacombs of West Norwood Cemetery. On the day of Hannen's funeral, Lord Coleridge said, when sitting in the divorce court, 'If there has been a greater English judge during the seventy-three years of my life than Lord Hannen, it has not been my good fortune to see him or to know him.' He went on to describe Hannen as 'a man of great ability, of remarkable learning, of an intellect strong, capacious, penetrating, powerful, with a singular grasp of facts, and a great power of dealing with them when they were grasped like a master'.

Hannen married in 1847, but Lady Hannen predeceased him in 1872.

COLIN BLACKBURN, PC, BARON BLACKBURN OF KILLEARN (1813–1896)

Blackburn was born on 18th May 1813 in Killearn, Stirlingshire, the son of John and Rebecca Blackburn. He was educated at Eton, and Trinity College, Cambridge. He graduated with a BA in 1835 (and an MA in 1838). He was admitted to Lincoln's Inn in April 1835 and, after moving to Inner Temple, was called to the Bar in November 1838. He was not immediately successful on the Northern Circuit: his obituary in *The Times* commented 'he does not appear at any time to have commanded a large practice'. Nevertheless, his reputation for legal scholarship grew particularly with the publication in 1845 of a text book of the law of sale which remained the standard text in this area for 25 years.[32] He also collaborated in law reporting (on what was the *Ellis & Blackburn Reports* for eight years with a ninth (1858) as the *Ellis, Blackburn & Ellis Reports*).

In 1859 Lord Campbell,[33] a fellow Scot, is said to have informally consulted with Blackburn as to who might be suitable to fill a vacancy for a judge in Queen's Bench. On Blackburn mentioning a few names, Campbell dismissed them, 'I do not think Mr Blackburn, that any of these gentlemen would make so good a judge as yourself'. The subsequent appointment of Blackburn did not meet with universal approval. Campbell's diary records of this issue, 'I have already got into great disgrace by disposing of my judicial patronage on the principle detur digniori'.[34] Much was made of the fact the Blackburn had not yet taken silk, but Campbell defended his appointment, disavowing any friendship or knowledge of the new judge's politics and declaring that he believed him to be 'a sound, good and able lawyer – one of ablest in Westminster Hall'.

When in 1876 Blackburn became one of the first Lords of Appeal in Ordinary in the House of Lords[35] there was apparently no longer any doubt over his promotion or his ability, 'the approval of the profession was as emphatic as its disapproval of his original appointment'. Of his seven years in Queen's Bench his obituarist declared him to have been a learned and capable judge, observing that he 'learnt more from reporting [cases] than others do from practice'. *The Spectator* obituary for Lord Chief Justice Cockburn alludes to Blackburn's presence in court alongside him, 'In Banc [Cockburn] had the good or bad fortune to sit for years side by side with the greatest living master of the Common Law' – high praise for the authority that Blackburn had attained.

Blackburn retired from his position of Law Lord in December 1861. Other honours he had received were a knighthood in April 1860 and being

Appendix II

made an Honorary Bencher of the Inner Temple in April 1877. He died at home at Doonholm in Ayrshire on 8th January 1896. He never married.

His obituary did not mention his role in *Banks v Goodfellow*, but highlighted two cases described below both of which were Victorian *causes célèbres*.

With Sir John Mellor, Blackburn presided in Manchester at the trial of the Manchester Martyrs in 1867, a contentious trial carried out in a volatile atmosphere, which resulted in guilty verdicts and the execution of three of the principals. Almost 2,000 troops together with armed police were used to guard the courtroom. Blackburn pronounced the death sentences on three members of the Irish Republican Brotherhood for the murder of Police Sergeant Brett.

In 1868 Blackburn played a part in the legal aftermath of the 1865 Morant Bay Rebellion in Jamaica. This began when, on 11th October, several hundred black Jamaicans protested against poverty, injustice and lack of representation. Matters escalated and the Governor, Edward John Eyre,[36] suppressed the rebellion with use of troops. The death toll is known to exceed 400, with many of the dead having committed no offence – the troops shot people indiscriminately. A further 350 people were arrested and executed without trial. An additional 600 men and women were flogged or received prison sentences. Many more were made homeless after the deliberate burning of houses. George William Gordon, a businessman, magistrate and politician of mixed race, was, despite not being at Morant Bay, tried under martial law and executed.[37] This matter understandably became a *cause célèbre* in England and Jamaica, with pressure for Eyre and Brigadier Nelson to be put on trial. The matter came before Blackburn, who held that relevant statutes were applicable and that Eyre could be indicted, but the grand jury refused the bill against Eyre. Eyre never was prosecuted for his actions in Jamaica.

A small sample of Blackburn's cases that are of continuing legal interest includes:

- *Tweddle v Atkinson*,[38] which until reform in 1999 remained the standard case on privity of contract;
- *Smith v Hughes*[39] on mistake and contract and the principle of *caveat emptor*;[40]
- *Rylands v Fletcher*,[41] a seminal judgment in the tort of nuisance;
- *Speight v Gaunt*[42] on a trustee's duty of care, which is still cited today;
- *Hughes v Metropolitan Railway Co Ltd*[43] on promissory estoppel.

SIR ALEXANDER JAMES EDMUND COCKBURN QC, 12TH BARONET (1802–1880)

Alexander Cockburn was born on 24th December 1802 in Alţâna in Transylvania, then part of the Habsburg Empire, but today in central Romania. His father, from a Scottish family, was the British Consul to the Hanse towns, based in Hamburg. His mother was Yolande de Vignier, a daughter of the French Viscomte de Vignier. Alexander was one of three children. His two sisters were Louisa Clemence and Yolande Bridget. Cockburn was privately educated both abroad and in England. The overseas education, and perhaps his mother's French origins, led to his facility with foreign languages and his affection for continental Europe. He spoke French excellently and was also well versed in Spanish, German and Italian.

He matriculated at Trinity Hall, Cambridge on 14th September 1822, was made a scholar 24th October 1823 and elected a fellow 26th May 1828. He was elected president of the Cambridge Union for Easter term 1824. He gained a first in civil law and graduated with an LLB (Bachelor of Law) in 1829, winning at least one academic prize along the way. On graduating he was elected a fellow of Trinity Hall, which he remained until 1850. In 1874 he was awarded an honorary DCL (Doctor of Civil Law) by Oxford University.[44]

On 19th November 1825 Cockburn was admitted to the Middle Temple and was called to the Bar in 1829. He became a Bencher in 1841, the same year he took silk, and later became Treasurer of Middle Temple in 1853. After being called, Cockburn joined the Western Circuit and quickly developed a sizeable practice at the Bar, although his London work was much slower to develop.

After the passage of the Great Reform Act 1832,[45] Cockburn collaborated with William Rowe to report the decisions on disputes that had arisen in elections after the reforms. The published collected decisions were reckoned to be 'of great and substantial merit' and helped to further his practice in representing individuals before Parliament in election disputes. At this time parliamentary disputes were not heard in a court of law, but by Parliament itself. His reputation for able parliamentary work soon also included representing railway companies when their Parliamentary Bills for authority for the construction of railway lines were being examined by Parliament. He was appointed Recorder of Southampton (1840–46) and later Recorder of Bristol (1854–56).

Cockburn's practice increased in scope, as did his liking for high profile cases. In 1843 his successful defence of Daniel M'Naghten helped to change the course of criminal law on culpability and partial insanity. In 1846 he successfully defended Lt Henry Hawkey, who was accused of murdering James Seton, the last Englishman killed in a duel in England. In 1852 he unsuccessfully defended John Henry Newman[46] against a charge of libel, but the judgment against Newman is widely considered to be a travesty.

By 1847 his growing interest in politics led Cockburn to stand successfully for Parliament as the Member for Southampton. He remained the MP for this constituency until his appointment to the Bench. As a parliamentary orator he showed great skill – to match his reputation for courtroom oratory. The first occasion on which his parliamentary talent came to national prominence was the defence of Lord John Russell's Liberal Government over the Don Pacifico affair.[47] Cockburn's speech, reckoned at the time one of the finest heard that century, helped to prevent a motion of no confidence in the government being passed. In 1851 the new Prime Minister Lord Aberdeen appointed Cockburn Solicitor-General in his government, with the usual knighthood that accompanied the post. The following year Cockburn was appointed to the office of Attorney-General, an office he held, with a minor interruption, until he was appointed to the Bench.

One of the functions of the Attorney-General was to lead for the Crown in court in all poisoning cases.[48] In 1856 Cockburn led the prosecution of William Palmer (also known as the Rugeley Poisoner). Cockburn's forceful and effective cross-examination of the defence witnesses was a major factor in Palmer's conviction. Palmer, a keen race-goer (but poor backer of horses), credited Cockburn's skill in court with his conviction; using a turf expression, he said of it, 'It was the riding that did it'.

In 1856 Cockburn was appointed as Chief Justice of the Court of Common Pleas. In 1859 he was appointed Chief Justice of Queen's Bench and in 1875 the first Lord Chief Justice of England – a position he still held at his death. In 1857 he was appointed to the Privy Council and later, in March 1876, he was given the freedom of the City of London.

It was said of Cockburn that he used his position as Chief Justice to ensure that he sat in the high-profile cases and as a consequence he was much in the public eye (and press reports).

Cockburn died on 28th November 1880 at his house at 40 Hertford Street, Mayfair.[49] He was buried in his family vault at Kensal Green, London. All courts adjourned for the day of his funeral, and many members of the Bench and Bar attended.

Although he inherited his family's baronetcy in 1858 at first glance it looks unusual that, with his career and social and political connections, further honours were not awarded, apart from his knighthood on becoming Attorney-General. Several Prime Ministers had considered him for a peerage and he accepted an offer in 1864. The proposed peerage was refused by the Queen, 'this peerage has been more than once previously refused upon the ground of the notoriously bad moral character of the Chief Justice' based on his well-known reputation as a womaniser.

In personal appearance Sir Alexander Cockburn was of small stature, but with a large head. He had a dignified appearance and carried himself so well that to most he did not appear small. A colleague, and later a Lord Chief Justice, Lord Russell of Killowen, wrote of his 'voice of great beauty'[50] and, on his death, *The Spectator* wrote of his manner and voice being 'as near perfection as such things can well be'. He was fond of yachting and in his last years kept his yacht *Zouave* at Ryde on the Isle of Wight. He was also fond of field sports and was engaged in writing a series of articles on the history of the Chase in the nineteenth century at the time of his death.

He delighted in London society, and was described as being throughout his life, away from court, addicted to frivolities 'not altogether consistent with advancement in a learned profession, or with the positions of dignity which he successively occupied'.[51] He was a *bon viveur* with a wide circle of friends and a fondness for food, society and concerts. He was described as 'A man of the widest culture and of excellent literary taste'.[52] Cockburn was said to be an admirable raconteur and host (and, unlike many supposed raconteurs, a good listener). No doubt this side of his character helped in establishing his close friendship with Charles Dickens. At the farewell dinner at Freemasons Hall in London for Dickens, before he left for America in November 1865, Cockburn and Lord Lytton escorted Dickens in to the dinner.

The Times obituary refers to Cockburn 'distinguished courtesy (which he maintained to the last upon the Bench, even when wearied to the utmost by the persistency of an advocate)'. One has the sense of a man of ability who had great faith, perhaps even a degree of arrogance, in his own abilities. He was also at home in his chosen environments of university, the Bar, the Bench and Parliament, as well as London society.

There seems little doubt that Cockburn was one of the most effective advocates of his time, both for and against a cause. A contemporary drew attention to his 'great synthetical and analytical power'[53] in his presentation of a case and he was also noted for his fluency and persuasiveness (no bad skills for counsel to develop). He was particularly able in his retention and marshalling of facts – something that carried through to his career on the Bench with his marathon summing up in the Tichborne claimant case, *R v Castro*.[54]

Of his reputation as a judge there are conflicting views. Lord Westbury said of him that he was a first-rate judge only because he sat so often in

Appendix II

Queen's Bench alongside Blackburn.[55] On the other hand, and making due allowance for a tendency towards *de mortuis nil nisi bonum*, he had the respect of his contemporaries and was praised as an effective lawyer in his obituaries. He was, with some justification, proud of his written style.

Counsel

Counsel for Edward Barron Goodfellow

SIR JOHN HOLKER QC (1828–1882)[56]

John Holker was the son of Samuel Holker, a manufacturer of Bury, and his wife Sarah. He born at Bury in 1828 and educated at Bury Grammar School. At first destined for holy orders, he was instead articled to a solicitor in Kirkby Lonsdale, Westmoreland. In 1851 he was entered as a student at Gray's Inn and was called to the Bar there in 1854. He became a bencher in 1868, and in 1875 Treasurer of his Inn.

After being called, Holker spent a short time in London before he joined the Northern Circuit and settled in Manchester. His practice did not prosper quickly and this might not have been helped by becoming known, from his appearance, as Sleepy Jack Holker. He was, all his life, a 'tall, plain, lumbering Lancashire man, who never seemed to labour a case nor to distinguish himself by ingenuity or eloquence, but through whom the justice of his cause appeared to shine as through a somewhat dull but altogether honest medium'. Perhaps this was an aspect of his presentation that helped to sway the jury in *Banks v Goodfellow* with his appeal to common sense. Another description applied to him was his 'faculty of quietly but unerringly weaving a coil around the malefactors with whom he has to do'. The two descriptions give a picture of an effective barrister, but one not given to flashy court performances. After ten years of growing a miscellaneous practice, Holker attracted praise for his success before a parliamentary committee considering the Stalybridge and Ashton Waterworks Bill, when he was left alone to deal with matters by no less than three different leaders. He returned to London in 1864 and took silk in 1866 and at once stepped into a leading position on his circuit. Thereafter, patent cases took up a large part of his practice. In 1872 the Tichborne claimant case involved many of the best-known leaders at the Bar of the time. Holker, however, was not instructed in that case, and the unavailability of other seniors who were involved created an opening for him to significantly further his reputation. Persuasiveness, shrewdness, and tact were characteristics said to have made him extraordinarily successful in winning verdicts.

In 1872 he successfully stood as a Conservative at the Preston by-election. This was one of the first elections in England which used a secret ballot (as required by the Ballot Act 1872). He represented this constituency until his death. He was appointed Solicitor-General by Disraeli in 1874, and received the customary knighthood that went with this office. In November 1875, Holker became Attorney-General.[57] In that role he appeared for the Treasury in the second inquest into the death of Charles Bravo in 1876.[58] In the same year he also successfully led for the Crown in the prosecution of Henry Wainwright for the murder of his mistress Harriet Lane.[59] His practice at the Bar had by now prospered greatly and it is said that his income during two consecutive years was £22,000pa – an exceptional income for that time. In the House of Commons he had proved to be a successful law-officer.

While on the Italian Riviera at San Remo (for health reasons) in January 1882, he was appointed by Gladstone as a Lord Justice of Appeal. He sat in that court for only a few months – although long enough to make some mark – before being compelled to resign by reason of failing health on 19th May. He had said, when he accepted, that with his appointment Gladstone had 'done something to smooth the pillow of a dying man'. He died at his home in Devonshire Street, Portland Place, on 24th May, and was buried on 30th May in his mother's grave at Lytham, Lancashire. *The Times* ascribed his death to a degeneration of the kidneys, although he had also suffered for some time from a weakness of the heart.

He was married, first, to Jane, daughter of James Wilson of Eccles, Lancashire, and, secondly, in 1874, to Mary Lucia, daughter of Patrick McHugh of Cheetham Hill, Manchester, but he left no issue from either marriage. In his will he left his estate to his widow, but added a non-binding wish that, when she died, she should bequeath what was left of the estate to Gray's Inn. On her death, her will specified that Gray's Inn should hold the estate upon trust and apply the income of the trust for the purpose of awards to be called The Lord Justice Holker awards (these are still available to students today).

Counsel for John Banks the younger

JOHN BRIDGE ASPINALL QC[60] (1818–1886)

John Aspinall was born in 1818, the son of the Reverend James Aspinall MA, rector of Althorpe, and grandson of Mr JB Aspinall (who was mayor of Liverpool in 1813). Aspinall was educated at Rugby and, instead of going up

Appendix II

to university, he spent time travelling in Europe before being admitted to Middle Temple on 6th January 1838. He was called to the Bar on 19th November 1841 and thereafter joined the Northern Circuit. He made progress with his practice, principally as a criminal lawyer, and was appointed Recorder of Liverpool in 1861.[61] In July 1864 Aspinall took silk and in the autumn of the same year became a Bencher of the Middle Temple. Later he was appointed the Autumn Reader in Middle Temple in 1868, and then elected Treasurer for 1877/88. In 1872 he was appointed Attorney-General of the County Palatine of Durham. In 1880 he was appointed a commissioner for the commission set up to enquire into corrupt election practices in Great Britain.

In 1843 Aspinall married Bertha Wyatt in Liverpool. In 1847 he became a member of the Roman Catholic Church. In politics, he was a staunch Whig (Liberal) throughout his life. Aspinall died at his London residence, 64 Queen's Gardens, after prolonged ill health, on 5th February 1886. He was survived by his widow, three sons and a daughter.

SIR HENRY MANISTY QC (1808–1890)[62]

Manisty was the second son of James Manisty, BD, the vicar of Edlingham, in Northumberland. He was born on 13th December 1808 and educated at Durham Cathedral Grammar School. Afterwards he was articled at Messrs Thorpe & Dickson, attorneys of Alnwick, Northumberland.

Manisty was admitted as a solicitor in 1830, and practised as such for twelve years, as a member of Messrs Meggison, Pringle, & Manisty, of Bedford Row, London. On 20th April 1842 he became a student of Gray's Inn, and he was called to the Bar on 23th April 1846. He became a Bencher there in 1859, and treasurer in 1861.

After being called, Manisty joined the Northern Circuit, where he quickly developed a substantial practice and on 7th July 1857 he took silk. While developing a reputation in mercantile cases, he continued with more routine circuit cases. His entry in the *Dictionary of National Biography*[63] notes that his opinions on points of law were always held in especial esteem, and his obituary in *The Times* wrote that 'he knew much of which more brilliant men were ignorant' and describes him as not illustrious but an excellent craftsman. Somewhat late in his career, after Lord Blackburn left the High Court for the House of Lords, Manisty was made a judge of Queen's Bench,[64] and was knighted on 28th November 1876. He fell ill with paralysis while in court 30th January 1890, and died the following day at his house at 24A Bryanston Square, London. He was buried on 5th February, at Kensal Green cemetery.

Manisty was married twice, first, in August 1831 to Constantia Dickson, the daughter of a Berwick-on-Tweed solicitor. Secondly, following the death of Constantia in August 1836, he married Mary Ann Stevenson, the daughter of a Berwick-on-Tweed surgeon in May 1838. There were four sons and three daughters from the second marriage, and a daughter from the first marriage.

APPENDIX III

The Judgment in Queen's Bench

BANKS
— v —
GOODFELLOW

Court of Queen's Bench

Judgment given on 6th July 1870
(hearings on January 11th and May 13th 1870)

An appeal from a jury trial before Brett J at
Cumberland Spring Assizes 17th and 18th February 1869

The Court:
Cockburn CJ,
Blackburn J
Mellor J
Hannen J

COCKBURN CJ (on behalf of the court):[1]

Introduction and Facts

[1]   This is an action brought by the plaintiff, as heir at law of John Banks, to try the validity of a will made by the latter in favour of one Margaret Goodfellow; of whom, she having died since the decease of the testator, the defendant is the heir. The question in issue at the trial was the capacity of the testator to make a will.

[2] Instructions for the will, taken by the attorney who prepared it, were signed by the testator and attested by witnesses in his presence, on the 2nd of December, 1863; the will, formally prepared from such instructions, was duly executed on the 28th of the same month. The question is, whether on both or either of those days the testator was of sound mind, so as to be capable of making a will.

[3] It is a fact beyond dispute that the testator, John Banks, had at former times been of unsound mind. He had been confined, as far back as the year 1841, in the county lunatic asylum; discharged, after a time, from the asylum, he remained subject to certain fixed delusions. He had conceived a violent aversion towards a man named Featherstone Alexander, and notwithstanding the death of the latter some years ago, he continued to believe that this man still pursued and molested him; and the mere mention of Featherstone Alexander's name was sufficient to throw him into a state of violent excitement. He frequently believed that he was pursued and molested by devils or evil spirits, whom he believed to be visibly present. Besides these delusions, which were spoken to by two witnesses whose evidence was above suspicion, the one a medical man who attended him from 1856 to the end of 1862, the other the clergyman of the parish in which the testator resided, there was a body of evidence which, if believed, was strong to establish a case of general insanity. The jury, however, found in favour of the will, and therefore must have believed this evidence to be greatly exaggerated, or must have come to the conclusion that the will was made during a lucid interval.

[4] From September, 1863, he had a succession of epileptic fits, and a blister was applied to his head, and the medical man who attended him throughout this period, deposed that his mental power, such as it was, suffered from the fits, and that he considered him insane, and incapable of transacting business during the whole time.

[5] On the other hand, it appeared that the testator managed his own money affairs (which, however, were on a limited scale), and was careful of his money. According to the evidence of a witness named Tolson, who had acted as his agent in receiving the rents of some cottage property at Keswick, amounting to about £80 a year, the testator had not only always shewed himself capable of transacting business with him, but had also on the last occasion of Tolson's coming to pay the rents, suggested to him to take a lease of the cottages in question, so as to relieve him (the testator) from all risk or trouble in the matter. He had also desired Tolson, when he came to pay over the next half-year's rents, to bring with him a Mr. Ansell, an attorney of Keswick, as he wanted to see him about making a will. On the 2nd of December, 1863, Tolson went to Arkleby, where the testator lived, taking

Ansell with him. On their arrival, the testator, according to the statement of Ansell and Tolson, told Ansell he wished to make his will. He fetched from his room a will which he had made in 1838, in favour of his sister, who had since died, and said he wished to give all his property to his niece, Margaret Goodfellow, in the same way. On Mr. Ansell asking who should be the executors, the testator turned to his niece, who was present, and asked who she thought should be executors; whereupon she desired that Tolson should be one, and asked who should be the other, when the name of the other executor, Thirlwall, was suggested by a person present, and assented to by the testator. The instructions thus received by Ansell were put down by him on paper, and having been read over to the testator, were, by the desire of Ansell, signed by him, and his signature was formally attested by two witnesses, so as to make the paper a sufficient and valid will, although it was intended that a more formal document should afterwards be prepared and executed; the reason given by Ansell for such signing and attestation of the instructions being, that he always pursued this course when his clients lived at a distance from him, and time would be required between the taking the instructions and the final completion of the will. The distance between Keswick and Arkleby is about twenty miles, and the road was said to be bad.

[6]   After the matter of the will had been disposed of, a conversation took place concerning the proposed lease to Tolson. The testator calculated the amount of the rents, and finding that they came to £80, offered Tolson a lease of the cottages for seven years, at a rent of £76 a year. This being agreed to by Tolson, Ansell was instructed to prepare a lease on these terms; and the instructions, having been reduced to writing, were signed by the testator and Tolson. After this, Tolson proceeded to settle with the testator for the rents received by him, which amounted to £40. 7s. 4d. Of this Tolson produced £29. in cash, and offered his cheque for the remainder, but the testator observed that a cheque would be of no use to him, as there was no bank near, and desired Tolson to pay the balance into a bank at Keswick, at which the testator had an account. After this, a conversation ensued with a Mrs. Routledge, at whose house the testator lodged, as to the amount which he should pay her weekly for his board and lodging combined, which, if truly reported, tended strongly to shew that he was then capable of managing his affairs.

[7]   On the 28th of December Tolson took over the will and lease, which had been prepared by Ansell, to the testator, who, having read them two or three times, said they were all right, after which both instruments were executed by him, and the will was duly attested.

[8] The testator lived till July, 1865. His niece, Margaret Goodfellow, survived him, but died in 1867, under age and unmarried. She was his heir at law. He had other nephews and nieces, to whom he is said to have been attached. The effect of the will, if valid, is, that the property goes to the defendant, who is no relation in blood to the testator, as the heir at law of Margaret Goodfellow, instead of to any relative of the testator. This possible consequence of Margaret Goodfellow dying without issue and intestate, does not, however, appear to have presented itself to the mind of any of the parties at the time of making the will.

[9] Upon this evidence, the learned judge left it to the jury to say, 'whether, on the 2nd of December, 1863, or on the 28th of December, 1863, or on both, the testator was capable of having such a knowledge and appreciation of facts, and was so far master of his intentions, free from delusions, as would enable him to have a will of his own in the disposition of his property, and act upon it;' the learned judge telling the jury that 'the mere fact of his being able to recollect things, or to converse rationally on some subjects, or to manage some business, would not be sufficient to shew he was sane; while, on the other hand, slowness, feebleness, and eccentricities would not be sufficient to shew he was insane'; with the further direction that 'the whole burden of shewing that the testator was fit at the time was on the defendant.' The jury returned a verdict for the defendant, saying that they found that the will 'was a good and valid will.'

Basis of Appeal

[10] The present rule was applied for and obtained on two grounds, first, that the judge misdirected the jury; secondly, that the verdict was against the weight of the evidence. The alleged misdirection is that the learned judge, in leaving to the jury the question whether at the time of making the will the testator was free from delusions, did not proceed to tell them that though the delusions, under which the testator had undoubtedly before laboured, might not have been present to his mind at the time of making the will, yet, if they were latent in his mind, so that, if the subject had been touched upon, the delusions would have recurred, he was of unsound mind and therefore incapable of making a will.

[11] We must take it, for the present purpose, as a fact, that the testator, though generally of weak intellect, was able to manage his own affairs, and, apart from the delusions under which he laboured, was, at all events at the time of executing one or both of the testamentary instruments in question, of sufficient testamentary capacity. We must also take it that no delusion

manifested itself at the time of making the will. On the other hand, there is ample proof that the delusions existed in the interval between the making of the will and the death of the testator, as they had done before; and it is therefore quite possible that these delusions may have remained, at the time of making the will, uncured and latent in the testator's mind, and capable of being evoked and reproduced at any moment, if anything had occurred to lead his thoughts to the subject.

[12]   The inquiry not having been directed to this point, it is quite possible that all that the jury meant in finding in the affirmative of the question whether the testator was 'free from delusions' at the time of making his will, was that the delusions were not present to his consciousness, not that they were eradicated from his mind; and that if the question had been specifically put to them whether the delusions still remained latent in the testator's mind, and his mind was to the extent of these delusions unsound, they would have found in the affirmative.

[13]   It therefore becomes necessary to consider how far such a degree of unsoundness of mind as is involved in the delusions under which this testator laboured would be fatal to testamentary capacity; in other words, whether delusions arising from mental disease, but not calculated to prevent the exercise of the faculties essential to the making of a will, or to interfere with the consideration of the matters which should be weighed and taken into account on such an occasion, and which delusions had in point of fact no influence whatever on the testamentary disposition in question, are sufficient to deprive a testator of testamentary capacity and to invalidate a will.

[14]   We must assume, for the present purpose, that the testator laboured under the insane delusions ascribed to him; but, on the other hand, that these delusions had not, nor were calculated to have, any influence on him in the disposal of his property; and that, irrespective of these delusions, the state of his mental faculties was such as to render him capable of making a will. For, whatever may have been the evidence as to general insanity, the verdict of the jury, which there was ample evidence to support, and in which the learned judge who presided at the trial states that he concurs, establishes that at the time of making the will, irrespectively of the delusions referred to, the testator was sufficiently in possession of his faculties.

Rejection of *Waring v Waring*

[15]   The question whether partial unsoundness, not affecting the general faculties, and not operating on the mind of a testator in regard to the particular testamentary disposition, will be sufficient to deprive a person of

the power of disposing of his property, presents itself here for judicial decision, so far as we are aware, for the first time. It is true that, in the case of *Waring v. Waring*[2], the Judicial Committee of the Privy Council, and, in the more recent case of *Smith v. Tebbitt*[3] Lord Penzance, in the Court of Probate, have laid down a doctrine, according to which any degree of mental unsoundness, however slight, and however unconnected with the testamentary disposition in question, must be held fatal to the capacity of a testator. But in both these cases, as we shall presently shew, the wide doctrine embraced in the judgment was wholly unnecessary to the decision, and we therefore feel ourselves warranted, and indeed bound, to consider the question as one not concluded by authority, and on which we are called upon to form our own judgment. The question is one of equal importance and difficulty, and we have given it our best consideration.

[16] The text-writers throw no light upon the point. They content themselves with stating in general terms that to be capable of making a will a man must be of sound disposing mind and memory, and that persons non compotes cannot make a will; but they are silent as to the degree of mental disturbance which will amount to a want of disposing mind and memory. The cases prior to *Waring v. Waring*, in which the law on the subject of mental unsoundness, as affecting the capacity to make a will, has come into question, are by no means numerous. It may be as well to pass them in review.

[17]   In *Combe's Case*[4] it is said to have been agreed by the judges, 'that sane memory for the making of a will is not always where the party can in some things answer with sense, but he ought to have judgment to discern and to be of perfect memory, otherwise the will is void.' So, again, in the *Marquis of Winchester's Case*[5], 'By the law, it is not sufficient that the testator be of memory, when he makes the will, to answer familiar and usual questions, but he ought to have a disposing memory, so as to be able to make a disposition of his estate with understanding and reason.' In the case of *Greenwood v. Greenwood*[6], an action brought to recover estates under a will, the validity of which was disputed, the principal indication of insanity relied on being a strange aversion on the part of the testator towards his only brother, his heir at law, and a groundless suspicion of the latter having attempted to poison him, Lord Kenyon, in charging the jury, said: 'I take it a mind and memory competent to dispose of property, when it is a little explained, perhaps may stand thus:—having that degree of recollection about him that would enable him to look about the property he had to dispose of, and the persons to whom he wished to dispose of it. If he had a power of summoning up his mind, so as to know what his property was, and who those persons were that then were the objects of his bounty, then he was competent to make his will.'

In other cases, such as the well-known case of *Dew v. Clark*[7], the insane delusion had a direct bearing on the provisions of the will. In such cases, the delusion being once proved, and its connection with the will being manifest, there could be no difficulty in setting aside the will. Cases of this description afford little or no assistance towards the solution of the question before us. Again, other cases occurring prior to the case of *Waring v. Waring*, such as *The Attorney General v. Parnther*[8] and *Cartwright v. Cartwright*[9], had reference to the effect to be given to a lucid interval at the time of making the will, rather than to the degree of mental unsoundness which would constitute testamentary incapacity. The judgment in the latter case is, however, not unworthy of attention. The case was a remarkable one, from the fact that the will had been made by a person actually confined in a lunatic asylum, and who was undoubtedly insane both before and after the making of the will; nevertheless it was upheld. Sir William Wynne, the then Judge of the Prerogative Court of Canterbury, in giving judgment, uses language tending strongly to shew that, in his opinion, the rationality of the act done affords an effectual test of the mental capacity of the party doing it. He says: 'I think the strongest and best proof that can arise as to a lucid interval is that which arises from the act itself: that I look upon as the thing to be first examined, and if it can be proved and established that it is a rational act rationally done, the whole case is proved. What can you do more to establish the act? Because, suppose you are able to shew that the party did that which appears to be a rational act, and it is his own act entirely, nothing is left to presumption in order to prove a lucid interval. Here is a rational act rationally done. In my apprehension, where you are able completely to establish that, the law does not require you to go further, and the citation from Swinburne (Swinburne, part ii s.3) states it to be so. The manner he has laid it down is (it is in the part (2) in which he treats of what persons may make a will): "If a lunatic person, or one that is beside himself at some times, but not continually, make his testament, and it is not known whether the same were made while he was of sound mind and memory or no, then, in case the testament be so conceived as thereby no argument of phrensy or folly can be gathered, it is to be presumed that the same was made during the time of his calm and clear intermissions; and so the testament shall be adjudged good, yea, although it cannot be proved that the testator useth to have any clear and quiet intermissions at all, yet, nevertheless, I suppose that if the testament be wisely and orderly framed, the same ought to be accepted for a lawful testament."' 'Unquestionably,' Sir William Wynne continues, 'there must be a complete and absolute proof the party who had so framed it did it without any assistance. If the fact be so that he has done as rational an act as can be, without any assistance from another person, what there is more to be proved, I don't know, unless the gentlemen could prove by any authority, or law, what the length of the lucid interval is to be, whether an hour, a day, or a month. I know no such law as that. All that is wanting is, that it should be of sufficient length to do the rational act intended. I look upon it, if you are able to establish the fact that the act done is perfectly proper, and that the party who is alleged to have done it was free from the disorder at the time, that is completely sufficient.'

[18] Without going to the length of adopting to its full extent what is here said as to the effect of the rational character of the will, or at all saying that effect can be given to the rationality of the disposition beyond, that which is due to it as evidence of the sanity of the testator, we advert to this case and the judgment of Sir William Wynne as shewing that a more indulgent view of the effect of insanity, as affecting testamentary incapacity, was then taken than has latterly prevailed.

[19] We come now to the case of *Waring v. Waring* (since followed by that of *Smith v. Tebbitt*) in which the doctrine now contended for on behalf of the plaintiff was for the first time laid down. It may be shortly stated thus: To constitute testamentary capacity, soundness of mind is indispensably necessary. But the mind, though it has various faculties, is one and indivisible. If it is disordered in any one of these faculties, if it labours under any delusion arising from such disorder, though its other faculties and functions may remain undisturbed, it cannot be said to be sound. Such a mind is unsound, and testamentary incapacity is the necessary consequence.

[20] As has already been observed, neither in *Waring v. Waring* nor in *Smith v. Tebbitt*, was the doctrine thus laid down in any degree necessary to the decision. Both these were cases of general, not of partial, insanity; in both the delusions were multifarious,—and of the wildest and most irrational character, abundantly indicating that the mind was diseased throughout. In both there was an insane suspicion or dislike of persons who should have been objects of affection; and, what is still more important, in both it was palpable that the delusions must have influenced the testamentary disposition impugned. In both these cases, therefore, there existed ample grounds for setting aside the will without resorting to the doctrine in question. Unable to concur in it, we have felt at liberty to consider for ourselves the principle properly applicable to such a case as the present. We do not think it necessary to consider the position assumed in *Waring v. Waring*, that the mind is one and indivisible, or to discuss the subject as matter of metaphysical or psychological inquiry. It is not given to man to fathom the mystery of the human intelligence, or to ascertain the constitution of our sentient and intellectual being. But whatever may be its essence, everyone must be

conscious that the faculties and functions of the mind are various and distinct, as are the powers and functions of our physical organization. The senses, the instincts, the affections, the passions, the moral qualities, the will, perception, thought, reason, imagination, memory, are so many distinct faculties or functions of the mind. The pathology of mental disease and the experience of insanity in its various forms teach us that while, on the one hand, all the faculties, moral and intellectual, may be involved in one common ruin, as in the case of the raving maniac, in other instances one or more only of these faculties or functions may be disordered, while the rest are left unimpaired and undisturbed;—that while the mind may be overpowered by delusions which utterly demoralize it and unfit it for the perception of the true nature of surrounding things, or for the discharge of the common obligations of life, there often are, on the other hand, delusions, which, though the offspring of mental disease and so far constituting insanity, yet leave the individual in all other respects rational, and capable of transacting the ordinary affairs and fulfilling the duties and obligations incidental to the various relations of life. No doubt when delusions exist which have no foundation in reality,—and spring only from a diseased and morbid condition of the mind, to that extent the mind must necessarily be taken to be unsound; just as the body, if any of its parts or functions is affected by local disease, may be said to be unsound, though all its other members may be healthy, and their powers or functions unimpaired. But the question still remains, whether such partial unsoundness of the mind, if it leaves the affections, the moral sense, and the general power of the understanding unaffected, and is wholly unconnected with the testamentary disposition, should have the effect of taking away the testamentary capacity. [21] We readily concede that where a delusion has had, as in the case of *Dew v. Clark*, or is calculated to have had, an influence on the testamentary disposition, it must be held to be fatal to its validity. Thus if, as occurs in a common form of monomania, a man is under a delusion that he is the object of persecution or attack, and makes a will in which he excludes a child for whom he ought to have provided; though he may not have adverted to that child as one of his supposed enemies, it would be but reasonable to infer that the insane condition had influenced him in the disposal of his property. But, in the case we are dealing with, the delusion must be taken neither to have had any influence on the provisions of the will, nor to have been capable of having any; and the question is, whether a delusion, thus wholly innocuous in its results as regards the disposition of the will, is to be held to have the effect of destroying the capacity to make one.

Consideration of the Foreign Law

[22] The state of our own authorities being such as we have shown, we have turned, to the jurisprudence of other countries, as on a matter of common juridical interest, to see whether we could there find any assistance towards the solution of the question. We have, however, derived but little advantage from the inquiry. The Roman law, the great storehouse of juridical science, is as vague and general on the subject as our own. The madman (*furiosus*), and the person of defective intelligence (*mente captus*), are declared incapable of making a testament; but as to what shall constitute madness or defectiveness of intelligence, sufficient to prevent the exercise of the testamentary right, the authorities are silent. The continental codes are equally general in their terms, simply providing, either that persons must be of sound mind to make a will, or that persons of unsound mind shall be disabled from doing so. The older writers appear not to have been alive to the distinction between total and partial unsoundness as affecting testamentary capacity. In recent times, however, the question has been mooted by eminent and distinguished jurists, but unfortunately with a marked discordance of opinion. M. Troplong, in his well-known work, '*Le Droit Civil Explique*' (Commentaire sur le donations entre vifs et testaments, tom. ii 451–7), and M. Sacase, in a treatise entitled '*La Folie considered dans ses rapports avec la Capacité*' p.16, have adopted the doctrine of the unity and indivisibility of the mind, and the consequent unsoundness of the whole if insane delusion anywhere exist. Writers equally entitled to respect have maintained the contrary view. Legrand du Saulle, in a very able work, entitled '*La Folie devant les tribunaux*' p.146 contends that 'hallucinations are not a sufficient obstacle to the power of making a will, if they have exercised no influence on the conduct of the testator, have not altered his natural affections, or prevented the fulfilment of his social and domestic duties; while, on the other hand, the will of a person affected by insane delusion ought not to be admitted if he has disinherited his family without cause, or looked on his relations as enemies, or accused them of seeking to poison him, or the like. In all such cases, where the delusion exercises a fatal influence on the acts of the person affected, the condition of the testamentary power fails: the will of the party is no longer under the guidance of reason, it becomes the creature of the insane delusion' M. Demolombe, in his great work, the '*Cours de Code Napoleon*' (Traité des donations entre vifs et testaments Liv. iii tit. 2 ch. ii), M. Castlenau, in his treatise, '*Sur l'Interdiction des Alienes*,' and Hoffbauer, in his remarkable work on Medical Jurisprudence relating to Insanity, have maintained the doctrine that monomania, or partial

insanity, not affecting the testamentary disposition, does not take away the testamentary capacity. Mazzoni, in a recent work, entitled '*Istituzioni di diritto civile Italiano*' (Liv. iii tit. 2, s 3), lays it down that 'monomania is not an unsoundness of mind which absolutely and necessarily takes away testamentary capacity, as the monomaniac may have the perfect exercise of his faculties in respect of all subjects beyond the sphere of the partial derangement.'

[23] None of these writers, however, have gone very deeply into the subject, or considered it with reference to the principles on which mental alienation should be held to form a ground for taking away testamentary capacity. The older jurists were content to say that an insane person was incapable of making a testament, because he has no mind, '*quia mente caret*,' as it is said in the Institutes (Instit. Lib. II. Tit. 12, 1); or because he could not have a will, and therefore was incapable of declaring his ultimate will as to the disposal of his property—positions obviously unsatisfactory when the fact becomes recognized that a man may labour under harmless delusions, which leave the other faculties of his mind unaffected, and leave him free to make a disposition of his property uninfluenced by their existence. In our day the doctrine has sprung up of the unity and indivisibility of the mind, but the ground on which insanity should cause incapacity appears to have been overlooked in the reasoning on which it is founded. It is important to recall it.

[24] The law of every civilized people concedes to the owner of property the right of determining by his last will, either in whole or in part, to whom the effects which he leaves behind him shall pass. Yet it is clear that, though the law leaves to the owner of property absolute freedom in this ultimate disposal of that of which he is thus enabled to dispose, a moral responsibility of no ordinary importance attaches to the exercise of the right thus given. The instincts and affections of mankind, in the vast majority of instances, will lead men to make provision for those who are the nearest to them in kindred and who in life have been the objects of their affection. Independently of any law, a man on the point of leaving the world would naturally distribute among his children or nearest relatives the property which he possessed. The same motives will influence him in the exercise of the right *of* disposal when secured to him by law. Hence arises a reasonable and well warranted expectation on the part of a man's kindred surviving him, that on his death his effects shall become theirs, instead of being given to strangers. To disappoint the expectation thus created and to disregard the claims of kindred to the inheritance is to shock the common sentiments of mankind,

and to violate what all men concur in deeming an obligation of the moral law. It cannot be supposed that, in giving the power of testamentary disposition, the law has been framed in disregard of these considerations. On the contrary, had they stood alone, it is probable that the power of testamentary disposition would have been withheld, and that the distribution of property after the owner's death would have been uniformly regulated by the law itself. But there are other considerations which turn the scale in favour of the testamentary power. Among those, who, as a man's nearest relatives, would be entitled to share the fortune he leaves behind him, some may be better provided for than others; some may be more deserving than others; some from age, or sex, or physical infirmity, may stand in greater need of assistance. Friendship and tried attachment, or faithful service, may have claims that ought not to be disregarded. In the power of rewarding dutiful and meritorious conduct, paternal authority finds a useful auxiliary; age secures the respect and attentions which are one of its chief consolations. As was truly said by Chancellor Kent, in *Van Alst v Hunter*[10], 'It is one of the painful consequences of extreme old age that it ceases to excite interest, and is apt to be left solitary and neglected. The control which the law still gives to a man over the disposal of his property is one of the most efficient means which he has in protracted life to command the attentions due to his infirmities.' For these reasons the power of disposing of property in anticipation of death has ever been regarded as one of the most valuable of the rights incidental to property, while there can be no doubt that it operates as a useful incentive to industry in the acquisition of wealth, and to thrift and frugality in the enjoyment of it. The law of every country has therefore conceded to the owner of property the right of disposing by will either of the whole, or, at all events, of a portion, of that which he possesses. The Roman law, and that of the Continental nations which have followed it, have secured to the relations of a deceased person in the ascending and descending line a fixed portion of the inheritance. The English law leaves everything to the unfettered discretion of the testator, on the assumption that, though in some instances, caprice, or passion, or the power of new ties, or artful contrivance, or sinister influence, may lead to the neglect of claims that ought to be attended to, yet, the instincts, affections, and common sentiments of mankind may be safely trusted to secure, on the whole, a better disposition of the property of the dead, and one more accurately adjusted to the requirements of each particular case, than could be obtained through a distribution prescribed by the stereotyped and inflexible rules of a general law.

The Test Set Out

[25] It is unnecessary to consider whether the principle of the foreign law or that of our own is the wiser. It is obvious, in either case, that to the due exercise of a power thus involving moral responsibility, the possession of the intellectual and moral faculties common to our nature should be insisted on as an indispensable condition. *It is essential to the exercise of such a power that a testator shall understand the nature of the act and its effects; shall understand the extent of the property of which he is disposing; shall be able to comprehend and appreciate the claims to which he ought to give effect; and, with a view to the latter object, that no disorder of the mind shall poison his affections, pervert his sense of right, or prevent the exercise of his natural faculties—that no insane delusion shall influence his will in disposing of his property and bring about a disposal of it which, if the mind had been sound, would not have been made.*[11]

Reconsideration of Basic Principles

[26] Here, then, we have the measure of the degree of mental power which should be insisted on. If the human instincts and affections, or the moral sense, become perverted by mental disease; if insane suspicion, or aversion, take the place of natural affection; if reason and judgment are lost, and the mind, becomes a prey to insane delusions calculated to interfere with and disturb its functions, and to lead to a testamentary disposition, due only to their baneful influence—in such a case it is obvious that the condition of the testamentary power fails, and that a will made under such circumstances ought not to stand. But what if the mind, though possessing sufficient power, undisturbed by frenzy or delusion, to take into account all the considerations necessary to the proper making of a will, should be subject to some delusion, but such delusion neither exercises nor is calculated to exercise any influence on the particular disposition, and a rational and proper will is the result; ought we, in such case, to deny to the testator the capacity to dispose of his property by will?

[27] It must be borne in mind that the absolute and uncontrolled power of testamentary disposition conceded by the law is founded on the assumption that a rational will is a better disposition than any that can be made by the law itself. If therefore, though mental disease may exist, it presents itself in such a degree and form as not to interfere with the capacity to make a rational disposal of property, why, it may be asked, should it be held to take away the right? It cannot be the object of the legislator to aggravate an affliction in itself so great by the deprivation of a right the value of which is universally felt and acknowledged. If it be conceded, as we think it must be, that the only

legitimate or rational ground for denying testamentary capacity to persons of unsound mind is the inability to take into account and give due effect to the considerations which ought to be present to the mind of a testator in making his will, and to influence his decision as to the disposal of his property, it follows that a degree or form of unsoundness which neither disturbs the exercise of the faculties necessary for such an act, nor is capable of influencing the result, ought not to take away the power of making a will, or place a person so circumstanced in a less advantageous position than others with regard to this right.

[28] It may be here not unimportant to advert to the law relating to unsoundness of mind arising from another cause—namely, from want of intelligence occasioned by defective organization, or by supervening physical infirmity or the decay of advancing age, as distinguished from mental derangement, such defect of intelligence being equally a cause of incapacity. In these cases it is admitted on all hands that though the mental power may be reduced below the ordinary standard, yet if there be sufficient intelligence to understand and appreciate the testamentary act in its different bearings, the power to make a will remains. It is enough if, to use the words of Sir Edward Williams, in his work on Executors, 'the mental faculties retain sufficient strength fully to comprehend the testamentary act about to be done.' (Williams on executors 6th ed. Vol.1 p37, n.x) '*Non sani tantum,*' says Voet in his Commentary on the Pandects (Lib. 28, tit. I, s.36), founding himself on the language of the Code, Book 6, tit. 23,1.15, '*sed et in agone mortis positi, seminece ac balbutiente lingua voluntatem prornentes, recte testamenta condunt, si modo mente adhuc valeant.*'

US Decisions on Sound and Disposing Mind

[29] This part of the law has been extremely well treated in more than one case in the American Courts.

[30] In the case of *Harrison v. Rowan*[12], in the United States Circuit Court for the district of New Jersey, the law was thus laid down by the presiding judge: 'As to the testator's capacity, he must, in the language of the law, have a sound and disposing mind and memory. In other words, he ought to be capable of making his will with an understanding of the nature of the business in which he is engaged, a recollection of the property he means to dispose of, of the persons who are the objects of his bounty, and the manner in which it is to be distributed between them. It is not necessary that he should view his will with the eye of a lawyer, and comprehend its provisions in their legal form. It is sufficient if he has such a mind and memory as will enable him to

understand the elements of which it is composed, and the disposition of his property in its simple forms. In deciding upon the capacity of the testator to make his will, it is the soundness of the mind, and not the particular state of the bodily health, that is to be attended to; the latter may be in a state of extreme imbecility, and yet he may possess sufficient understanding to direct how his property shall be disposed of; his capacity may be perfect to dispose of his property by will, and yet very inadequate to the management of other business, as, for instance, to make contracts for the purchase or sale of property. For, most men, at different periods of their lives, have meditated upon the subject of the disposition of their property by will, and when called upon to have their intentions committed to writing, they find much less difficulty in declaring their intentions than they could in comprehending business in some measure new.'

[31]   In the case of *Den v. Vancleve*[13] the law was thus stated: 'By the terms "a sound and disposing mind and memory" it has not been understood that a testator must possess these qualities of the mind in the highest degree; otherwise, very few could make testaments at all; neither has it been understood that he must possess them in as great a degree as he may have formerly done; for even this would disable most men in the decline of life; the mind may have been in some degree debilitated, the memory may have become in some degree enfeebled; and yet there may be enough left clearly to discern and discreetly to judge, of all those things, and all those circumstances, which enter into the nature of a rational, fair, and just testament. But if they have so far failed as that these cannot be discerned and judged of, then he cannot be said "to be of sound and disposing mind and memory".'

[32]   In the subsequent case of *Stevens v. Vancleve*[14] it is said: 'The testator must, in the language of the law, be possessed of sound and disposing mind and memory. He must have memory; a man in whom the faculty is totally extinguished cannot be said to possess understanding to any degree whatever, or for any purpose. But his memory may be very imperfect; it may be greatly impaired by age or disease; he may not be able at all times to recollect the names, the persons, or the families of those with whom he had been intimately acquainted; may at times ask idle questions, and repeat those which had before been asked and answered, and yet his understanding may be sufficiently sound for many of the ordinary transactions of life. He may not have sufficient strength of memory and vigour of intellect to make and to digest all the parts of a contract, and yet be competent to direct the distribution of his property by will. This is a subject which he may possibly have often thought of, and there is probably no person who has not arranged

such a disposition in his mind before he committed it to writing. The question is not so much what was the degree of memory possessed by the testator? as this: Had he a disposing memory? was he capable of recollecting the property he was about to bequeath; the manner of distributing it; and the objects of his bounty? To sum up the whole in the most simple and intelligible form, were his mind and memory sufficiently sound to enable him to know and to understand the business in which he was engaged at the time he executed his will?'

[33]   This view of the law is fully adopted by the Court in the case of *Sloan v. Maxwell*[15], and is there stated to have been approved by Chancellor Vroom in a case as to the will of Tace Wallace, which, however, is not reported. It appears to have had the sanction of Chancellor Kent, in the case of *Van AM v. Hunter*[16], already referred to.

[34]   In a case of *Harwood v. Bolter*[17], before the Judicial Committee of the Privy Council, in which case a will had been executed by a testator on his deathbed, in favour of a second wife, to the exclusion of the other members of his family, he being in a state of weakened and impaired capacity from disease producing torpor of the brain, and rendering his mind incapable of exertion unless roused, Erskine, J, delivered the judgment of the Court in these terms: (3 Moo PC at 291) 'Their Lordships are of opinion that, in order to constitute a sound disposing mind, a testator must not only be able to understand that he is by his will giving the whole of his property to one object of his regard, but he must also have capacity to comprehend the extent of his property, and the nature of the claims of others, whom by his will he is excluding from all participation in that property; and that the protection of the law is in no cases more needed than it is in those where the mind has been too much enfeebled to comprehend more objects than one; and more especially, when that one object may be so forced upon the attention of the invalid as to shut out all others that might require consideration. And, therefore, the question which their Lordships propose to decide in this case is, not whether Mr. Baker knew, when he executed this will, that he was giving all his property to his wife, and excluding all his other relations from any share in it, but whether he was at that time capable of recollecting who those relations were, of understanding their respective claims upon his regard and bounty, and of deliberately forming an intelligent purpose of excluding them from any share of his property. If he had not the capacity required, the propriety of the disposition made by the will is a matter of no importance. If he had it, the injustice of the exclusion would not affect the validity of the disposition, though the justice or injustice of the disposition might cast down some light upon the question as to his capacity.'

Consideration of a Redefined Test

[35] From this language it is to be inferred that the standard of capacity in cases of impaired mental power is, to use the words of the judgment, the capacity on the part of the testator to comprehend the extent of the property to be disposed of, and the nature of the claims of those he is excluding. Why should not this standard be also applicable to mental unsoundness produced by mental disease?

[36] It may be said that the analogy between the two cases is imperfect; that there is an essential difference between unsoundness of mind arising from congenital defect, or supervening infirmity, and the perversion of thought and feeling produced by mental disease, the latter being far more likely to give rise to an inofficious will than the mere deficiency of mental power. This is, no doubt, true, but it becomes immaterial on the hypothesis that the disorder of the mind has left the faculties, on which the proper exercise of the testamentary power depends, unaffected, and that a rational will, uninfluenced by the mental disorder, has been the result.

[37] It is said, indeed, by those who insist that any degree of unsoundness should suffice to take away testamentary capacity, that where insane delusion has shewn itself, it is always possible, and indeed may be assumed to be probable, that a greater degree of mental unsoundness exists than has actually become manifest. But this view, which is by no means universally admitted, is unsupported by proof, and must be looked upon as matter of speculative opinion. It seems unreasonable to deny testamentary capacity on the speculative possibility of unsoundness which has failed to display itself, and which, if existing in a latent and undiscovered form, would be little likely to have any influence on the disposition of the will. No doubt, where the fact that the testator has been subject to any insane delusion is established, a will should be regarded with great distrust, and every presumption should in the first instance be made against it. Where insane delusion has once been shewn to have existed, it may be difficult to say whether the mental disorder may not possibly have extended beyond the particular form or instance in which it has manifested itself. It may be equally difficult to say how far the delusion may not have influenced the testator in the particular disposal of his property. And the presumption against a will made under such circumstances becomes additionally strong where the will is, to use the term of the civilians, an inofficious one, that is to say, one in which natural affection and the claims of near relationship have been disregarded. But where in the result a jury are satisfied that the delusion has not affected the general faculties of the mind, and can have had no effect upon the will, we see no sufficient reason why the testator should be held to have lost his right to make a will, or why a will

made under such circumstances should not be upheld. Such an inquiry may involve, it is true, considerable difficulty, and require much nicety of discrimination, but we see no reason to think that it is beyond the power of judicial investigation and decision, or may not be disposed of by a jury directed and guided by a judge. In the case before us two delusions disturbed the mind of the testator, the one that he was pursued by spirits, the other that a man long since dead came personally to molest him. Neither of these delusions—the dead man not having been in any way connected with him—had, or could have had any influence upon him in disposing of his property. The will, though in one sense an idle one, inasmuch as the object of his bounty was his heir at law, and therefore would have taken the property without its being devised to her, was yet rational in this, that it was made in favour of a niece, who lived with him, and who was the object of his affection and regard. And we must take it on the finding of the jury that irrespectively of the question of these dormant delusions, the testator was in possession of his faculties when the will was executed.

[38] Under these circumstances, we see no ground for holding the will to be invalid. If, indeed, it had been possible to connect the dispositions of the will with the delusions of the testator, the form in which the case was left to the jury might have been open to exception. It may be, as was contended on the part of the plaintiff, that in a case of unsoundness, founded on delusion, but which delusion was not manifested at the time of making the will, it is a question for the jury whether the delusion was not latent in the mind of the testator. But, then, for the reasons we have given in the course of this judgment, we are of opinion that a jury should be told, in such a case, that the existence of a delusion, compatible with the retention of the general powers and faculties of the mind, will not be sufficient to overthrow the will, unless it were such as was calculated to influence the testator in making it.

[39] This, in effect, disposes of the question of misdirection. As, for the reasons we have given, we are of opinion that if the testator was, at the time of making the will, of capacity to make a will as defined by the learned judge, the existence of mental disease, if latent, so as to leave him free from the consciousness and influence of delusion, there having been a total absence of all connection between the delusion and the will, would not overthrow the will, it follows that there can have been, practically speaking, no misdirection in not leaving the question of latent delusion to the jury. Where delusions are of such a nature as is calculated to influence the testator in making the particular disposition, as was the case in *Waring v. Waring*[18], and in *Smith v. Tebbitt*[19], a jury would not in general be justified in coming to the conclusion that the delusion, still existing, was latent at the time, so as to leave the

testator free from any influence arising from it; but in the present case the disposition was quite unconnected with the delusions, and consequently there is no reason to suppose that the omission to call the attention of the jury to this specifically can have affected the verdict.

[40]   Looking to the evidence given on the trial, and to the verdict of the jury, it appears to us that if this case were submitted to another jury, whatever they might find as to the existence of latent delusion, their decision must be in favour of the will as to the absence of all connection between the delusions and the disposition made by the testator. It would, consequently, be worse than useless to put the parties to the expense of a new trial, when in our judgment the only proper or possible result must be a second verdict establishing the will.

Counsel and attorneys:
Manisty Q.C, Aspinall Q.C. and Kemplay, for the plaintiff.
Holker, Q.C. and O. Button, for the defendant
Attorney for plaintiff: J.G. Waugh.
Attorneys for defendant: Nethersole & Speechley.

Endnotes

Introduction

1   The opening line of *The Go Between* (published 1953).

Chapter One

1   Jacob Banks is referred to as Jacob Banks the elder in order to differentiate him from the eldest son of his first marriage, Jacob Banks the younger.
2   John Banks, the main subject of the book, is referred to as John Banks the elder in order to differentiate him from his half-nephew John Banks the younger, the challenger to John Banks the elder's will.
3   *Jollie's Guide* of 1811, quoted in 'The Characters and Events that Shaped Keswick's Pencil Industry' by Dr Roger Asquith in the February 2011 issue of *The Journal of Lorton & Derwent Fells Local History Society*.
4   *Carlisle Journal*, 14th March 1847.
5   The will contained the following bequest:

> I give and devise unto my said son John Banks and his Heirs all that my freehold Messuage and Tenement consisting of two dwelling houses situate in the main street of Keswick aforesaid with the several dwelling houses or cottages Shops Warehouses Outbuildings and the piece or parcel of Ground immediately behind and adjoining the same now in the occupation of Joseph Banks Mary Fisher Edward Wilson Hugh McClain(?) John Williamson Joseph Wright and Henry Stoddart as Tenants and all other the Hereditaments and premises Which I lately purchased of John Ashburner To hold the same with all and every the Rights Members (?) and Appurtenances thereunto belonging unto and to the use of my said Son John Banks and his Heirs and Assigns forever.

Chapter Two

1   The term 'schizoid' was not coined until 1908 (by Eugen Bleuler), but 'psychosis' dates from 1841 (KF Canstatt). However, no medical witnesses at trial applied this term to John – a country doctor at this time would most probably not be familiar with it.

2   The literacy rate for Great Britain in 1870 has been estimated at 76%, and this was up from 52% fifty years previously (https://ourworldindata.org/literacy/ this period covers approximately John's life).

3   These were a copy of his brother-in-law Thomas Goodfellow's will and a covering letter.

4   Edward Highton was shown in the 1871 census as a 'schoolmaster and organist', living at Brigham School. His son, Thomas Edward Highton, was later headmaster at this school from 1880 to 1907. Thomas Edward Highton is also commemorated by a memorial window at St John's Church, Keswick (where he was superintendent of the Sunday school).

5   See https://en.wikipedia.org/wiki/United_Kingdom_Census_1841.

6   This property is described now, on one letting agency's website, as a large period property. A 1787 map by James Clarke (in *A Survey of the Lakes of Cumberland, Westmoreland and Lancashire* published in 1787) shows a property called Shooly Crow in this position on Penrith Road in Keswick.

7   Affidavit of William Robinson a miner, probably of graphite, of Keswick, dated 18th April 1868, National Archives C 16/398.

8   Evidence of Grenip Cartmel, 18th April 1868, National Archives C 16/398.

9   Act to regulate the care and treatment of insane persons within England 1828.

10 Affidavit of Edward Highton, dated 20th April 1868, National Archives C 16/398.

11 Affidavit of William Robinson of Keswick, dated 18th April 1868, National Archives C 16/398.

12 It was in Asylum Lane, which is now Dunston Road, Gateshead. The asylum is long since demolished. It was classed as a 'Licenced House', i.e. premises licensed to receive lunatics by Parliamentary Act.

13 The premises were licensed on 3rd January 1831: *Return of Public and Private Asylums or Houses Licensed for the Reception of Lunatics*, 22nd March 1831 (published by order of the House of Commons, 25th March 1831).

14 There were also private asylums at Wrekenton, Bensham, the Fell and Spittal Tongues in the same locality as Dunston.
15 http://studymore.org.uk/4_09.htm#COMMENDED.
16 Published by Neill & Co, 1847.
17 Metropolitan Report, pp 6–7.
18 Metropolitan Report, p 7.
19 Metropolitan Report, p 88.
20 Metropolitan Report, pp 54–55.
21 Metropolitan Report, p 189.
22 Metropolitan Report, p 54.
23 Metropolitan Report, p 55.
24 Pussin (1746–1811) was a tanner by trade, but after being treated for scrofula at Bicêtre he was employed on the hospital staff.
25 Bicêtre was at various times, sometimes simultaneously, a general hospital, a state prison, a mental hospital and a hospice. It is a hospital today (http://hopital-bicetre.aphp.fr/44-2/). It was the scene of a massacre of prisoners in September 1792, during a counter-revolutionary scare. The Marquis de Sade is probably the most infamous of the inmates of Bicêtre, being sent there by Napoleon in 1803.
26 Pinel (1745–1826) came from a family of doctors and, unlike Pussin, was a qualified medical practitioner.
27 Metropolitan Report, p 54.
28 Hippocrates, a physician of the Greek Classical Age, postulated that there were four bodily fluids (blood, yellow bile, black bile and phlegm) which gave rise to different types of ill humours in a person when one fluid was out of balance with the others. Correcting the ill humour, or illness, could be carried out by removing the excess of the particular fluid, thereby re-balancing the person's natural fluids.
29 In some defence of leeches, it should be added that that their use did continue for genuine reasons, not connected to insanity. The absence of antibiotics until the 1940s meant that treatment for infected tissue could be limited. Leeches were sometimes used to drain and clean the infected areas with beneficial effect. Sir Nigel Gresley (1876–1941) locomotive engineer of the LNER (and designer of the *Mallard*) was treated successfully for an infected wound on his leg in 1910 by the application of leeches to clean the wound. The alternative for him would have been amputation of his leg (Don Hale, *Mallard* (Aurum Press, 2005)).

30 Peter R Henriques *Realistic Visionary: A Portrait of George Washington* (University of Virginia Press, 2006), p 202. Britain had a similar event in 1817 with Princess Charlotte of Wales (daughter of the Prince Regent), who died following complications in childbirth that were quite possibly survivable, but for the medical treatment during pregnancy of an inadequate diet, bleeding, and incompetent medical supervision during and after labour. The child was stillborn and, if these deaths had not changed the succession, Victoria may well not have acceded to the throne (Helen Rappaport, *A Magnificent Obsession* (St Martin's Press, 2011), p 105). Thomas Dormandy in *The White Death* (Hambledon Press, 1999), p 15, gives an extraordinary example told by Colonel George MacDonald of the Coldstream Guards, after Waterloo. He observed an army surgeon, on the battlefield, who carefully attempted to open a vein to let blood from a wounded soldier, while the soldier was bleeding to death from a severed femoral artery.

31 In *The Times* on 23rd September 1856 a letter was published supporting the verdict of the grand jury and regretting that the paper had published its previous editorial. It also objected to the paper having used the expression 'cruel usage' to describe the fatal treatment. The letter also revealed that Mr Snape had tried the shower bath for himself and stood under it for forty-five minutes without harm. It was written by one who had stood bail for Mr Snape.

32 A Quaker retreat opened in 1796 in response to Hannah Mills' death in the York Asylum in 1790. After her death her fellow Quakers, who had been refused admission to see Hannah, discovered that the patients were treated worse than animals.

33 Sarah Wise, *Inconvenient People: Lunacy, Liberty and the Mad-Doctors in Victorian England* (Vintage, 2012) provides a highly disturbing, yet fascinating, account of what was not part of the medical profession's finest hour.

34 Wilkinson was not medically qualified. *The London Gazette* of 31st May 1867 shows the bankruptcy of John Etridge Wilkinson and Mary Marvel (Victuallers and Co-partners) later of Roker, Sunderland. The name might indicate that this was either the former asylum keeper or a son.

35 This would have been a charge paid by whichever local council was responsible for the pauper being incarcerated.

36 The control of the asylum passed to Cornelius Garbutt, who died in November 1865. He was later succeeded by his sons William and

Cornelius. William was also Wilkinson's son-in-law: J Bath and RF Stevenson, *The Gateshead Book of Days* (The History Press, 2013).

37   Gateshead Libraries Collection ref AR000006. *The Gateshead Book of Days* (*op cit*) gives a different version, putting the publication of the Report in 1853. The patient was named Gibson and he was horsewhipped for an alleged attack on Wilkinson, with his teeth later being removed to prevent biting. In April 1852, Wilkinson had indicated that he no longer wanted to take patients from Cumberland and Westmoreland, thereby precipitating the planning for a new asylum for those counties. The date seems to indicate a connection between this and the imminent loss of his licence (http://archaeologydataservice.ac.uk).

38   *Cumberland Pacquet*, 12th January 1858.

39   *The Times*, 20th February 1869.

40   Authored by JC Bucknill and DH Tuke (published 1858).

41   This drug has unpleasant side effects and is now little used. Administration by injection, both intramuscular and intravenous, can have serious side effects, and administration by mouth produces a strong burning taste. In all cases it can produce foul-smelling breath. Chlorpromazine discovered in 1952 proved to be a major breakthrough in treating schizophrenia, and similarly with lithium carbonate's effect as a mood stabiliser for bipolar disorder in 1948. But this was nearly a century after John's death.

42   In the *Seventh Annual Report of the Crichton Royal Institution for Lunatics, Dumfries*, November 1846.

43   Witness statement of Elizabeth Routledge, 14th July 1868, National Archives C 16/398.

44   Bill of Complaint filed 11th November 1867, para 9.

45   Joseph Usher and his wife, Mary, both gave evidence for the plaintiff at the trial. Given that Thomas Goodfellow was also a grocer he may well have helped arrange matters with the Ushers.

46   Superintendent Isaac Bird was a local policeman. According to the 1861 census, he and his wife Margaret lived at Market Hill, Wigton. They had three children aged six or under at this time, but were not deterred by this from accepting John as a lodger – they had other lodgers at the same time.

47   The census entry is for 'Thomas Banks', aged 48, born in 1813 in Keswick, and he is again shown as a 'proprietor of houses'. The Christian

name given must be an error, given the other details. Residence at Bassenthwaite also matches the reported evidence of Mrs Bird at the trial.

48 'Gilfort Cottage' in the 1861 census is believed to be an error. The property was built c1847. An 1860 conveyance shows the sale to William Thirlwall of 'a dwellinghouse, shop and premises complete with the shelves, pigeon cotes, counters, beams, nails, cupboards and other fixtures in and about the said shop' (information from the current owner of the property). William Thirlwall was the brother-in-law of James Routledge and was also an executor of John Banks' will.

49 In the nineteenth century 'idiot' was used in relation to a person with severe intellectual disability, while 'lunatic' was an older term for one who is mentally ill (derived the Latin *luna* and the belief that changes in the moon could trigger madness).

50 The Poor Law Amendment Act 1834 created a system of boards of guardians within a parish or groups of parishes. They were elected by those individuals – property owners – who were required to pay the poor rate. They were responsible for the local administration of relief of the poor.

51 1844 Welsh Report, p 59. Ashley, *Hansard*, 23rd July 1844.

52 http://historyofwages.blogspot.co.uk/2011/02/agricultural-labourers-wages-1850-1914.html.

53 Rates were a property tax in Britain, probably originating out of the Poor Law Act 1601, which introduced a rate or levy for relief of the poor within a parish. Each property was ascribed a value for this purpose and the rate was effectively a percentage of that value assessed annually. It was the forerunner of the current Council Tax introduced in 1993.

54 Harriet Martineau, *A Complete Guide to the English Lakes* (Whittaker and Co, 1855).

55 See https://en.wikipedia.org/wiki/Souther_Fell or https://esmeraldamac.wordpress.com/2011/01/19/the-ghostly-procession-at-souther-fell/.

56 The *Paisley Herald and Renfrewshire Advertiser*, 27th February 1869 (the same report had appeared in the *Glasgow Daily Herald* on 20th February 1869). These were presumably syndicated reports and look to be taken from a longer report in the *Cumberland Pacquet* on 23rd February 1869.

57 The *Cumberland Pacquet*, 23rd February 1869.

58 *The Times*, 20th February 1869.

Endnotes

59 This was when Dr Jones first arrived in Aspatria as assistant to a Dr Elliot. Dr Elliot retired at Christmas 1863, after which Dr Jones was the sole practitioner until taking a partner in February 1868.

60 Affidavit of William Jones, dated 6th April 1868, National Archives C 16/398.

61 From the website of the Foundation for Brain Injury Explanation (www.braininjury-explanation.com/causes-disorders/brain-injury-by-stroke/left-sided-hemiparesis).

62 The word 'schizophrenia' was not coined until 1908, by the Swiss PE Bleuler. It was previously known as *dementia paecox*, a term introduced by BE Morel in France in 1852 but given a definition in 1893 by Emil Kraepelin.

63 According to the NHS website: 'Someone who develops psychosis will have their own unique set of symptoms and experiences, according to their particular circumstances. However, four main symptoms are associated with a psychotic episode. They are: hallucinations; delusions; confused and disturbed thoughts; lack of insight and self-awareness' (www.nhs.uk/Conditions/Psychosis/Pages/Symptoms.aspx).

64 The middle name Bird is unusual and probably shows a connection with the police superintendent, Isaac Bird, or his wife, Margaret, who gave evidence against the will. Isaac Bird was from Arkleby and is buried, together with his wife, in Plumbland churchyard.

65 Crosthwaite Parish Register 1865, entry 996.

66 Crosthwaite Parish Register 1847, p 282, entry 2255.

Chapter Three

1 As required by the original Wills Act 1837, s IX. At the time of writing, the Law Commission is undertaking a review of some aspects of this Act.

2 This Act came into force on 1st January 1838 and, although it has since been amended in part, it is still in force and is the basis of the modern law of wills. That it is still in force to today (with minor amendments) is a tribute to the quality and clarity of the original drafting.

3 At this time 'attorney' referred to a lawyer who practised in the common law jurisdiction, while 'solicitors' were lawyers practising within the equity jurisdiction. The Supreme Court of Judicature Act 1873 merged the courts of equity and the common law and, as part of this, s 7 abolished the use of the designation 'attorney' and replaced it with 'solicitor'.

4   Affidavit of Joseph Tolson, dated 25th January 1868, National Archives C 16/398.
5   This property was built c1847. It was purchased by William Thirlwall in 1860, who was therefore his sister's landlord (information from the current owner).
6   These figures are for current daylight at Carlisle for this time of year (www.timebie.com/sun/carlisleuk.php). At this time there was no daylight-saving adjustment to the clocks in winter, and it would therefore have been darker in the evening one hour later than it would be today and conversely lighter one hour later in the morning.
7   The Lake District is probably the wettest part of England (www.metoffice.gov.uk/learning/rain/how-much-does-it-rain-in-the-uk). While first drafting this part of this chapter in December 2015, the Lake District had just suffered record rainfall with significant flooding in Keswick. Honister Pass leading into Borrowdale established a UK rainfall record in the twenty-four hours up to 5th December 2015, during which 13.4 inches (341.4mm) was recorded.
8   *Banks v Goodfellow* (1870) LR 5 QB 549 at 553.
9   On a modern map Keswick to Arkleby via Bassenthwaite (A591/A595) is sixteen miles. Travelling up the western side of Bassenthwaite Lake by A66 then going east to join the A591/A595 route is nineteen miles. Going via Cockermouth on the A66/A595 is about twenty-one and a half miles. These distances are based on modern road plan which can be very different to that of the mid-nineteenth century. That the court worked on the basis of basis miles might imply that the Cockermouth route would be a better, but longer route, with possibly less gradient.
10 Tarmac as we know it today was an invention of Edgar Pooley in 1902.
11 National Archives C16/398.
12 This style of writing was still used in the nineteenth century for transcribing wills at the Probate Registry (*Jowett's Dictionary of English Law*, volume 1, 3rd edition (Sweet & Maxwell, 2010), p 807).
13 The risk of a testator's death between giving instructions and execution of a will has long been recognised. However, it was not until the House of Lords' judgment in *White v Jones* [1995] 1 All ER 691 that a solicitor could be found liable for losses caused to prospective legatees when death occurred before the will was executed and where the delay in preparation was found to be excessive (Martyn Frost, Penelope Reed QC and Mark Baxter, *Risk and Negligence in Wills Estates and Trusts*, 2nd edition (OUP, 2014)). In being conscious of the difficulties caused by death

before the will was executed, Ansell was being conscientious, although at that time no liability would attach to him for any delay.
14 *Carlisle Patriot*, 19th February 1869.
15 *Burgess v Hawes* [2012] WTLR 423; *Re Ashkettle, Ashkettle v Gwinnett* [2013] WTLR 1331.
16 Scarman J in *Re Fuld (No 3)* [1968] P 675.
17 If not a doctor as well, although the so-called 'Golden Rule' of Templeman J in *Re Simpson* (1977) 121 Sol Jo 224 requiring the presence of a medical practitioner is now considered not to be a rule, but instead guidance as to good practice.

Although *Banks v Goodfellow* predates *Parker v Felgate* (1883) LR 8 PD 171, the principle in that decision could have saved the second will even if John Banks lacked capacity at the time of executing it, as long as he understood that he was executing a will that he had earlier given valid instructions for: see *Perrins v Holland* [2010] EWCA Civ 840 for a review of the earlier authorities on which *Parker v Felgate* was based.
18 A niece of the whole blood is a child of a person who is a full brother or sister (siblings 'of the whole blood') of the deceased, as opposed to being of the half-blood if the niece was a child of a half-brother or half-sister ('siblings of the half-blood'). The descriptions 'full blood' and 'half-blood' are still used today to describe such relationships when dealing with inheritance on intestacy (Administration of Estates Act 1925, s 46).
19 *Banks v Goodfellow* (1870) LR 5 QB 549 at 554.
20 *Jarman on Wills*, 8th edition (Sweet & Maxwell, 1986), p 439:

> The doctrine [of lapse] applies indiscriminately to gifts with and gifts without words of limitation. Thus, if a devise be made to A and his heirs or to A and the heirs of his body and A die in the lifetime of the testator, the devise absolutely lapses and the heir, special or general (as the case may be) of A takes no interest in the property, he being included merely in the words of limitation, i.e. in the terms which are used to denote the quantity or duration of the estate to be taken by the devisee, through whom alone any interest can flow to such heir.

21 The modern approach is that the making and the revocation of a will both require the same level of mental capacity: *Re Sabatini* (1970) 114 SJ 35; i.e. the test established in *Banks v Goodfellow* (1870) LR 5 QB 549 applies to both. However, this point does not appear to have been specifically considered by a court before 1970.

22 Evidence for the plaintiff of Mary Thwaite, John Banks' landlady in Bassenthwaite, quoted in *Cumberland Pacquet*, 23rd February 1869. She also said that on other occasions he mentioned going to a foreign country to escape the spirits.

Chapter Four

1 Stapleton is about sixteen miles north east of Carlisle.
2 Presumably, just below the bridge that today carries St Aidan's Road over the Eden.
3 The taxation of tea, the East India Company's monopoly on the importation of tea to Britain, the large-scale smuggling of tea and the consequences of these factors for the American colonies is a complex story that ended with the loss of those colonies.
4 And native Indian tea shrubs were also discovered shortly afterwards in Assam.
5 1864, when the Aerated Bread Company began to serve tea with its food (www.britainexpress.com/History/tea-in-britain.htm).
6 *Cutty Sark* is probably the best remembered of this type of vessel.
7 Complicated in this case by an epileptic fit.
8 In *Northanger Abbey*, Jane Austen even poked fun at the literary convention of heroines having mothers who died in childbirth. The book opens:

> No one who had ever seen Catherine Morland in her infancy would have supposed her born to be an heroine. Her situation in life, the character of her father and mother her own person and disposition, were all equally against her. Her father was a clergyman, without being neglected, or poor and a very respectable man ... Her mother was a woman of useful plain sense, with a good temper, and, what is more remarkable, with a good constitution. She had three sons before Catherine was born; and instead of dying in bringing the latter into the world, as anybody might expect, she still lived on – lived to have six more children – to see them growing up around her, and to enjoy excellent health herself.

Clearly, Jane Austen thought that death in childbirth was already becoming rather over-used.

9 The frequency that Dickens alone used orphanhood in his plots is astonishing (e.g. *David Copperfield, Edwin Drood, Great Expectations, Our Mutual Friend, Oliver Twist, Nicholas Nickleby, The Old Curiosity Shop*).

10 See further details at www.workhouses.org.uk/Drouet/.
11 Geoffrey Chamberlain, 'British Maternal Mortality in 19th and early 20th Centuries', in *Journal of the Royal Society of Medicine*, November 2006.
12 Geoffrey Chamberlain, 'British Maternal Mortality in 19th and early 20th Centuries', in *Journal of the Royal Society of Medicine*, November 2006.
13 From the introduction to Irvine Loudon, *The Tragedy of Childbed Fever* (OUP, 2000).
14 With obstetric haemorrhage the second most common cause and toxaemia/eclampsia the third.
15 Irvine Loudon, *The Tragedy of Childbed Fever* (OUP, 2000), p 6.
16 The use of chloroform was developed in England by Professor James Young Simpson. Chloroform was administered to Queen Victoria by Dr John Snow. Snow's later career in medicine was remarkable, particularly his work with establishing the cause of cholera (see Sandra Hempel, *The Strange Case of the Broad Street Pump* (University of California Press, 2007)).
17 Prince Leopold, Duke of Albany (1853–84) was Queen Victoria's eighth son. She was a carrier of the gene responsible for haemophilia in male issue. Albany was the only male child of hers to suffer from haemophilia. Leopold died from uncontrolled bleeding after a fall. His posthumous child, Charles, who was not a haemophiliac, inherited his maternal uncle's title of Duke of Saxe-Coburg Gotha in 1900 and rose to the rank of general in the German Army in the First World War. After the Armistice he lost his British titles and his German Dukedom. He was later a supporter of Hitler and an Obergruppenführer in the SA, and died in poverty in 1954.
18 The association of this surgical intervention with Julius Caesar, or his ancestors, goes back to Roman times, but the tradition that it relates to Julius Caesar is almost certainly false. The name of his presumed son by Cleopatra, is usually given as Caesarion (a nickname meaning Little Caesar) and this has no connection with the Caesarean procedure.
19 https://en.wikipedia.org/wiki/Caesarean_section#History.
20 Although I have referred to a doctor, it is possible that Margaret was attended by a local midwife for some stages of the birth, but given Margaret's pre- and post-natal illnesses she would have also been attended by a doctor.
21 KC Carter and BR Carter, *Childbed Fever: A Scientific Biography of Ignaz Semmelweiss* (Transaction Publishers, 2005).

22 Justus von Liebig developed and marketed Liebig's Soluble Food for Babies. Humanity owes him additional debt, as his discovery that yeast could be concentrated is claimed to have paved the way for Marmite.

23 His name appears as such in a notice regarding by-laws in the *Cumberland Pacquet*, 8th November 1853.

24 The Temperance movement was relatively new in England having started in the early part of the nineteenth century. It was often identified with the non-conformist religious groups.

25 The date of death was published as 8th April – a printer's error.

26 This middle name is interesting, as the rent collector for John Banks, and executor of his will, was Joseph Tolson. He was described in the Probate as a grocer and a cousin of Thomas. Also, John Goodfellow's death later was registered by Daniel Tolson of Ulscar Above Derwent.

27 His death certificate shows the cause of death as being from rheumatic fever with 'numerous abscesses'. The cause of death is certified as preceding death for three weeks. As abscesses are not today recognised as a symptom of rheumatic fever, if rheumatic fever was indeed the correct diagnosis, there will have been some other cause of the abscesses. Today, rheumatic fever is rarely a cause of death in the developed world, but this is largely due to the treatment of it with antibiotics – an unknown treatment in 1865.

28 Dedicated to St Kentigern (known as St Mungo in Scotland), the churchyard is notable for the grave of Robert Southey (1774–1843), a long time Keswick resident, who was one of the Lake Poets and Poet Laureate (1813–43). Thomas Goodfellow's grave is only a few steps away from Southey's grave. This church was the parish church for Keswick until 1838 when St John's was completed.

29 See Chapter Five on the witnesses at the trial, where evidence was given by a Murray relative.

30 In 1848 in Bristol. In *Keswick and Its Neighbourhood – A Handbook* (1852) at p 13, Mr (sic) Dallow is described as a minister of the Plymouth Brethren. Their services were held at the High Street Chapel in Keswick ('a neat little building'). Services were 'well attended' and there was a Sunday School.

31 Later the founder of the Keswick Convention in 1875, which is still held annually in Keswick for evangelical Christian groups.

32 Letter of 29th January 1850 (www.biblicalstudies.org.uk/pdf/cbrfj/14_11.pdf).

Endnotes

33 John was buried in Crosthwaite churchyard (see Crosthwaite Parish Register, 1865, p 122, entry 975) on 24th March 1865, but the location of his burial is not known.

34 Edward Barron died September 1860, and his executrix was Frances. It appears that his wife had died in 1853 or 1859. Frances was most likely the sole heir. Although Edward was described as the assistant overseer for Keswick, he was by trade a flour merchant. The overseers of the poor were responsible for administering relief for the poor under the Poor Law. Their position was unpaid and therefore the appointees were usually men of at least modest wealth.

35 John Stuart Mill (1806–1873) was a philosopher, political economist, MP, reformer and liberal. This is from his essay *The Subjection of Women* from 1869.

36 Henry Hunt MP had lodged a petition calling for votes for women in 1832, but this pre-dated the founding of the Women's Suffrage Committee.

37 Representation of the People (Equal Franchise) Act 1928.

38 For example, rape within marriage could not be prosecuted as a crime in England until after R v R [1991] UKHL 12; statutory reform followed in the Criminal Justice and Public Order Act 1994 and the Sexual Offences Act 2003. Imprisonment of a wife by her husband was found to be unlawful in R v Jackson [1891] 1 QB 671, CA, in which there was *obiter* to the effect that a husband's right to beat his wife, if it ever had existed, no longer did so.

39 Elizabeth Garrett Anderson (1836–1917) was the first female doctor to qualify in England, in 1865. The first women barristers were called to the bar in 1922. The Women's Police Service was founded in 1914. There were signs of change in 1869 as women telegraphists were employed by the General Post Office thus becoming the first female civil servants. There were women schoolteachers, but only for as long as they remained unmarried.

40 National Archives C 16/344/G98.

41 Adrian Gallop, *Mortality Improvements and Evolution of Life Expectancies*: (UK Government Actuaries Department, January 2006).

42 Plumbland Parish Register, entry 670.

43 There is, however, a prominent marker just inside the churchyard gate to Superintendent Isaac Bird and his wife Margaret. John was their lodger for a time and they both gave evidence for the plaintiff against the will.

44 Probably by train from Aspatria station (1.3 miles from Arkleby) as it would have been too far to walk from Arkleby to Carlisle.
45 First identified by Robert Koch in 1882 – he received the Nobel Prize for physiology (medicine) in 1905 for this discovery.
46 A graphic portrayal of which is presented in Ken Russell's film of DH Lawrence's *Women in Love* with the death of the mine owner Thomas Crich.
47 Today, the World Health Organisation estimates that 66% of those with latent tuberculosis (TB) who do not seek treatment will die eventually from the disease. It is estimated that today one-third of the world's population are infected with TB, albeit most commonly latent TB (www.healthline.com/health/ pulmonary-tuberculosis#Overview1).
48 Katherine Byrne, *Tuberculosis and the Victorian Literary Imagination* (CUP, 2013).
49 Thomas Dormandy, *The White Death* (The Hambledon Press, 1999), p 22.
50 Prior to this and as far back as Aristotle, the accepted view was that it was infectious.
51 The brutal effect of consumption on a family can be illustrated by the Brontë siblings (their birth dates make them near-contemporaries of John Banks and his sister):

- Maria (23/4/1814 to 6/5/1825) consumption, aged eleven.
- Elizabeth (?/1815 to 15/6/1825) consumption, aged ten.
- Charlotte (21/4/1816 to 31/3/1855) consumption, possibly aggravated by typhoid fever, shortly before her thirty-ninth birthday.
- Patrick Branwell (26/6/1817 to 24/9/1848) consumption, delirium tremens, addiction to opium(?), aged thirty-one.
- Emily Jane (30/7/1818 to 19/12/1848) consumption, aged thirty.
- Anne 17/1/1820 to 28/5/1849) consumption, aged twenty-nine.

Haworth was a dreadfully unhealthy place in the mid-nineteenth century with cholera and typhoid epidemics brought on by appallingly insanitary conditions. In 1838 the average age at death in Haworth was 19.6 years.

52 Thomas Dormandy, *The White Death* (The Hambledon Press, 1999), chapter 2.

Chapter Five

1. A not uncommon reaction to unexpected devolution in a will even today (or where a husband leaves all of his estate to his second wife to the exclusion of the first wife and/or his children by the first marriage).

2. John Romilly, 1st Baron Romilly PC QC (1802–74), MP for Bridport (1832–35 and 1846–47) and later Devonport (1847–52); he was Solicitor-General and then Attorney-General before his appointment to the Bench. He was Master of the Rolls 1851–73.

3. *Jowett's Dictionary of English Law*, 3rd edition (Sweet & Maxwell, 2010).

4. The Court of Appeal was not created until 1875, following the reforms of the Judicature Acts.

5. *Simon v Byford* [2013] WTLR 1615, ChD and [2014] WTLR 1097, CA.

6. Queen's Counsel (QC) (KC, King's Counsel, in the reign of a King); the name 'silk' is taken from the silk gown worn by a QC in court. Silks are more senior, and more distinguished members, of the Bar. Appointment as QC is by individual application, and from the applications an independent panel selects annually those to be appointed. Since 1995 solicitors who have gained rights of audience in higher courts can also put their names forward for consideration of an appointment.

7. Brett J had no civil business to hear in Appleby, only two cases of theft, one relating to linen sheets (not guilty) and the other a silver watch (four months in prison with hard labour for the pickpocket); three hours' business in total.

8. Presumably, this was by the Eden Valley Railway to Penrith and then on the Lancaster & Carlisle Railway to Carlisle. The current Appleby station, on the Settle–Carlisle line, was not opened to passengers until 1876. Appleby is now a small market town, near to Penrith, that is famous for its annual horse fair.

9. The Office of High Sheriff for an English county is thought to be the oldest surviving secular office of the Crown. Mr Ewart and his fellow High Sheriffs for the other counties for 1869, had attended Queen Victoria at Osborne House, Isle of Wight, on 4th February 1869: *The London Gazette*, 5th February 1869.

10. A hammercloth is a cloth, usually ornamented and fringed that covers the coach box or driver's position.

11. 'Drab' is not used in a pejorative sense, but to describe a colour, most likely a light brown.

12 *Cumberland and Westmoreland Advertiser and Penrith Literary Chronicle*, 23rd February 1869.
13 *Cumberland and Westmoreland Advertiser and Penrith Literary Chronicle*, 23rd February 1869.
14 The Cathedral Church of the Holy and Undivided Trinity – the second smallest cathedral in England (after Christ Church Cathedral in Oxford).
15 Matthew 6: 19.
16 In theory, a man could bring such an action for a woman's breach of promise, but this was rare.
17 Charles Dickens, *The Posthumous Papers of the Pickwick Club* (1836); Gilbert & Sullivan, *Trial by Jury* (1875): both works that launched their creators' careers.
18 *Maidstone Telegraph*, 20th February 1869.
19 Offences against the Person Act 1860, s 60:

> If any woman shall be delivered of a child, every person who shall, by any secret disposition of the dead body of the said child, whether such child died before, at, or after its birth, endeavour to conceal the birth thereof, shall be guilty of a misdemeanour, and being convicted thereof shall be liable, at the discretion of the court, to be imprisoned for any term not exceeding two years, with or without hard labour.

20 Garlands Hospital (the Cumberland and Westmorland Asylum) had been opened seven years earlier in Carlisle.
21 *Dew v Clark and Clark* (1826) 162 ER 410, (1826) 5 Add 79 was a will made as a result of the testator's insane delusion about his daughter. The court held that where the element of partial insanity directly affected the terms of the will it would find against the will, no matter how rational the testator's mind might be on all other issues.
22 As we do not know where John lodged between March 1854 and August 1859, he could have gone to Bassenthwaite at any time during this period. However, as Gibson took up his post in 1855, the period during which he had dealings with John would have been fairly short, and it is therefore more likely that it refers to when he started lodging with Isaac Thwaites in Bassenthwaite in October 1860.
23 The story of throwing the inkwell at the Devil is now thought to be apocryphal, although it has been widely told. However, Luther's belief that he was visited by the Devil and evil spirits throughout his life is more widely credited.

Endnotes

24 Women did not serve on court juries in England and Wales at this time.
25 Forster and Short of Scotch Street, Carlisle were wholesale grocers, tea dealers and tallow chandlers. Their business was established in Botchergate in 1858 by Richard Forster and Thomas Short. In 1872 the firm moved to Scotch Street (www.carlislehistory.co.uk). Being a grocer in Carlisle, which is where Thomas Goodfellow was before moving to Keswick, makes one wonder if Thomas Short knew Thomas and his family.
26 *Constable v Tufnell* (1833) 4 Hag Ecc 465; *Hastilow v Stobie* (1865) 1 P & D 64.
27 As originally enacted, s 9 reads as follows:

> And be it further enacted, That no Will shall be valid unless it shall be in Writing and executed in manner herein-after mentioned; (that is to say), it shall be signed at the Foot or End thereof by the Testator, or by some other Person in his Presence and by his Direction; and such Signature shall be made or acknowledged by the Testator in the Presence of Two or more Witnesses present at the same Time, and such Witnesses shall attest and shall subscribe the Will in the Presence of the Testator, but no Form of Attestation shall be necessary.

For the current text of s 9, see www.legislation.gov.uk/ukpga/Will4and1Vict/7/26/section/9.

28 There is no affidavit from this witness in the trial papers in the National Archives, and his remark is taken from the press report.
29 There are no affidavits from these witnesses in the trial papers in the National Archives.
30 Brett J was probably thinking of *The Attorney-General v Parnther* 3 Bro CC 441, where a will was made by a patient confined in a lunatic asylum; see later in this chapter on Cockburn's judgment and the *Parnther* case.
31 This is based on an extract from Brett J's directions that is taken from the headnote to the case report, (1870) LR 5 QB 549, although most of it also appears in the main text of the judgment. In part it is augmented by the press report of the summing-up from the *Cumberland Pacquet* of 23rd February 1869.
32 The Juries Act 1870 permitted food and drink for a jury at their own expense.

33 Presided over by Sir Alexander Cockburn CJ, with Blackburn, Mellor and Hannen JJ; see Appendix II at the end of this work for biographical notes on these distinguished judges.

34 Supreme Court of Judicature Act 1873; the title Queen's Bench was probably retained for the new Division of the High Court because it had the greater preponderance of work by the time of the merger. In 1882 the Court of Queen's Bench was moved to the new Royal Courts of Justice. At the time of this appeal, the Court was located in Westminster Hall, part of the Palace of Westminster.

35 Now a Lord Justice of Appeal.

36 *Kostic v Chaplin* [2007] EWHC 2298 (Ch) at [200]; the Court of Appeal also called it 'a decision which has stood the test of time' in *Sharp v Adam* [2006] EWCA Civ 449 at [66].

37 *Banks v Goodfellow* (1870) LR 5 QB 549 at 563.

38 (1848) 6 Moo PC 341, [1848] EngR 693, heard by the Privy Council as an appeal from the decision of the Church of England's Prerogative Court of Canterbury; see also *Smith v Tebbitt* (1867) LR 1 P & D 437, which followed the *Waring* judgment.

39 Henry Peter Brougham, 1st Baron Brougham and Vaux (1778–1868) was a Scottish lawyer, noted early in his career for his defence of Queen Caroline in the Prince Regent's attempt to divorce her. A noted Whig and opponent of slavery, he was Lord Chancellor (1830–34) and later, as a Privy Councillor, heard cases referred to it.

40 [1848] EngR 693 at 715.

41 Lord Brougham observed ([1848] Eng R 693 at 718) of this word that it was used:

> on the supposition of its being confined, which it rarely is, to a single faculty, or exercise of the mind; a person shall be of sound mind, to all appearance, upon all subjects save one or two; and on those he shall be subject to delusions, mistaking for realities suggestions of the imagination.

42 [1848] Eng R 693 at 719.

43 [1848] Eng R 693 at 720.

44 *Rex v Teal* (1809) 11 East 307.

45 Sir JP Wilde, 1st Baron Penzance (1816–99) QC PC, lawyer and rose grower, was appointed a Baron of the Court of Exchequer. Later he presided over the Court of Probate and Divorce (1863–72). In 1875 he

was appointed Dean of Arches (who presides over the Court of the Archbishop of Canterbury).

46 *Combe's Case* (1604) Moore KB 759; *Marquis of Winchester's Case* (1598) 6 Co Rep 23a; *Greenwood v Greenwood* (1790) 3 Curt App 30; *Dew v Clark* (1826) 3 Add 79; *Attorney-General v Parnther* (1792) 3 Bro CC 441; *Cartwright v Cartwright* (1793) 1 Phill Ecc 90.

47 While the wording is exactly that of the judgment, I have laid it out in a different manner to simplify understanding of it. The manner in which later courts have applied this test is not part of the subject of this book. For those who might be interested, a more detailed commentary on the court's application of the test can be found in Martyn Frost, Stephen Lawson and Robin Jacoby, *Testamentary Capacity: Law Practice and Medicine* (OUP, 2015).

48 This term was coined by the German physician Johann Christian Bell in 1808. The forerunner of the Royal College of Psychiatrists was founded in 1841 (Royal Charter 1926).

49 It has recently been augmented by the decision of Briggs J (as he then was) in *Re Key, Key v Key* [2010] WTLR 623 with regard to decision-making capabilities.

50 Then a Lord Justice of Appeal (retired in 1982).

51 (1800) 27 St Tr 1282. Sir William Follett (1792–1845).

52 He also successfully represented Louisa Nottidge, in *Nottidge v Ripley* (1849), who had been abducted, falsely certified insane and confined in an asylum – matters arising out her connection to the activities of the Reverend Henry Prince and the Somerset religious community of Agapemone (Abode of Love). At the trial Baron Pollock said in his summing-up:

> It is my opinion that you ought to liberate every person who is not dangerous to himself or others. If the notion got abroad that any person may be confined in a lunatic asylum or a madhouse who has absurd or even mad opinion upon any religious subject, and is safe and harmless upon every other topic, I altogether and entirely differ with such an opinion; and I desire to impress that opinion with as much force as I can in the hearing of one of the Commissioners.

53 In the newly opened Broadmoor Asylum.

Chapter Six

1. Samuel Ladyman's *Thoughts and Recollections of Keswick during Sixty Years* (privately published Keswick, 1885) lists Jacob Banks senior and junior both as pencil manufacturers 'sixty years ago', i.e. c1825.
2. *Pigot's Directory of Cumberland* (1834) shows Jacob Banks (the younger) as a pencil manufacturer at that time.
3. National Archives C 16/398.
4. The National Portrait Gallery has a portrait of Francis William Newman (1805–97), younger brother of Cardinal John Henry Newman (1801–90), that is signed 'J Banks Ambleside'. The portrait, in the view of the Gallery, appears to have been drawn from a photograph. It is possible, but only on a very speculative basis, that this could be the work of John Banks the younger.
5. There is nothing particularly unusual in this as it was a time of considerable emigration from Europe to North America.
6. Evidence for the plaintiff of Mary Thwaite, John Banks' landlady in Bassenthwaite, quoted in the *Cumberland Pacquet*, 23rd February 1869.
7. And charged during this period with 20/- per week annuities to his three sisters.
8. This is the Californian company that owned the Central Pacific Railroad, which was the western part of the first Transcontinental Railroad in the USA. It linked up to the eastern portion of the railroad, the Union Pacific Railroad, at Promontory Point Utah on 10th May 1869 (approximately six years after the Central Pacific was started). The CPR ceased independent operation by a *de facto* merger with the Southern Pacific Railroad in 1885. The shares remained in issue until 1959, as the Southern Pacific technically only leased the track from the existing shareholders until then.

Chapter Seven

1. The age of majority was reduced to eighteen by Family Law Reform Act 1969, s 1.
2. Edward Goodfellow was nineteen and therefore still a minor; his affidavits in the court case were sworn by this aunt.
3. Built in 1866, the hotel still exists (see www.lakedistricthotels.net/borrowdalehotel/index.php).

Endnotes

4   Benjamin, his wife and son are buried in Borrowdale (see http://cumbriafamilycom.ipage.com/peoplepages/armstrong.htm).
5   This condition was first described by Johannes Fabry in 1898 in Germany and by William Anderson in England and is also known as *angiokeratoma corporis diffusum*.
6   Benjamin was described as the postboy at the hotel in the census.
7   As cited in ES Turner, *Roads to Ruin: The Shocking History of Social Reform* (Michael Joseph, 1950).
8   Her mother was the Duke of Wellington's sister, and because this was a voidable marriage the Duke of Wellington was resolutely opposed to it.
9   In addition to the male heir the marriage also produced six daughters.
10 1 Moo PC 397.
11 See Leonard Shelford, *A Practical Treatise of the Law of Marriage and Divorce* (John S Little, 1841), p 154.
12 Marriage Act 1835, s 2.
13 Two of the Pre-Raphaelite painters, William Holman Hunt and John Collier, solved the problem in this way.
14 William Bell, *A Dictionary and Digest of the Law of Scotland* (John Anderson, 1838), pp 629–30.
15 'The usual punishment for incest is the performance of public penance on a Sunday, during divine service' (Leonard Shelford, *A Practical Treatise of the Law of Marriage and Divorce* (John S Little, 1841), p 154).
16 *Jowitt's Dictionary of English Law*, 3rd edition (Sweet & Maxwell, 2010); incest became a matter for the criminal law after the Punishment of Incest Act 1908.
17 The Act took effect on 1st September 1835.
18 The Preamble to the Act refers to the purpose of the Act being to make such marriages 'ipso facto void and not merely voidable'.
19 Mrs Colin Mackenzie, *May A Man Marry His Deceased Wife's Sister* (Hatchards, 1880), p 5.
20 John Stuart Blackie (1809–95) a Scottish scholar and intellectual, and Professor of Greek at Edinburgh University at the time he made this comment.
21 Bill of Rights 1689 and Act of Settlement 1701; it also ignored the House of Stuart whose claim to the English throne was by descent from Henry VII not Henry VIII. It also ignored the awkward point that Henry's affair

with Mary Boleyn, before his marriage to Anne, placed marriage to Anne in breach of the rules of affinity also.

22 *Iolanthe* opened in London in November 1882; the quotation is from the Queen of the Fairies' curse on the House of Lords at the end of Act I ('Every bill and every measure that may gratify his pleasure …').

23 From an address to a meeting of Scottish Churchmen in Edinburgh on 28th November 1882 by Lord Forbes.

24 Quoted in Simon Bradley, *The Railways* (Profile Books, 2015).

25 ES Turner, *Roads to Ruin: The Shocking History of Social Reform* (Michael Joseph, 1950).

26 Marriage to a divorced wife's sister had to wait until 1960. In the House of Lords in 1949, Lord Mancroft, a Conservative peer, spoke for this reform and dealt with the temptation to murder a wife in order to marry a sister (*Hansard*, Marriage Enabling Bill, Second Reading, HL Deb, 24th March 1949, vol 161, c 693):

> I can hardly believe that such an argument could have been seriously put forward, but nevertheless it was. I have carried out exhaustive inquiries and I can find no example in this country of such a murder. Admittedly, I have found one case which occurred in America fifteen years ago. A man's wife died in circumstances which later proved to be murder. The man then married his sister-in-law, killed her too, and burned down the house for the insurance money. I hardly think that your Lordships would like to take that as a normal case, even by the possibly more elastic standards which prevail across the Atlantic.

27 By a strange coincidence, Brett J who presided at the trial of John Banks' will in 1869, is recorded as last having contributed to a debate in the House of Lords in July 1898 when the Colonial Marriages (Deceased Wife's Sister) Bill was under consideration. He spoke in favour of the Bill. Cockburn, who heard the appeal in this case, had spoken in the Commons (before he resigned his seat on being appointed to the Bench) in favour of reform.

28 The Deceased Brother's Widow's Marriage Act did not follow until 1921.

29 Although ecclesiastical marriages licences originate in the fourteenth century, they were provided for as a matter of statute law by Lord Hardwicke's Marriage Act 1753, which required either the reading of banns or a licence for a legally valid marriage.

30 Marriage Act 1836, s 6:

> ... that he or she believeth that there is not any impediment of kindred or alliance, or other lawful hindrance to the said marriage ...

31 Marriage Act 1836, s 19:

> That every person who shall wilfully make a false oath or declaration, or who shall knowingly sign any false Certificate required by this Act, for the purpose of procuring any Marriage, shall be deemed guilty of perjury and punished accordingly.

32 Currently, Perjury Act 1911, s 3 provides for the same maximum of seven years' imprisonment on conviction for making a false declaration knowingly and wilfully to procure a marriage.

33 Steerage was the cheapest and most basic passenger accommodation on nineteenth- and early twentieth-century ships. It takes its name from the steering equipment which traditionally ran through this part of the ship.

34 Later designated RMS *Doric* (not to be confused with the White Star liner of the same name launched in 1922). There were sister ships, the *Coptic* and the *Ionic*. The three sister ships were the first steel ships built by Harland & Wolff.

35 Later the owners of RMS *Titanic*.

36 The SS *Doric* was withdrawn from service in 1906 and later sold to the Pacific Mail Steamship Company, which changed the name to *Asia*. The ship was wrecked at Finger Rock on the China Coast in 1911.

37 The *New Zealand Times*, 10th December 1887, carried a report that the Shaw, Savill & Albion Line calendar for 1888, supplied to contacts in New Zealand:

> has two pretty scenes depicted, one being of the great London docks with the s.s. Arawa and several of her sister ships alongside. The other is a view of the s.s. Doric arriving in harbor at sunset.

38 *Evening Post* (New Zealand), 21st December 1887.

39 'Produce – Butter: Prices remain unaltered. Very heavy shipments will be made per Doric and Kakoura, for London, early next month, both of which vessels have cool chambers': the Auction and Produce Report in the *Taranaki Herald*, 17th December 1887.

The *Wairarapa Daily* for 27th December 1887 carried a report of increased production of cheese and of a proposed shipment of five tons via the *Doric* given the profit made on the previous season's shipment. In London, 6d per lb. could be obtained against 4½d locally; despite the shipping costs, the margin was sufficient for a worthwhile profit:

> ... the colonial companies are beginning to regard with much hope the export market and there is no doubt that ... a large and profitable trade will be done.

40 Various goods were advertised as having arrived on the *Doric*. Examples are: two cases of guns and one bale of fishing lines; a small shipment of best English apples containing Russets, Blenheim Oranges, Wellingtons and King Pippins; 'fresh' frozen salmon; haberdashery; and rabbit-proof fencing (for the Hurundi Rabbit Board).

41 The first transatlantic cable was laid in 1866, by the SS *Great Eastern*. Later, Bombay (Mumbai) was linked to England by cable. Australia was linked to Bombay, via Singapore, in 1872 and New Zealand was joined to this in 1876. The network of undersea cables was actively encouraged by the British Government in order to promote the governance and trade of the Empire.

42 *Otago Daily Times*, 22nd December 1887 – Portobello is only 1.5 miles across the bay from Port Chalmers.

43 *McAndrew's Hymn*, notes by Alastair Wilson (www.kiplingsociety.co.uk/rg_mcandrew1.htm). This poem was started in 1893 and published in 1894. The poem, in the form of a dramatic monologue, is related by the old marine engineer standing watch at night musing on his life, his engines and the hand of God.

   Kipling left Cape Town on the *Doric* on 25th September 1891 and arrived in New Zealand on 18th October. After travelling in New Zealand, he later went on to Samoa to visit Robert Louis Stevenson.

44 In 1885 it was still possible for the so-called Independent State of the Congo to be the personal fief of King Leopold II of Belgium. His personal ownership of the country and all that was in it produced a regime that was one of the utmost cruelty. International pressure brought his personal rule to an end in 1908. The death toll of his rule is horrific and some estimates of the deaths are as high as 20% of the population.

45 Although the Suez Canal had opened in 1869, the ships on the New Zealand route were slow to use this route (https://teara.govt.nz/en/the-voyage-out/page-6).

Endnotes

46 Adjacent to Victoria Dock, the Royal Albert was closed for shipping in the 1980s. It is now the site of London City Airport and Gallions Reach Marina.
47 'We are indebted to Mr W.L. Walters, who, with his accustomed courtesy, had the report ready for the press representatives', *The Press*, 23rd December 1887. While this practice assisted reporters, it would also have been good PR for the shipping line (although the term 'PR' (public relations) was not used then).
48 A French island (Ouessant) approximately 30 miles north-west of Brest that is a key feature of the Channel Approaches.
49 A promontory on the coast south of Dunedin.
50 In 1883 when the *Doric* started on this route the advertised passage was 45 days.
51 Lyttleton owes its development to having the natural harbour which Christchurch, 12 miles away, lacks.
52 In 1850 a transatlantic immigrant passage was ten days and cost £4. For New Zealand the voyage took between seventy-five and one hundred and twenty days and cost £15 (www.teara.govt.nz/en/the-voyage-out/page-1); the advent of steamers reduced this time to around fifty days, depending upon the weather.
53 According to www.teara.govt.nz/en/the-voyage-out/page-1:

> Reports of the dreadful conditions on board, from those who had made it to the other side of the world, put many people off. In the early 1870s a Wellington immigration officer informed the agent-general in London that
>
>> 'letters written home by immigrants who have been made miserable throughout the passage by causes entirely remediable, do more to retard emigration than all the costly advertisements, peripatetic lecturers, and highly paid agents do to advance it'.

54 Built in 1904 by William Hamilton and Company of Port Glasgow, the *Moshulu* is now a floating-restaurant at Penn's Landing, Philadelphia, USA. The *Moshulu* can be seen in *The Godfather II* as the immigrant ship bringing Vito Corleone to New York.
55 Eric Newby, *The Last Grain Race* (Folio Society, 2001 (originally published in 1956)). Eric Newby was nineteen when he completed this voyage. The *Moshulu* took ninety-one days to reach Queenstown (Cobh) Ireland from

Australia and was the winner of the last race of the square-riggers to get the first of the Australian grain harvest to Europe.

56 Just outside Port Chalmers Harbour is the island Kamau Taurua. The alternative name for this island is Quarantine Island. It was used for quarantine for ships' crew and passengers between 1863 and 1924. In 1996 the island's Maori name was restored – it means place of the nets.

57 *Otago Times*, 26th December 1887.

58 British sovereignty was declared here in 1840. Wellington, the new capital, had a population of 4,900 (Keswick at the same time had a population between 2,500 and 3,000).

59 There are some problems with this census entry. The surname Ballential reads like an error in transcription – there is no one of this name recorded as being born in 1826 in Richmond, Yorkshire, as he claimed, nor anyone else in the 1881 census with this surname. The original entry for occupation was 'Jockey' and this is overwritten in another hand with 'Hunstman'. It is not wholly clear if the words 'Coachman not dom' added in the same handwriting on the line above are part of the same amendment for Ballential or a correction to the entry of 'Postboy' for the nineteen-year-old Benjamin Armstrong.

60 Which translates from Maori as, curiously, 'scraps from an earth oven'.

61 Now Paekakariki, which translates from Maori as 'perching place of the kakariki' (green parrot).

62 Evidence of Mr Harrison to the Coroner's inquest, 17th February 1903, New Zealand National Archives J46 Box 254 – COR1903/178.

63 Evidence of the Reverend Pargiter to the Coroner's inquest, 17th February 1903, New Zealand National Archives J46 Box 254 – COR1903/178.

64 Evidence of Timothy O'Rourke to the Coroner's inquest, 17th February 1903, New Zealand National Archives J46 Box 254 – COR1903/178.

65 William Walter Harrison told the inquest that he thought that William was aged between forty-five and fifty.

66 Mary Mitchinson Goodfellow (1851–1930), who married George Renton (1846–1937) on 11th June 1878.

Chapter Eight

1 According to the 1851 census, where they are both shown as house servants. An Armstrong genealogy site (http://cumbriafamilycom.ipage.

com/index.html) records them as having married in 1852, first at Gretna Green and then in St Cuthberts, Carlisle.
2. The 1861 census shows him an innkeeper at the Lodore.
3. On 22nd May 1873, and he was buried in Borrowdale churchyard.
4. His paternal grandfather Benjamin Armstrong (1851), two uncles Joseph and William (1849) and aunt Sarah Armstrong (1851) are also known to have died from the same cause (http://cumbriafamilycom.ipage.com/index.html).
5. In 1877, when there was a reported dispute over fishing rights in Derwentwater, Edward Goodfellow was described as the 'landlord' and 'lessee' of the hotel, not the owner: *Carlisle Patriot*, 13th July and 14th September 1877.
6. See http://cumbriafamilycom.ipage.com/index.html for details of the genealogy of the Armstrong family together with some family photographs.
7. At Carleton near Carlisle, this asylum was built to cater for the needs of both Cumberland and Westmorland. It was opened in 1862 and closed in 1999.
8. This life interest would cease should she remarry – which she did not.

Appendix I

1. *Keswick and Its Neighbourhood: A Handbook* (1852) at p 18 gives the population of Keswick in 1851 as 2,618, up from 1,350 in 1803.
2. Harriet Martineau, *A Complete Guide to the English Lakes* (Whittaker & Co, 1855), p 72.

Appendix II

1. Towards the end of his life he was made an honorary fellow of this college.
2. His *Times* obituary records that he was three times in the winning crew of the Boat Race, but his name only appears as part of the 1839 Boat Race eight in the list of Cambridge crews (https://en.wikipedia.org/wiki/List_of_Cambridge_University_Boat_Race_crews). *The Times* appears to have been mistaken over the 1837 and 1838 races against Leander.

3   The *Dictionary of National Biography*, 1901 supplement (Oxford, 1901) states that he was called to the Bar in 1846, and this was confirmed by enquiry of Lincoln's Inn. Other sources show 'likely 1840'.
4   At this time the Bar was a wholly male preserve.
5   The Northern Circuit included both Liverpool and Manchester.
6   Created around 1200, this Court was abolished by the reforms of the Supreme Court of Judicature Act 1873 when the High Court of Justice was created.
7   By the Judicature Act 1873 – it first sat in 1875.
8   Sir George Jessel (1824–83) was a distinguished chancery barrister, Solicitor-General and, in 1873, Master of the Rolls. He was known for his speed in clearing cases and his practical ability during a period of law reform. He made his mark, in particular, on equity. He was the first Jew to be in government (Solicitor-General), a regular member of the Privy Council and a member of the Bench. When he started his career he should have been unable to practise as a barrister because of his religion (but no one ever raised this point against him).
9   The Master of the Rolls is today the third most senior judge after the President of the Supreme Court and the Lord Chief Justice. He presides over the Civil Division of the Court of Appeal. The title goes back to the late 1200s, but its functions then were not the same as today.
10 Later 1st Earl of Halsbury, Lord Chancellor 1885–86, 1886–92 and 1895–1905 – at this time the appointment as Lord Chancellor was a political one and not a permanent judicial post.
11 Ernest Bowen-Rowlands, *Seventy-two Years at the Bar: A Memoir* (Macmillan, 1924).
12 Barrister from 1851 to 1895.
13 Lord Coke (1552–1634). Esher's obituary gives details of several longer-serving judges before him.
14 1829–1896; artist and one of the founders of the Pre-Raphaelite Brotherhood.
15 One modern website confuses this point by listing William Brett as the illegitimate issue of Napoleon!
16 Napoleon was back in Paris from Russia, minus his Grande Armée, on 18th December 1812, although he left for the 1813 campaign on 15th April before returning to Paris shortly after the disaster at the Battle of the Nations at Leipzig in mid-October 1813. At the end of January 1814 he was campaigning in eastern France and in April he abdicated at

Fontainebleau and left for Elba. These timings fit for him being in Paris at the right time, but there is really little evidence for the claim of his paternity.
17 After the commencement of the Universities Act 1871.
18 A Recorder was a judge who presided on a part-time basis in a particular borough. Appointees by this time were usually barristers. An appointment as a Recorder was a mark of prestige.
19 His obituary in *The Times* of 28th April 1887 suggests that his retirement may have been prompted by increasing deafness.
20 Taylor (1806–1880) was well-known for his work on toxicology and had helped to convict the notorious poisoners Dr William Palmer (the Rugeley Poisoner) in 1856 and Dr John Smethurst in 1859. What he knew of mental illness is unclear.
21 In *Famous Trials of the Century* (Herbert S Stone, 1899).
22 Probably a pulmonary oedema.
23 Kingsdown had a lifeboat station between 1866 and 1927.
24 Serjeant Ballantine, *Some Experiences of a Barrister's Life* (Richard Bentley & Sons, 1883).
25 Sir Cresswell Cresswell PC (1794–1863), the first judge of the new Probate Divorce and Matrimonial Cause Court, who did much to establish the early law on divorce – an interesting appointment for a bad-tempered and childless bachelor.
26 Sir James Wilde, 1st Baron Penzance (1816–1899), a noted nineteenth-century judge with much experience of wills and probate issues.
27 (1868) 1 P&D 481.
28 (1873) LR 3 P&D 64.
29 (1879) 5 PD 84.
30 (1883) 8 PD 171; see *Re Perrins (deceased), Perrins v Holland* [2010] WTLR 1415 for the endorsement of the modern Court of Appeal on the correctness of this judgment.
31 A judicial enquiry set up by the government into the alleged crimes of the Irish parliamentarian Charles Parnell Stewart after *The Times*, in 1887, tried to link him to the assassinations of the Chief Secretary for Ireland and his Permanent Under Secretary in Phoenix Park in May 1882. Parnell was found to be innocent. The work of the Commission was widely recognised by both sides as having been fair and properly conducted.

32 *Treatise on the Effect of the Contract of Sale on the Legal Rights of Property and Possession of Goods, Wares and Merchandise* (eight volumes) (William Benning & Co, 1845).
33 John Campbell, 1st Baron Campbell PC QC (1779–1861) was Chief Justice of Queen's Bench 1850–59 and Lord Chancellor 1859–61.
34 Let it be given to the more worthy.
35 A judicial appointment to the House of Lords by way of a life peerage to increase the membership of the Judicial Committee of the House of Lords.
36 1815–1901. In an entirely different context, Eyre is famous for his explorations of Australia between 1839 and 1841. In 1854 he was appointed Governor of Jamaica and several other islands.
37 In 1969 he was declared a National Hero of Jamaica. This is the highest of the five Jamaican Orders of the Societies of Honour. He was also depicted on the Jamaican 10c coin and $2 bill.
38 (1861) 1 B&S 393.
39 (1871) LR 6 QB 597, heard in Queen's Bench by Cockburn CJ, Blackburn J and Hannen J.
40 Buyer beware.
41 (1868) LR 3 HL 330.
42 (1883) 9 App Cas 1.
43 (1877) 2 AC 438, involving Brett J in Queen's Bench, Mellor J in the Court of Appeal and Blackburn in the House of Lords.
44 Details of Cockburn's academic career at Cambridge are courtesy of the Trinity Hall Archivist.
45 A landmark in Parliamentary reform that abolished the rotten boroughs, created new, more representative, constituencies and extended the franchise.
46 John Henry Newman (1801–1890), later Cardinal Newman, was a national figure in his early thirties. He founded the Oxford Movement within the Church of England but in 1845 joined the Roman Catholic Church. He was beatified in 2010. In 1852 the Attorney-General could still practise law privately. This ceased in 1890.
47 An episode of Palmerstonian gunboat diplomacy in 1849–50; Alexander Cockburn's speech is reported at length in *The Times*, 29th June 1850.
48 This continued until the Homicide Act 1957.
49 Today, the site of the Embassy of Panama.

Endnotes

50 *North American Law Review*, 1894.
51 *Encyclopaedia Britannica*, vol 6 (1911).
52 *The Spectator*, 28th November 1880.
53 Lord Russell, *North American Law Review*, September 1894.
54 LR 9 QB 360.
55 Richard Bethell, 1st Baron Westbury (1800–1873) and Lord Chancellor (1861–65): see *Harvard Law Review*, vol 14, no 2 (June 1900), p 88, where the author says this remark was 'characterized by his usual keenness in disparagement' (Westbury was well known for such disparagement).
56 Represented Edward Barron Goodfellow at both trials.
57 Illustrating the small world of the English judiciary at that time, a draft codification of the English criminal law was prepared. The committee appointed to review it included Lord Blackburn. The merits of the draft code were roundly and publicly attacked by Cockburn LCJ. Attorney-General Holker immediately withdrew his support and no more was heard of the proposal (Ernest Bowen-Rowlands, *Seventy-two Years at the Bar: A Memoir* (Macmillan, 1924), p 304).
58 A Victorian *cause célèbre*, involving a murder by arsenic (although no one was charged with it) that disgraced and ruined the widow, Florence Bravo, because of her extra-marital affair with Dr James Gull, an exponent of hydropathy, with substantial society connections.
59 Known as the Whitechapel Murder, this case attracted much publicity, although it is now far less well known than the later Whitechapel murders of Jack the Ripper (1888).
60 He represented John Banks the younger at both trials.
61 *The Times* obituary says 1862, but Middle Temple records show 1861.
62 He represented John Banks the younger at the second trial.
63 Volume 36 (Oxford, 1885–1900).
64 *The Times* obituary suggests, instead, that he was one of the two judges appointed to replace the recently deceased Archibald J and Quain J.

Appendix III

1 Sub-headings and paragraph numbers in this text were added by the author.
2 6 Moo PC 841.
3 Law Rep 1 P & M 398.
4 Moore 759: s.c. 8 Vin Abr 43, No 22.

5   6 Rep 23.
6   3 Curt App 30.
7   3 Add 79: Haggard's Report of Judgment, p 19.
8   3 Bro CC 441.
9   1 Phillim 90, 100.
10 5 Johnson NY Ch Rep at p 150.
11 Author's added emphasis.
12 3 Washington, at p 585; referred to in *Sloan v Maxwell*, 2 HW Green (New Jersey Ch Rep) at p 570.
13 12 Southard at p 660.
14 4 Washington at p 267.
15 2 HW Green (NJ Chan R) 563.
16 5 Johnson NY Ch Rep at 159.
17 3 Moo PC 282.
18 6 Moo PC 341.
19 Law Rep 1 P & M 398.

Index

References are to page numbers.

Ansell, George   24, 47, 69–71, 178–179
  John Banks's wills
    accusations against   70–71, 115–117
    1838 will   49
    1863 will instructions   51–55, 67, 69, 110, 111
    1863 'draft will'   56–61
    1863 engrossed will   61, 63, 64
Albuminuria   146–147
  diabetes   146–147
  Fabry disease   147
  Stroke   147
Alexander, Featherstone   25, 27, 31–33
Arkleby   24, 25, 27, 29, 36, 40, 45–46, 51–55, 58, 60–62, 65, 90, 93, 95, 100, 110–112, 114, 115–116, 119, 129, 178,188, 206, 207, 232n
Armstrong
  Benjamin   145, 169–170, 250n
  Hannah   146–147
  illness and death   146–147
  marriage   145, 169–171
  Joseph   145, 169–170
  Mary (the elder)   145, 169–170, 172
  Mary (the younger) (see under Goodfellow, Mary (née Armstrong))
  Martha   145
Askew, Mr   172–173
Aspinall, John Bridge, QC   106–107, 111–112, 114–115, 118, 120–124, 202–203
Asylums
  abuse of committal process   20
  Bethlem hospital   20
  Bicêtre hospital   16, 227n
  Cumberland and Westmoreland   12
  Dunston   11–13, 14, 17, 18, 20–21, 22–25, 112
  'Farming out'   28–29
  Lincoln   17
  Salpêtrière hospital   16
  Surrey County   19–20

Asylums *(continued)*
  treatments
    bleeding, blisters and setons
      17, 18
    cold showers   19–20
    emetics   19–20
    opiates   19
    restraints   16, 17–18, 23
    sedatives   22
    sympathetic environment
      22–23
  West Auckland   16
  Wreckenton   16

Ballential, William   165, 250n
Banks
  Jacob (the elder)
    business   1–2, 3, 47, 137
    issue   3
    marriages   3
    will   3–5, 25, 225n
  Jacob (the younger)   3, 4, 137–138
  John (the elder)
    behaviour   10, 11, 23, 26, 30, 35, 36, 41, 52, 56, 110, 112, 113, 114–115, 118–120, 177–178
    violence   11, 12, 23, 36
    birth and childhood   3, 8, 9
    death and burial   3, 7, 45–47, 66
    financial position   6, 9, 11, 22, 25–26, 29–30, 41, 65–66, 94, 118, 119, 177–180
    lease of properties   65–66, 117
    language   32, 37
    literacy   8, 49–50

lodgings   26–27, 240n
mental asylum   11–13, 22–25, 74, 108–109, 112, 115
mental illness   7, 8, 10, 22, 25–26, 31–42, 56, 60–61, 74, 108–109, 125–126
  hallucinations/delusions   10, 25, 30–34, 38, 42, 70, 125–126
  Featherstone
    Alexander   25, 31–34, 35, 36, 37, 42, 112, 115
    Joseph Dallow   33–34, 88
  'Spectral army'   34
  spirits   34
  the Devil   31, 32, 35, 36, 37, 42, 115
  Thomas Goodfellow   25, 33, 42, 112
  hitting head   36, 36, 43
  hydatid cyst   43
  modern diagnosis   42–45
  rational   9, 26, 35, 39, 41, 51–52, 58–62
  schizoid personality   8
  schizophrenia   42–43
  syphilis, tertiary   43
  treatment   18
mother's drapers shop   11
physical health   7, 36, 41, 44
  epilepsy   19, 37–40, 43–44, 51, 108, 112
  exercise   7, 34, 36, 52
  stroke   38, 40–41, 44, 45, 52

Index

teetotal 7
watchers 11, 31
wills 74, 109, 138
   1838 49–50, 59, 67
   1863 will instructions
     50, 51
   1863 'draft will' 55–61,
     66–71
   1863 'engrossed will'
     61–64, 66–71
   probate 101
John (the younger) 66, 68–71,
   100–101, 103, 138–142,
   175
Margaret (the elder) 3, 5, 10,
   25, 27
Margaret (the younger) (see
   under Goodfellow,
   Margaret)
Barron, Frances 89, 145, 237n
Bassenthwaite 7, 24, 36, 52, 112
Beaufort, 7th Duke of 149
Bible, the
   Deuteronomy 152
   Ephesians 151–152
   Leviticus 151–152
Bipolar disorder 42
Bird
   Isaac 27, 28, 32, 36, 229n,
     231n
   Margaret 27, 28, 32, 33, 35–
     36, 40, 118
Blackburn, Mr Justice 196–197
Blackie, Professor JS 151, 245n
Blencathra 34, 187
Borrowdale Hotel 145–148, 156,
   165, 169–173, 174, 188, 251n
Brett, Mr Justice 105, 106, 114,
   117, 119, 121–124, 126, 133,
   189–192, 241n

Bridekirk coursing 55–56
Bronte sisters 97, 238n
Brougham, Lord 123, 126–129,
   132–133, 242n

Cartmel, Grenip 35, 177
Cartmel, Mary 35
Catherine of Aragon, Queen 152
Childbirth,
   bacterial infections 81–84
   caesarean section 80–81, 235n
   chloroform 80
   death 77–79, 234n
   dehydration 79–80
   orphans 77–78, 234n
   puerperal fever 83–84
   literary device 78
Cholera 21
Christopherson, Charles 119
Church of England
   churching of women 78
   incestuous relationships 150,
     245n
   resistance to reform 153–154
   rules of affinity 149–150
Clark, Jane 25, 32, 36, 40, 62, 114
Cockburn, Sir Alexander, Chief
   Justice 124–136, 198–201
Coleridge, Samuel Taylor 1
Commissioners in Lunacy
   Cumberland 14
     1846 report 14–16, 17, 19,
       20
   Metropolitan Report 1844 13,
     15, 17, 18, 20
Cook, Thomas 1
Crosthwaite Parish Church 3, 46–
   47, 86, 141, 145

Dalhousie, Earl of 151

Dallow, Rev Joseph   32–33, 87–88, 94
Deceased wife's sister, marriage to   149–155, 174–175, 245n, 246n
Dewey, Sarah   137
Dolley, Daniel   19–20
Doric, SS   156–165
Drouet, Bartholomew   78
Drummond, Edward   134

Edward VII, King   149
Ewart, John, High Sheriff   105

Garbutt, Cornelius   21, 228n
Gibson, Mr   30, 112–113
Gill, John   69, 180
Gladstone, William Ewart   154
Goodfellow
   Clara Frances Barron   148, 156
   Edward Barron
      birth and childhood   86, 145, 244n
      Borrowdale Hotel   145, 170–173, 251n
      children   148, 156
      death and inquest   166–168
      inheritance   66, 101, 102, 103, 106, 143–145, 175, 176
      marriage to Hannah Armstrong   145, 169
      marriage to Mary Armstrong   147–154, 171, 174–175
      perjury   155
      sails to New Zealand   156–157
      time in New Zealand   161–162, 165
   John   156
   John Tolson   86, 88, 101, 236n
   Margaret   10
      birth   3, 73–75
      death   47, 50, 66, 77, 79–84
      inheritance   5, 67–68
      marriage   3, 32–33, 73–75
   Margaret Banks   46, 57–59, 61–63, 66–71, 73–76, 90, 100, 107–108, 176
      birth   77, 84–85
      death   88, 90, 138, 139
      education   89
      finances   92, 94, 102, 138, 144–145, 179–180
      guardianship   91–92, 102
      health   70, 84, 92, 93
      isolation   92–93
   Mary (née Armstrong)
      marriage to Edward Goodfellow   147–154, 156, 171, 173, 174–175
      children   148, 156
      move to Workington   156
   Mary Mitchinson   86, 101, 167
   Sarah   26, 85–86, 89
   Thomas   5, 26, 27, 28, 31, 32, 34, 67, 75, 79
      business   76–77, 85
      death and burial   86–88, 141
      marriage to Margaret   73–75, 77
      marriage to Sarah   85–86
      will   87, 88–89, 94
Gordon, Alexander   83

Hammond, Ann   119
Hannen, Mr Justice   193–195
Harland & Wolff   157
Hartford-Battersby, Rev   88
Henderson, Mr Justice   125

Henry VIII, King   152
Highton, Edward   9, 39, 102, 113, 117, 226n
Hindmoor, Ann   11,
Hodgson, John   99
Holker, Sir John, QC   106–110, 112–114, 117, 118, 119, 120–121, 201–202
Holmes, Oliver Wendell, Snr   83
Hope, James   99
Hurstfield, Martha   3

Iolanthe   153, 246n

Jones, Dr William   37–39, 40, 44, 120, 126

Keswick   1, 2, 53, 188, 251n
Kipling, Rudyard   158, 248n

Lake District
  pencil manufacture   2, 137
  tourism   1
  weather   47, 53, 187–188, 232n
Law Commission   125
Litigation
  breach of promise   106
  common law courts   100
  costs   103, 141–142
  Chancery, Court of   102
  Cumberland Spring Assizes 1869   105–124
  debts of John Banks' estate   103
  ejectment   103–104
  evidence of mental incapacity   99–100
  guardianship   102
  jury   100, 123
  next friend   102
  Queen's Bench   124–136
Lodore Hotel   169
Lush, Mr Justice   105
Lush, Senior Judge   125
Luther, Martin   9, 113, 240n
Lyndhurst, Lord   149–150

M'Naghton, Daniel   134–135
McVitie, William Hall   148
McVitie, Mary   148
Manisty, Henry QC   203–204
Mellor, Mr Justice   192–193
Marriage Act 1835   149–150, 158
Murray, John   87
Murray, Mary   40, 114

National Society for Promoting Religious Education   61
New Zealand
  British Empire and   158–159
  emigrants   159, 162–164
  Port Chalmers Garrison Band   164
  trade with UK   157–158, 164
Newby, Eric   163

Parsonby   36, 46–47, 52, 54, 61–63, 90, 111, 188
Peel, Sir Robert   134
Pendlebury, Richard   141
Penzance, Lord   129, 130, 132, 242n
Perjury Act 1728   155
Pinel, Philippe   16–17, 227n
Plymouth Brethren   88
Psychiatry   13
Pussin, Jean-Baptiste   16–17, 227n

Roads   54

Robinson
  Ann   137
  William   139
  William (miner)   10, 12, 34, 138, 177
Romilly, Lord, Master of the Rolls   103–104
Routledge
  Elizabeth   24, 28, 29–30, 33, 36, 39, 40, 54, 55–61, 65, 90, 94, 102, 114–117, 177, 178–180
  Hannah   39
  Isaac   45
  James   27, 28, 45–46, 55, 102, 118

Scambler, John   87, 94
Scott, John   12
Semmelweiss, Dr Ignaz   82–83
Shakespeare, William   152
Shaw, Savill & Albion Line   157
Short, Thomas   114, 241n
Showley Crow, Keswick   10, 226n
Skiddaw   7, 34, 187
Snape, Charles   19–20
Southey, Robert   1
Stoddart, John   12

Tea   76–77
Thirlwall, William   9, 51–52, 55, 57, 58, 59, 90, 102, 120
Thwaites
  Isaac   24, 27, 28
  Mary   25, 119

Tolson
  Jane   41, 61–62
  Joseph   9, 24, 32, 41, 53–55, 55–61, 61–64, 111–112, 178–179
  collection of rents   30, 51–52, 65–66, 178
Tuberculosis   86, 95–97
Tuke, William   17
Tweddle, Dr John   40, 112

Usher
  Joseph   8, 26, 28, 31, 88, 118
  Mary   26, 27, 28, 29, 31, 36, 118, 178

Victoria, Queen   80, 119, 149, 152

Washington, George   18
Watson, George   89
Watson, Rev Sheppley Watson   119–120, 126
White Star Line   157
Wilkinson, John Etridge   20–21, 228n, 229n
Wills
  formal validity   110, 114–117
  testamentary capacity   109–110, 120–123, 126
  unity and indivisibility of the mind   126–131
Wilson, Miles   170–171
Women in 19th century   90–91
Wordsworth, William   1